DATE DUE			

Semiotics and Thematics in Hermeneutics

Semiotics and Thematics
in
Hermeneutics

T. K. SEUNG

COLUMBIA UNIVERSITY PRESS
New York   1982

Library of Congress Cataloging in Publication Data

Seung, T. K., 1930–
Semiotics and thematics in hermeneutics.

Includes bibliographical references and
index.
1. Semiotics.   2. Hermeneutics.
3. Criticism.   4. Speech acts (Linguistics)
I. Title.
P99.S443   808'.00141   82-4345
ISBN 0-231-05410-6   AACR2

COLUMBIA UNIVERSITY PRESS
NEW YORK   GUILDFORD, SURREY

*Clothbound editions of Columbia University Press books are
Smyth-sewn and printed on permanent and durable acid-free paper.*

For
my tutors and mentors
from
New Haven to Austin

Irwin C. Lieb

George A. Schrader

Judson Neff

Contents

Preface

SINCE the emergence of the New Criticism, the text has become the sole focus of textual interpretation. This textual obsession has made us overlook and even forget the role of context, and this contextual oversight has lately led us to experience some acute interpretive uncertainties and methodological anxieties. These uncertainties and anxieties are now becoming the new syndrome of a post-New Critical malaise. As a remedy for this malady, it is necessary to recall our attention to the problem of contextual understanding. This book is my response to that recall.

My objective is to reinstate contextual understanding as the foundation of all our interpretive activities, as installed long ago in the German hermeneutic tradition. In this restoration attempt, I will show how the recent developments in linguistics and semiotics can be used for the articulation of various contexts. I will further show the indispensability of contextual articulation for the thematic explication of textual meaning. Thus I shall demonstrate the contextual nexus between semiotics and thematics.

This contextual nexus is essential not only for determining the meaning of a text (signification), but also for assessing its meaningfulness (significance). For it alone can situate a text and its meaning in a historical context of human existence, the ultimate ground for all meanings and meaningfulness. This contextual approach goes against the textual approach of formalist programs, especially the New Criticism and French structuralism, which have dominated the humanistic studies in our century. The formalists in general have operated with the confidence that their textual analyses are performed in a timeless perspective that transcends all contextual distortions. But their vaunted timeless perspectives have been no more than their synchronic perspectives in disguise, and can never fully capture the existential relevance and historical significance of their texts. The relevance and significance of those texts are inexorably diachronic and historical, because they are products of human existence and historical experience.

The meaningfulness of a text becomes drastically thinned out when it is filtered through the synchronic meshes of formalist analysis. This attenuation of its significance is further aggravated by the distortion of its signification, when synchronic perspectives are wistfully mistaken for eternal perspectives. These two evils, of attenuation and distortion, cannot be avoided without appropriating historicism and existentialism into our experience of textual interpretation. With this appropriation, the limited method of formal–structural analysis can be expanded into a complete organon for fully disclosing textual meanings in contextual frameworks. This methodological expansion in hermeneutics is the ultimate objective for the composition of this volume.

In the composition of this volume, I have received precious help from many of my friends and colleagues. It is my regret that I cannot record them all. But I would like to mention at least the following: Aloysius Martinich's counsel on pragmatics, Herbert Hochberg's on semantics, David Francis' on Homeric epics, William Nethercut's on Vergil's epic, James Kinneavy's on Roman rhetoric, Alexander Mourelatos' and Paul Woodruff's on Greek philosophy, and Robert Palter's on the current issues in hermeneutics.

A few segments of this volume have already appeared in the following journals: chapters 2 and 3 in *Journal of Literary Semantics* in 1979 and 1980, chapter 7 in *Philosophy and Literature* in 1980, a part of chapter 8 in *Italica* in 1979, and chapter 11 in *International Philosophical Quarterly* in 1980. The last item had originally been sketched out ten years earlier, in my personal letter of September 21, 1970, to Chet Lieb, which I wrote during my one-year residence at the Institute for Ecumenical and Cultural Research, Collegeville, Minnesota. This clearly indicates the extent of his involvement in my thematic project, which I still remember in gratitude. Of course, I gratefully remember the lovely Institute and its gracious director, Kilian McDonnell. I am also grateful to the abovementioned journals for their kind permission for my use of those published articles in this volume.

This volume concludes the series that began with the publication of my *Cultural Thematics* in 1976. In that book, I demonstrated the role of cultural context in the explication of thematic meaning. I followed this work with my *Structuralism and Hermeneutics* in 1982, which exposed the danger of misinterpretation inherent in the formalist and post-formalist programs of interpretation, due to their disregard of contextual considerations. The first one was a constructive proposal, and the second a systematic critique. Both of them presupposed a set of theoretical assumptions and methodological commitments. These assumptions and commitments are fully elaborated in this final volume, *Semiotics and Thematics in Hermeneutics*.

I began my work on this trilogy in 1969. During the ensuing twelve years, I have received generous grants from the Society for Religion in Higher Education, American Council of Learned Societies, National Endowment for the Humanities, and the University of Texas at Austin Research Institute. I am grateful to these institutions. I am also happy to acknowlege the generous help from William Livingston, director of our University Research Institute, administrative assistance from Winifred Conlon, and editorial counsel from Trisha Ingman.

Finally, my deepest gratitude goes to John R. Silber, Stanley N. Werbow, and Robert D. King, the three successive deans of my college, who have firmly stood behind my uncertain project from its inception to its conclusion. The three volumes in this trilogy are no more than a series of humble testimonials to their profound understanding of my complex project and their awesome confidence in its eventual outcome. The twelve years I have given to this trilogy have thus turned out to be one continuous lesson and exercise in humility and understanding.

Semiotics and Thematics in Hermeneutics

CHAPTER ONE
Text and Context

THE notion of textual objectivity has been the central premise for the development of the New Criticism. During the past decade, this premise has been subject to a mounting critique from the champions of reader-response criticism. Stanley Fish, Norman Holland, and many others have not only exalted the role of the reader's response and experience, but have also proclaimed his subjective consciousness to be the only agency that constitutes the text itself. Apart from the subjective act of interpretive synthesis, Norman Holland maintains, a literary text is just "a certain configuration of specks of carbon black on dried wood pulp" devoid of all meanings and significances.[1] The textuality of a text is established only to the extent that its scripts are recognized and their meanings interpreted by a reader. But this act of a reader's recognition and interpretation is solely determined by his subjective psychological conditions, such as his memories and phobias, his fantasies and aspirations, his expectations and anxieties.[2] Prior to this act of interpretive synthesis, a text is only a tabula rasa.

The essential feature of Holland's position is his thoroughgoing subjectivism; he cannot accept anything objective as a fundamental datum for the act of subjective consciousness. From this position, he has even chided Stanley Fish for his initial assumption that the text can, on its own, act on the reader as much as the reader can act on the text.[3] This assumption of Stanley Fish's surely betrayed his belief in the objective existence of a text and its actions. Holland tries to expose the naiveté of this belief by pointing out that the text acts on the reader not on its own, but only by virtue of being recognized and interpreted by the reader himself. But Fish has already mended his position by admitting that the manipulative text is itself constituted by readers' interpretive strategies.[4]

Apart from the all-powerful, all-constituting acts of the reader's subjective synthesis, a text does not even exist; its constitution and operation as a text can take place only within the subjective domain of the reader. This position may be called textual subjectivism or solipsism; the objectivity of the text has been swallowed up into the subjectivity of the reader. This spirit of textual solipsism is graphically represented by the title of one of Holland's many works, *Poems in Persons*, and the title of one of Fish's essays, "Literature in the Reader."[5] It is the central credo of textual subjectivism that the text of a literary work can exist and operate only in the subjectivity of its readers.

There is an incomparable advantage to being a textual solipsist; there is absolutely no way for him to suffer from the anxiety of misreading or misinterpreting a text. For every text he reads and every meaning he construes is constituted by the very act of his reading. No external constraints can ever intervene between his act of reading and his text. Hence Stanley Fish proclaims that every act of reading is an act of writing. In the world of textual solipsism, reading and writing are identical acts. A textual solipsist can enjoy all the prerogatives of the divine subject, who is sometimes said to be reading only what he is writing in the composition of his cosmic volume.

While some champions of reader-centered criticism have been vaunting the newly discovered almighty power of the reading subject, some progeny of the New Criticism have been haunted by an overwhelming sense of their own impotence in the search for textual objectivity. In one of his despairing moments, Harold Bloom says, "There are no interpretations but only misinterpretations." Geoffrey Hartman echoes the same note of despair and impotence: "Nothing hits the mark, or the right mark in *Hamlet*—except the play." Hartman goes on to compare our interpretive enterprise to Jacob's angelic wrestling, indeed a poignant analogy for describing the incomparable disparity between the puny subjective power of the reader and the forever-elusive objective reality of the text.[6]

Despite the obvious disparity between Jacob and his angel, the analogy of his wrestling is too majestic and too reassuring to portray Hartman's own doubtful struggle. Jacob at least had the assurance of grabbing the divine messenger with his hands, but this assurance is never available to Hartman and his fellow skeptics. Even their sense of struggle with the objective reality of the text may be no more than a subjective illusion, for there is no assured way to prove that we have established our contact with the text in its objective reality. Hartman describes the pathos of this self-doubt: "I see the angel struggling ('you must bless me before dawn') but he has many wings and at cockcrow I find scattered feathers only, a barnyard token."[7] Our presumed angelic struggle with the textual reality may be just a wrestling with a couple of domestic fowls flapping around in the barnyard of our subjective ideas.

The reader can never reach out and grasp the text as an objective reality; the domain of textual objectivity is a never-never land lying well beyond the reach of any reader. This position may be called textual agnosticism. The objectivity of the text has been totally alienated from the subjectivity of the reader. In his tormenting awareness of this total alienation, the agnostic reader can only brood over the ever-widening abyss between himself and his never-reachable text. Harold Bloom expresses this agnostic mood: "There is a dumbfoundering abyss between ourselves and the object, or between ourselves and other selves."

The textual agnosticism of these new New Critics appears to be diametrically opposed to the textual solipsism of reader-response critics. Whereas the textual solipsist admits the existence of the text only within the subjective consciousness of the reader, the textual agnostic locates the text emphatically beyond all possible reaches of his subjective consciousness. The former does not even recognize the possibility of misinterpretation; the latter is sure only of the inevitability of misinterpretation. For the former, the reader's response is always self-authenticating; for the latter, it is always self-defeating. Finally, the textual solipsist appears to be jubilant over his unlimited power of textual constitution and manipulation; the textual agnostic seems to be despondent over the irremediable inadequacy of his interpretive competence.

In spite of all these apparent differences, these two positions in textual criticism are really two opposite ways of expressing the same dialectical dilemma over the problem of textual objectivity. The textual agnostic claims that there is absolutely no way to know anything about the text as it truly is in its objective reality. This agnostic claim is being used as the foundation for textual solipsism. Since the objectively real text can never be known or even encountered, it can never beome the object of the reader's response in any form. The reader can respond to the text only as an object of his perception and recognition, that is, as an object of his own constitution. Since the reader is responding to the text as a product of his own constitutive act, the text lies securely within the domain of his subjectivity. Thus total textual agnosticism inevitably prepares the ground for the emergence of textual solipsism.

At this point it may be useful to introduce the distinction between the real text and the apparent text, the text as it truly is and the text as it appears to readers. The textual agnostic claims that the real text is never available to readers; the textual solipsist claims that the apparent text alone is accessible to readers. These two claims are not contradictory, but complementary. Although neither the agnostic nor the solipsist makes any knowledge claims of the real text, they show different attitudes toward the objective reality of the text. Whereas the textual solipsist resolutely disowns the old notion of textual objectivity, the textual agnostic cannot relinquish it.

This inability to relinquish the old notion of textual objectivity together with the overwhelming awareness of inability to know anything about it has generated interpretive anxiety, the anxiety of inevitable textual misinterpretation, among the practitioners of the new New Criticism. What Gerald Graff has called the hermeneutics of tragic angst or negative hermeneutics is the expression of this interpretive anxiety, which has been induced by their irresolvable ambivalence toward textual objectivity.[8] The solipsistic response-critics should be totally free of textual anxiety, since they have allegedly liberated themselves from the old mental shackle of textual objectivity. But their freedom from textual anxiety and their liberation from textual objectivity are only pretenses. Deep down in their hearts, they are not any better off than the anxiety-ridden new New Critics.

The notions of objective reality and textual objectivity can never be eradicated from the human mind, because they are firmly rooted in our inalienable sense of our own finitude. To be finite and to be aware of this finitude is to be related to something other than oneself. It is this sense of other-relation and of our own finitude that constitutes our ineradicable sense of objectivity. Only almighty God, in his infinite plenitude of self-relation, can dispense with the sense of objectivity, the awareness of something existing outside one's own being.

The textual solipsist is trying to play the role of almighty God with the mite of his text, but his role-playing consistently betrays his irrepressible sense of his own finitude and objectivity. He spares no effort in denying the objective existence of his text, but seldom thinks of denying the objective existence of other people around himself. In fact, the objective existence of other people is absolutely indispensable to his role-playing. It is to other persons and not to himself alone that he is denying the objective existence of his text. Again, it is to other persons' reading experiences and not to his own alone that his theory of reader-response is meant to apply. He even has to contend with other critics to maintain the objective validity of his own solipsistic theory.

Even if other persons are implicitly accepted as objective entities, they are still useless and meaningless to the textual solipsist's game unless they can identify and recognize the text he is talking about. For this reason, the other persons' references to the text inevitably creep into the discourse of the textual solipsist. But their references to the text must be objective, because they have no way of referring to the subjectively contituted text lying in the heart of the solipsist. In short, objective reference to the text constitutes an essential element in the solipsist's frame of textual constitution. The textual solipsist can deny the objective existence of a text only by presupposing it. If it were not presupposed, it could not even become the object of his denial. Thus, the game of textual solipsism turns out to be a most pathetic testimony in proof of textual objectivity.

The textual solipsist cannot relinquish the old notion of textual objectivity any more easily than can the textual agnostic. Hence the interpretive anxiety of the former is not any less acute than that of the latter. Their main difference lies in their way of coping with it. The textual agnostics try to turn interpretive anxiety into the inevitable fatal sickness in the world of readers and interpreters ("Every interpretation is a misinterpretation, and the fate of reading is the fate of misreading"); the textual solipsists try to talk themselves into believing in the nonexistence of that same anxiety ("There can be no objective interpretation because every reading is a subjective response to a subjectively constituted text"). The latter are fanatically suppressing thir anxiety complex, while the former are deliberately exaggerating its enormity. Neither of them appears to have found adequate ways to cope with their hermeneutic neurosis.

As a necessary preliminary to discovering an adequate remedy for this hermeneutic neurosis, it is time to attempt a reliable diagnosis of this malady. Like any other forms of anxiety, the anxiety of misreading and misinterpreting is a residual syndrome of separation trauma: in this case, the intellectual trauma of having been severed from the primal womb of textual objectivity. Both the textual agnostics and the textual solipsists had grown up in this primal womb during the heyday of the New Criticism. Unfortunately, the textual objectivity of the New Criticism was dialectically as unbalanced as the interpretive subjectivity of the textual agnostics and solipsists. The New Critics had tried to exorcise everything subjective from their textual objectivity—not only the readers' subjective responses but also the authors' subjective intentions. The new subjectivism of today is the inevitable dialectical reaction to this old objectivism. We must now examine the nature of this reaction.

Textual Intuition

"Back to the text"—this governing motto of the New Critics betrayed their innocent faith in textual objectivity, that is, the faith that every text is an objective fact in its very being. It was further assumed that this textual objectivity could be damaged or distorted only through the readers' subjective prejudices. All that was needed for its undistorted comprehension was our ability to approach the text with unprejudiced eyes and to survey it in its natural objectivity. When I. A. Richards distributed some sample poems to his students for their analyses, he took special pains to withold the titles and authorship of those poems.[9] This was meant as an aid in gaining naked perceptions of those poems in their objectivity. In its nakedness, a text was assumed to display fully its original objectivity, and thereby function as the demonstrative ground for objective analysis and exegesis.

The New Critics were not alone in espousing this innocent faith in the objectivity of their subject matter and in their capacity to get hold of it. They shared this blind faith with logical positivists and phenomenologists. For a long time, logical positivism stood on the unquestioned premise that the primitive (or atomic) facts constitute the obvious domain of ontological objectivity. For example, the *fact* that the meadow is green would retain its existence and self-identity, whether it is known or unknown, or whether it is described or undescribed. But it was soon realized that the very notion of fact is language-bound. For example, what counts as a meadow and what does not can be determined only in the context of a language whose lexicon includes the word "meadow" among other nouns; what should be called green and what should not be called green can only be settled in the context of a language whose lexicon includes the adjective "green" among other adjectives. The *fact* that the meadow is green is inconceivable outside a linguistic system. The very notion of 'fact' presupposes a system of language.

This is what W. V. Quine calls "ontological relativity"; that is, every ontology, including the ontology of facts, is relative to the linguistic framework that is implicitly or explicitly presupposed. According to him, every language has its own principle of individuation (its own way of distinguishing objects from one another and of establishing their identities) and its own method of reference.[10] It is this linguistic function of individuation and reference, together with the function of predication, that establishes the domain of facts. There may be facts, in the mental or the physical world, that are not yet caught in the meshes of any language; they may be called "bare facts" or "brute facts." But these brute or bare facts are unknown and unknowable. Hence there is no domain of facts that can function as the independent ground of uncontaminated objectivity. This realization shook up the very foundation of logical positivism by undermining its initial trust in the naked objectivity of facts.

While logical positivists placed their unquestioned trust in facts, phenomenologists placed theirs in "things themselves" (*die Sache selbst*). "To the things themselves!" was their governing motto. In hoisting this motto, they had assumed that the domain of things (*Sache*) was the ultimate ground of objectivity and certainty. Phenomenology was conceived as the new science of this objective domain; its proposed method was to establish a direct comprehension of objects in this domain. Such a direct comprehension was called the "phenomenological intuition." Since our subjective prejudices and presuppositions were assumed to be the only factors that could distort this phenomenological intuition, the first step in any phenomenological investigation was to gain freedom from these prejudices and presuppositions. Hence phenomenology was negatively characterized as the presuppositionless science, or the science free from all presuppositions.

The objectivity of phenomena and the subjectivity of presuppositions—these two ideas underlay the very conception of phenomenology as a new science. In the course of their maturing thoughts, however, phenomenologists came to realize that phenomena are constituted by the knowing subject in the same way that the fact of logical positivists are recognized to be constituted by the linguistic framework of the knowing subject. There are no phenomena prior to or independent of their constitution—this is Edmund Husserl's doctrine of phenomenological constitution. For this reason, the intuition of phenomena turns out to be the intuition, not of objectively existing phenomena, but of subjectively constituted ones.[11] In fact, the process of phenomenological intuition is a repetition of the original process of constitution.

This doctrine of phenomenological constitution undermines the initial faith in the primordial objectivity of phenomena, because the subjectivity of their constitution is now admitted as their ultimate ontological ground. Husserl tried to save the objectivity of phenomena by postulating the transcendental ego as the ultimate agent of constitution. The transcendental ego was now claimed to be the absolute subject that constitutes every entity in the world and the world itself. The individual subjects were said to have an objective intuition of phenomena only insofar as the former perceived the latter in the way the latter had been constituted in and by the absolute subject. The objectivity of phenomena is thus seen as grounded on the subjectivity of the transcendental ego.

Husserl's doctrine of absolute subject cannot be accepted as a product of phenomenological intuition, the intuition of the immediately given or evidently present. For it is a metaphysical dogma or postulate, whose truth is far from evident. But this dogmatic stance on the part of Husserl dramatizes the critical reversal in the conception of phenomena in phenomenology—as critical as the reversal in the conception of facts in logical positivism. Just as it was the naiveté of logical positivists that underlay the notion of objective facts, it was the naiveté of phenomenologists that underlay the notion of objective phenomena or *die Sache selbst*. In their naiveté, phenomenologists and logical positivists alike behaved as though they could and should have transcended the context of their subjectivity in order to reach the rainbow of objectivity. But this rainbow of objectivity is now seen as firmly rooted in the context of their own subjectivity. There is no way to step out of this pervasive context of subjectivity any more than to jump out of one's own consciousness.

This painful awareness of contextual subjectivity has marked the self-critical maturity of both phenomenology and logical positivism. It is this painful lesson that is now being appropriated by the avowed champions of subjectivity in the world of literary criticism, whether they assume the posture of textual solipsism or of agnosticism.

When the New Critics raised their banner "Back to the text," they were as blissfully devoid of contextual awareness as phenomenologists and logical positivists. They were confident of disclosing the meaning of a text as thoroughly as possible by observing and analyzing only what is in the text. Their method could have been called "textual intuition" in analogy to Husserl's method of phenomenological intuition. In truth, textual intuition can be regarded as a special instance of applying the method of phenomenological intuition to the domain of textual meaning.

This intuitive method is not meant to exclude the analytical method, although the word "intuition" often implies an opposition to the word "analysis." In phenomenology and the New Criticism, the method of analysis has been accepted as an integral feature of intuition. Their method is "intuitive" in the specific sense that what is analyzed and understood is an object of direct inspection and observation. Hence the word "intuition" mainly characterizes the relation between the knowing subject and the known object.

The nature of this intuitive relation between the knower and the known may be better explicated by contrasting it with their nonintuitive relation. If a nuclear physicist is reading a sheet of photographs from a high-powered particle accelerator in order to track down some hitherto unknown subatomic particle, he has an intuitive relation to the photograph itself, but not to the subatomic particle that is being sought. This particle is never open for direct inspection and observation; its discovery is made through a theoretical construction. Hence this nonintuitive relation between the knower and the known is called "constructivistic." It is an indirect relation.

The intuitive or direct relation between the knower and the known is generally limited to the present; even there it does not extend to the microphysical world, which escapes our direct observation and inspection. When it comes to the domain of the past, this relation can never obtain, whether it be on the microphysical or the macrophysical level. It is impossible to encounter directly the events and personages of the historical past. The objects belonging to the domain of historical evidence can be directly encountered; for example, we can directly inspect a Greek temple, a Roman coin, or a medieval lance. But the notion of historical evidence involves a far more complex relation than the intuitive or direct relation between the knower and the known. An object can be recognized as a Greek temple only through our notions of ancient Greece and its religious rites, which are our theoretical constructions about the ancient world. What is intuitively inspectable in historical evidence is only its present materiality; everything else is an object of constructivistic inference.

Since the intuitive method is available only where the object of analysis is intuitively present to the knowing subject, the doctrine of intuitive presence is an essential presupposition for the justification and application of the intuitive method. It was this doctrine of intuitive presence that underlay the New Critics' textual approach. They had assumed that the object of their textual analysis was intuitively present in the text itself. This assumption of intuitive presence gave them the confidence of fully disclosing the meaning of a text by observing and analyzing only what is in the text. All that was required for this intuitive analysis was to maintain a clear demarcation between what was present in the text and what lay outside it, and to forestall all confusion that might come about by carelessly mingling the two. This demarcation required the familiar distinction between what is intrinsic to the text and what is extrinsic to it. The motto "Back to the text" meant "Back to what is intrinsic to the text"; the textual criticism of the New Critics was known as intrinsic criticism.

What is really intrinsically and intuitively present in a text? The New Critics would have replied, "The textual meaning." But the textual meaning cannot enjoy such a presence, because the presence of meaning requires a context of meaning. For example, when we decode the meaning of a word or a sentence in a text, we can do so only within the context of its language. If its language is unfamiliar to us, the text in question would be no more than an assemblage of strange scripts. Even our recognition of its physical marks as an assemblage of scripts requires the context of our theoretical construction. What is intrinsically or intuitively present in the text is its physical properties. Even its textuality (the recognition of it as a text) goes well beyond the domain of intrinsic or intuitive presence.

One need not be a textual solipsist to say that a text is no more than a string of meaningless marks, if it is taken by itself. Every text is no more than a blank tablet unless and until it is interpreted in a proper context of signification. Every textual analysis presupposes a context of signification and communication. The question of meaning-context is neither extratextual nor intratextual. The distinction between intratextuality and extratextuality can arise only after the textuality of a text is established. But its textuality can be established only in a contextual framework.

Contextual Recognition

The context of meaning and understanding is such an integral feature of our very being as knowing subjects that we are usually not even aware of its presence and operation. It was only this natural absence of awareness that led the New Critics to assume that their textual analyses could be conducted in a direct confrontation with texts, that is, without the mediation of meaning-contexts. But every New Critic tended to read his texts in his own context under the blissful illusion that he was enjoying "the unmediated vision" of his texts, to borrow a metaphor from Geoffrey Hartman. This contextual illusion had a built-in ground for breeding contextual indeterminacy.

Two New Critics might claim their respective unmediated intuitions of a given text, and yet might be reading it in two different contexts. For example, one of them might read a Wordsworth poem in the context of vitalistic pantheism, while the other might respond to it in the context of mechanistic materialism. Unaware of this contextual difference, they might regard their interpretive differences as purely textual. This uncritical approach was always liable to induce contextual indeterminacy, which was usually mistaken for textual indeterminacy.

The New Critics never cared to make the distinction between textual and contextual indeterminacy. Such a distinction could have come about only at the frightful expense of losing their innocent comfort of textual immediacy. Moreover, very few of them ever developed a contextual sensitivity sharp enough to make such a distinction. Their ultimate concern was to obtain the highest possible degree of indeterminacy, whether it be the indeterminacy of a text or of its context. To be sure, they were not overly fond of the expression "the indeterminacy of meaning"; they would rather call it ambiguity, complexity, or even profundity. Since these were securely established evaluative terms in the so-called "intrinsic" criticism, every possibility of contextual indeterminacy was diligently sought under the pious guise of textual indeterminacy. Thus the problem of textual indeterminacy was aggravated by being unknowingly conflated with the problem of contextual indeterminacy, and the problem of textual meaning became highly volatile.

While the indeterminacy of meaning was heating up into exegetical volatility, some New Critics rejoiced in this transformation and even tried to justify it under the name of semantic or textual autonomy. But the word "autonomy" means the power of governing oneself and acting in independence of other agencies. Such a power can be exercised only by agents of action. Whereas an agent is a subject of action and reaction, a text can be only an object. It is an object conceived and produced by its author; it is an object to be interpreted and appreciated by its readers. The prerogative of autonomy cannot be attributed to such an inert object as a text. The meaning of a text is fixed and remains so once it is placed in a context. Even its textual indeterminacy remains fixed also, as long as it remains in the same context. The autonomy of a text has been a disguise for the autonomy of readers, especially autonomy in their se- lection of relevant meaning-contexts.

As soon as these disguises and delusions are seen through, the emer- gence of reader-response criticism turns out to be the most obvious and natural outcome. The dubious textual objectivity of the New Critics has now been recognized and accepted by the response-critics as the reader's subjectivity. Norman Holland says, "New Criticism turns out to have been Old Subjectivity."[12] Just like the response-critics, the New Critics had all along been preoccupied only with their own reading experiences, although these experiences were paraded as textual exegeses of objective meanings. After all, they took the initiative in banishing the authors from the texts in order to exercise their interpretive autonomy in the name of textual autonomy. The response-critics have simply accepted their de facto interpretive autonomy for what it was all along. In short, the rsponse-critics have every right to be called the true heirs of the New Critics—they have fully realized the true essence of New Criticism by liberating it from its false pretenses and dubious assumptions.

The dispute between the response-critics and the New Critics is mainly a dispute on labeling their works. Cleanth Brooks' textual analyses in his *The Well Wrought Urn* could have been called the analyses of reading experience; in fact, they were meant to be such.[13] Conversely, Stanley Fish's analyses of the reader's response or experience in his "Literature in the Reader: Affective Stylistics" could very well have been accepted as reputable textual analyses by any of the New Critics. Both of them have stressed the vitality of the reading experience. Whereas the New Critics had tended to attribute this vitality to the liveliness of the text, the response-critics unequivocally attribute it to the liveliness of the reader. The truth of the matter is that the lively reader and the lively text are the two essential partners in constituting a lively reading ex- perience. Hence the dispute between the response-critics and a New Critics is, at best, a dispute in emphasis.

In the meantime, some direct descendants of the New Criticism came to recognize the inadequacy of their elders' formalism. In "Beyond For- malism," for example, Geoffrey Hartman has demonstrated that most formalistic analyses are made from an ahistoristic perspective, blind to the historicity of literary forms.[14] Since every literary form has its own historical background, he has argued, its texture and function can never be fully comprehended by formalistic analyses unless they are placed in proper historical perspectives. Thus he has shown the urgent need to expand the formalistic approach of his elders.

Another conscientious offspring of the New Criticism, E. D. Hirsch, tried to overcome the inherently subjectivist tendency of New Criticism by importing some methods and principles from the German school of hermeneutics. The heart of this attempt was to propose the author's intention as the only principle for validating the interpretation of his text. He made this proposal by reviving the forgotten authority of Schleiermacher, the father of the German hermeneutic tradition.[15] But he gave no indication of how this proposal could be implemented.

If authorial intention were available for direct inspection and observation by readers, it could readily be used for settling the claims of competing interpretations. Unfortunately, authorial intention can be reached only through textual interpretations. The use of the former as the criterion for determining the validity of the latter would be placing the cart before the horse. Hence Hirsch's proposal cannot be accepted as an interpretive criterion; at best it can be accepted as one of the goals for our interpretations. Hirsch has overlooked the functional difference between a criterion to be used and a goal to be striven for in interpretation.

The problem of the interpretive criterion involves the problem of meaning-context to the extent that the meaning of a text and its interpretation are context-dependent. But Hirsch never directly raises the question of meaning-context. He tries to resolve the problem of textual indeterminacy by wrestling with the two variables of textual meaning and authorial intention. He seems to assume that the values of these two variables are context-independent. Thus he shows no inclination at all to provide a contextual account of authorial intention. In this context-free approach, he remains a true heir to the spirit of the New Criticism.

With Schleiermacher, however, the problem of context was the overriding concern. In his study of biblical exegeses, he was startled to discover what radically different interpretations of Paul's Epistles had been generated by the unconscious contextual transformations among its interpreters. Schleiermacher made the same discovery in his study of the history of interpreting Plato's dialogues. This overriding conern with the role of contexts induced him to devise the new science of hermeneutics. This contextual concern was given a concrete expression in his

Erster Kanon, which was intended to be the most important canon of interpretation: "Whatever in a given text requires a clearer determination, may be given such a determination only from the shared linguistic domain of the author and his original public."[16]

When Wilhelm Dilthey tried to revitalize this brainchild of Schleiermacher and to incorporate it into his theory of *Geisteswissenschaften* (human studies), he fully recognized the central importance of meaning-contexts in the science of hermeneutics. This is manifested in his various accounts of context (*Zusammenhang*): the life-context (*Lebenszusammenhang*), the experience-context (*Erlebniszusammenhang*), the meaning-context (*Bedeutungszusammenhang*), etc. He tried to bring together all these manifold functions of context into a unitary schema by appropriating Hegel's notion of objective mind (*objective Geist*) into his own hermeneutics. As a system of shared conventions, Dilthey's objective mind is the indispensable matrix for every act of communication and interpretation.

When E. D. Hirsch went to Europe to study the German hermeneutic tradition, he evidently had some reasons to bypass Dilthey and go straight back to Schleiermacher. However, to bypass Dilthey was to bypass this problem of contexts in hermeneutics. Although the importance of this problem was clearly seen by Schleiermacher, it was not given the same sort of extensive treatment in his hermeneutics as in Dilthey's. Consequently, Schleiermacher's hermeneutics can be taken as an instrument of textual intuitionism—at any rate, that was the way it was presented by Hirsch. He surely gave the impression that authorial intention could be captured by textual intuition alone. He reinforced this impression by taking seriously the divinatory (intuitive) phase of Schleiermacher's hermeneutics and by associating the notion of authorial intention with Husserl's notion of intentionality in eidetic intuitions.

In Gadamer's heremeneutics, Hirsch perhaps found a special reason to dissociate the notion of authorial intention from contextual considerations. Under the influence of Heidegger's existential phenomenology, Gadamer has transferred the role of context from the objective to the subjective domain. In the German hermeneutic tradition, the notion of context had been an indispensable medium for reconstructing and recognizing the object of cognition. In Gadamer's hand, it has become the circle of subjective finitude that locks in the intentionality of the cognitive subject.[17] Thus the notion of context has been transformed into the conceptual fountainhead of all the evils Hirsch was fighting against, that is, contextualism, relativism, subjectivism, and perspectivism. This may explain why he has decided to open a relentless battle against Gadamer, to bypass Dilthey completely, and go back to Schleiermacher's authorial intention.

But the problem of interpretive context cannot be bypassed, whether we like or dislike it. The question of recognizing or not recognizing meaning-contexts in the domain of interpretation is not a sensible one, because they are always and already there whether they are recognized or not. The only problem within our control is whether or not we should face squarely the reality of interpretive contexts. No doubt, the recognition of meaning-contexts in the domain of interpretation disrupts the idyllic relation between the interpreter and the text in intrinsic criticism. But this idyllic relation has been built upon the mythical foundation of the intuitive presence of textual objectivity, a myth of simple location.

With the dissolution of this myth, the seemingly intuitive relation between the interpreter and the text is now seen to be grounded on contextual mediation. Whereas a text is a tangible object, a context is an intangible one. You can hold a text in your hand, count its words, examine their syntax, turn over its pages, etc. But you can do none of these things with a context, even with the context in which you are talking and acting. Our access to the contexts of other ages and cultures can be established only through inference. Hence a context is a nebulous entity in comparison with the vivid entity called a text. To say that a text can become intelligible only by being placed in this nebulous entity means that the intelligibility of a text is not any less nebulous than that of a context despite its misleading appearance of vividness and distinctness.

Moreover, a context does not have the closure property that every finished text seems to have. Every context can be further clarified or amplified by being linked to, or placed in, other contexts. For example, Shakespeare's sonnets can be understood in the context of his plays, which can be amplified in the context of Elizabethan politics and religion, which can be further clarified in the context of the Renaissance ethos and economics, which can be placed in the context of the transition from medieval to modern Europe, and so forth. Every meaning-context is capable of generating an open-ended series of contexts, in which our text may seem to elude forever our grasp and recede into an infinite contextual abyss, the dumbfoundering abyss between the subject and the object, the interpreter and the text.

The recognition of this contextual abyss is bound to give us the Pascalian shock of the infinite void, especially if we have been brought up with the illusory sense of textual immediacy and security. It is this Pas-calian shock that has generated the interpretive anxiety underlying both textual solipsism and textual agnosticism. Lost in the ever expanding contextual abyss, one can easily dissipate one's interpretive energy in self-pity or self-glorification.

Recently, some critics have begun to behave as though our contextual abyss were a swamp of misfortune they had fallen into by some unfor-tunate accident. But this contextual or hermeneutic abyss is not a gift of accident, but our own achievement, which has been secured through our gradual realization of contextual significance. It is not a cognitive chaos that has been thrown over our fumbling intellect by some evil genius, but an epistemic space that has been created by our maturing contextual awareness. Only within this epistemic space may our "shuttle" of interpretation weave its web of recognition, to borrow another metaphor from Geoffrey Hartman. Hence it should never be allowed to be wasted by our hermeneutic anxieties or abused by Nietz-schean free plays. Either alternative would be a neurotic refusal to be weaned from the illusory comfort of textual immediacy, a childish per-petuation of our separation trauma.

Only through recovery of the hermeneutic abyss as our contextual space can our neurosis of hermeneutic anxiety be turned into a meaningful stage of necessary growth, that is, the critical transformation of textual obsession into contextual sophistication. And this transformation should mark the final transition from the old New Criticism to the new New Criticism.

CHAPTER TWO
Intention and Expression

MOST problems of interpretation seem to arise with those verbal expressions whose meanings are open to more than one possible reading. They are generally known as problems of textual ambiguity or indeterminacy. According to E. D. Hirsch, the aim of interpretation is to bring out the determinacy of verbal meanings from their indeterminacy.

> Meaning is not made determinate simply by virtue of its being represented by a determinate sequence of words. Obviously, any brief word sequence could represent quite different complexes of verbal meaning, and the same is true of long word sequences, though it is less obvious. If that were not so, competent and intelligent speakers of a language would not disagree as they do about the meaning of texts. But if a determinate word sequence does not in itself necessarily represent one, particular, self-identical, unchanging complex of meaning, then the determinacy of its verbal meaning must be accounted for by some other discriminating force which causes the meaning to be *this* instead of *that* or *that* or *that*, all of which it could be. That discriminating force must involve an act of will, since unless one particular complex of meaning is *willed* (no matter how "rich" and "various" it might be), there would be no distinction between what an author does mean by a word sequence and what he could mean by it. Determinacy of verbal meaning requires an act of will.[1]

Since the meaning of every verbal expression is by its nature indeterminate, Hirsch is arguing, it can be rendered determinate only by the determinate act of its author's will. For this reason, he proposes authorial intention as the ultimate principle for textual interpretation.

How can the indeterminate meaning of a verbal expression be made determinate by an act of will? This is the question that naturally arises in response to Hirsch's proposal. Suppose that I tell you, "I will give you a book next week." The meaning of this statement may be regarded as indeterminate in two respects; it is indeterminate what book I will give you, and what time next week I will give you that book. To avoid these two points of indeterminacy, let us suppose, I firmly fix in my mind the particular book I will give you and the particular time I will do so, while making the same statement. But to fix these things in my mind by an act of will does not seem to make the verbal meaning of my statement any more determinate than what it can mean on its own. It appears to be as impossible for an act of will to increase the determinacy of verbal meanings as to add one cubit to one's stature by one's anxious thought. Thus, Hirsch's proposal appears quite implausible.

This implausibility is further compounded by a contextual ambiguity, because Hirsch's proposal is meant to be accepted within either Husserl's or Schleiermacher's theory of language and verbal meanings. In both theories, to be sure, intention and thought play the central role in fixing the meanings of linguistic expressions. But the determinacy and indeterminacy of verbal meanings can pose quite different problems within these two theories, because they postulate different relations between intention and expression. Hence we cannot determine the normative role of authorial intention in textual interpretation without spelling it out in the context of Husserl's and Schleiermacher's theories of verbal expression and authorial intention.

Total Indeterminacy

In *Logical Investigations*, Husserl advocates an essentialist theory of verbal meanings: verbal signs (e.g., "horse" or "quadratic remainder") express the meanings of eidetic essences (e.g., the essence of horses or the essence of quadratic remainders).[2] In this essentialist theory of language and meaning, human intention or thought plays two related functions. First, it intuits the eidetic essences; second, it links up those essences with verbal expressions. Although both functions may be called intentional acts, they are quite different.

The first of these functions is the act of intuition; the second is the act of expression. The former is the act of comprehending meanings in the domain of eidetic essences; the latter is the act of conferring those meanings on verbal expressions (*der bedeutungverleihende Akt*).[3] If we take the example of the word "horse" and its meaning, the act of intuition is the act of comprehending the essential meaning of being a horse by intuiting the equine essence in the eternal domain of eidetic essences, and the act of expression is the act of conferring this eidetic meaning on a verbal expression such as the word *horse*, *Pferd*, or *equus*. The act of intuition is essentially nonverbal; it can take place without the aid of verbal signs. The act of expression is essentially verbal; it cannot take place without verbal signs.

In using verbal expressions, one has to perform these two acts conjointly; the act of intuiting the meaning-content of what one intends to say and the act of expressing this meaning-content by selecting an appropriate string of words. These two acts may be regarded as two inseparable functions of one speech act, which may correspond to what Hirsch calls an act of will. It is his central thesis that this act of will on the part of the author or the speaker is the ultimate determinant of verbal meanings. It is from this intentional act of the author or the speaker that every verbal expression receives its definite meaning. Every verbal expression is only a tabula rasa on which the intentional act inscribes its meaning by attaching it to a particular eidetic object. For example, the word "horse" could have been used to express any other eidetic essence (e.g., the eidetic essence of dogs, sadness, or brutality).

The claim that verbal expressions are totally devoid of all meanings apart from the meaning-conferring or meaning-fixing acts should be called the doctrine of total indeterminacy of verbal meaning, in distinction from that of partial indeterminacy, which we will shortly consider in its own right. According to the doctrine of total indeterminacy, every language is an arbitrary system of meaning conventions. For example, English has a different system of fixing verbal meanings from Korean, Chinese, or any other language, even though they may derive their meanings from the common source, the kingdom of eidetic essences.

This arbitrary differentiation of meaning conventions obtains not only between natural languages but also within the same natural language; for example, between the dialects of one natural language. This differentiation of meaning-fixing conventions need not stop at the level of dialects; even those who speak presumably the same dialect may be operating with different systems of fixing their verbal meanings. Perhaps the language of one human being is never identical with that of another human being. As a system of meaning-fixing conventions, Shakespeare's English is different not only from Chaucer's and Milton's, but also from Ben Jonson's and Francis Bacon's. By the same token, there is no reason to expect Shakespeare's English to retain the same system of meaning-fixing conventions throughout his numerous works, or even throughout any one of his plays.

According to the doctrine of the total indeterminacy of verbal meanings, every speaker or writer is forced into the position of Humpty Dumpty, and must make up his or her verbal signs to express exactly the meaning he or she decides to express.

> "You're holding it upside down!" Alice interrupted.
>
> "To be sure I was!" Humpty Dumpty said gaily, as she turned it round for him. "I thought it looked a little queer. As I was saying, that *seems* to be done right—though I haven't time to look it over thoroughly just now—and that shows that there are three hundred and sixty-four days when you might get un-birthday presents——"
>
> "Certainly," said Alice.
>
> "And only *one* for birthday presents, you know. There's glory for you!"
>
> "I don't know what you mean by 'glory,'" Alice said.
>
> Humpty Dumpty smiled contemptuously. "Of course you don't—till I tell you. I meant 'there's a nice knock-down argument for you!'"
>
> "But 'glory' doesn't mean 'a nice knock-down argument,'" Alice objected.
>
> "When *I* use a word," Humpty Dumpty said in rather a scornful tone, "it means just what I choose it to mean—neither more nor less."
>
> "The question is," said Alice, "whether you *can* make words mean different things."
>
> "The question is," said Humpty Dumpty, "which is to be master—that's all."
>
> Alice was too much puzzled to say anything.[4]

Every speaker or writer has to be the maker of his or her own language, if he or she is to be the master of language rather than its slave. To be the master of one's own language means to have one's own private system of meaning-fixing conventions, namely, a private language. If language is such a private or personal affair, it would be a mistake to regard it as a system of public meanings. Hirsch seems to have this point in mind.

> The idea of public meaning sponsored not by the author's intention but a public consensus is based upon a fundamental error of observation and logic.

It is an empirical fact that the consensus does not exist, and it is a logical error to erect a stable normative concept (i.e., *the* public meaning) out of an unstable descriptive one.[5]

There is a certain measure of truth in this statement. The individualities of speakers and writers seem to pervade their languages and make them more or less personal systems of expression and communication. This appears to be especially true of such inimitable writers as Dante and Shakespeare; they did not simply accept the prevailing languages of their communities, but more or less forged their own. For this reason, to understand their works, their ideas, and their styles is really to understand their languages in their unique mode of eminence. In spite of all this, however, the private dimension of language is only one of its two essential features; the other essential feature is its public dimension.

Without this public dimension, language would be totally useless as a medium of communication. Like Humpty Dumpty, let us suppose, I have decided to use the word "glory" to mean "a nice knock-down argument." This intentional act of meaning-fixing for the word "glory" can establish an efficacious meaning-convention in my language only if it is made known to my hearers and readers. Until and unless it is so known, my privately established convention is totally useless as a medium of communication. For its meaning is known to no one but my own private self. My hearer may ask me to explain its meaning, and I may comply with his request. But neither his request nor my compliance will be intelligible and communicable unless they are presented in the medium of conventions shared by both of us.

To be sure, I do not always have to spell out my private meaning of the word "glory" through the device of explicit definition to make it known to someone else. Instead, I can rely on the method of implicit definition, and let my hearers and readers figure out its meaning through the contexts of its use. Even there, the recognition of implicit meanings must be grounded in publicly shared conventions. Thus the public medium of meaning-conventions is the indispensable basis for endowing private languages with the power of communication. Without such a public medium, it would be impossible even to talk of the intelligibility or unintelligibility of private meaning-conventions.

When one thrusts oneself into an alien country and tries to learn its language simply by observing the linguistic behavior of its natives, one is still appealing to a set of such shared conventions as pointing at objects, speaking to someone, responding to the speaker, asking and answering questions, eating and sleeping, working and resting. Without sharing this large body of conventions, it must be impossible to learn another language by mere observation. This is why it has been exceedingly difficult to learn the presumably simple language of wolves, dolphins, and birds. As human beings, we share few conventions with those animals. But even in these cases of animal languages, the ultimate basis for figuring out their meanings is our knowledge of their fundamental conventions of eating and mating, working and playing, etc., which we, as animals, happen to share with them.

In his theory of verbal meanings, Husserl completely disregards the public dimension of linguistic signs. He opens his inquiry into the nature of verbal meanings by dividing all linguistic signs into two classes: the indication (*Anzeige*) and the expression (*Ausdruck*).[6] The examples of an indication or indicative sign are a brand as the sign of a slave, a flag as the sign of a nation, and smoke as a sign of fire. The common feature of indicative signs is the use of one object to indicate another, and the nature of every indicative relation is extrinsic and contingent. The bald eagle has no intrinsic property to stand as an emblem of the United States; some other bird could have been selected for that function. Likewise, something other than smoke could have been made a natural concomitant of fire. Every indicative relation rests on the contingency of natural association or cultural convention. Because of this contingency, Husserl maintains, indicative signs have no sense (*Sinn*) or meaning (*Bedeutung*).[7] Technically speaking, indicative signs do not mean; they only indicate.

An expression or expressive sign does not simply indicate another object, but expresses its meaning. An expression can be a word ("horse"), a phrase ("quadratic remainder"), a sentence ("Three perpendiculars of a triangle intersect in a point"), or a complex of sentences.[8] The meaning (*Bedeutung*) of an expressive sign is an ideal entity; as such it should be distinguished from its reference or its objective correlate, that is, the object referred to by that expressive sign.[9] For example, the expression "the natural satellite of the earth" refers to the moon, but its meaning is the idea of the celestial body orbiting around the earth. Meanings are abstract entities or universals; references are concrete entities or particulars.

The distinctive feature of meanings as eidetic objects is their absolute invariance and self-identity. For example, the expression "quadratic remainder" always has the selfsame meaning whenever it is uttered or by whomsoever it is uttered.[10] Everlastingly selfsame meanings are eternal or timeless entities; their self-identity is never affected by the contingency of the temporal world. In *Logical Investigations* Husserl calls these eternal objects "species"; in his later writings they are called "essences" or *eide*.[11] These eidetic essences are the objects of intellectual intuition; to apprehend the meaning of the expression "quadratic remainder" is to intuit the *eidos* or essence that is the meaning of that expression.[12] This intuition of essence is called essential or eidetic intuition (*Wesensanschauung*).

Whereas the indicative relation is extrinsic and contingent, Husserl maintains, the expressive relation is intrinsic and necessary. Of course, he does not mean that the word "horse" could not have been used to express any other eidetic essences than the equine essence; he is not claiming an essential or necessary relation between an expressive sign and its meaning, as it obtains in any language community. All he means is that one can be absolutely certain of the connective link between one's own expressions and their essential meanings, for this expressive relation is established and recognized by one's own act of intuition.

The essential relation between verbal expressions and their meanings holds only in the domain of subjective experience, that is, in the monologue of a solitary subject. In Husserl's view, all signs used in communication are not truly expressions but only indications; they indicate or intimate the speaker's thoughts to the hearer.[13] The relation between other persons' verbal signs and their meanings is as extrinsic and as contingent as the relation between the emblem of a nation and its symbolic meaning. One can never be certain of another person's verbal meaning. Even the doctrine of eidetic intuition is of no use in determining another person's verbal meaning, because there is no way to intuit the connection between that person's verbal signs and the eidetic meanings of those signs.

To use Hirsch's adjectives, only the relation between an expressive sign and its meaning is *determinate*, while the relation between an indicative sign and its meaning is *indeterminate*. Since the determinate relation of an expressive sign and its eidetic meaning obtains only within the subjective domain of a solitary individual, Husserl's theory of verbal meaning can offer no guide for determining the meanings of linguistic signs used in intersubjective communications. To be sure, his theory of eidetic essences was meant to assure the self-identity of verbal meanings not only in the subjective world of a single individual but also in the intersubjective world of different individuals. As we have seen, the eidetic essence of "quadratic remainder" was meant to secure the selfsame meaning of this expression "whenever it is uttered or by whomsoever it is uttered." But eidetic essences and their intuitions are useless in guaranteeing the intersubjective identity of verbal meanings, because their intuitions are the acts of subjective consciousness.

Two individual subjects, you and I, may be intuiting the same eidetic essence, e.g., the equine essence, but we may be using different verbal signs as the expressions of that eidetic meaning, e.g., *equus* and *Pferd*. The connection between your word and its eidetic meaning is determinate to you, but it is indeterminate and contingent to me. Likewise, the connection between my word and its eidetic meaning is determinate to me, but it is indeterminate and contingent to you. My intuition of eidetic essences and their connections with my verbal signs provides me with no assured way to figure out the meanings of your verbal signs, because I have no way to intuit the workings of your mind.

In order to overcome the indeterminacy in our intersubjective communication, you and I may agree on the selection of the same word as the expression of the same eidetic essence. But this agreement can be made only through the medium of intersubjective communication. Without such a public medium, you and I can never find out whether we are intuiting the same or different eidetic essences, or whether our words express the same or different ideal contents. According to Husserl, however, every medium of intersubjective communication is inevitably infected with the indeterminacy and contingency of indicative signs. Consequently, Husserl has no way to extricate his eidetic theory of verbal meanings from the tightly insulated world of subjective consciousness. He has established the permanent self-identity and determinacy of verbal meanings only by shearing them of their communicability.[14]

So far in this discussion, I have deliberately avoided the metaphysical issue of the existence of Husserl's eidetic essences. Since Aristotle's criticism of Plato's theory of Forms, many arguments have been advanced against the existence of those abstract entities. But there is no need to become entangled in those arguments, because Husserl's inability to account for the intersubjective communication cannot be mended by even the assured existence of eidetic essences. In his phenomenological writings, Husserl postulates the transcendental ego or subject as a metaphysical organ for intersubjectivity. The transcendental subject is not a private subject; it is supposed to be operative in every individual subject.

Insofar as the transcendental consciousness is operative in my own consciousness, I am aware not only of the eidetic objects that I am intuiting but also of the fact that they can be the objects of other individuals' eidetic intuitions. Transcendental consciousness is intersubjective consciousness.

The theory of transcendental consciousness is a far more dubious metaphysical theory than that of eidetic essences. I have no idea whether or not Hirsch would be willing to let his theory of verbal meanings be interpreted in the context of the transcendental subject. Despite these reservations, the theory of transcendental consciousness, if it is true, can indeed guarantee not only the determinacy of verbal meanings but also their communicability for all individual subjects who share the transcendental consciousness. In fact, this transcendental guarantee appears to be too good to be true; it would clearly forestall all the disputes arising from the indeterminacy of verbal meanings by assuring their everlasting self-identity for all individual subjects.

The indeterminacy of verbal meanings cannot even become a problem within Husserl's theory of the transcendental subject, whereas it surely is an insoluble one within his theory of the private, individual subject. For these reasons, Husserl's theory of verbal meanings can be of no use at all in resolving Hirsch's problem of indeterminacy. Now we have to see what Hirsch's proposal can amount to, if it is to be accepted within Schleiermacher's theory of language and meaning.

Partial Indeterminacy

In his *Hermeneutik*, Schleiermacher built his theory of interpretation on the demarcation between the public domain of language and the private domain of thought.[15] The two arts of expression and interpretation are said to operate in opposite directions. The art of expression is to move from the domain of inner thought to the domain of outer speech. The art of interpretation is to reverse this process; it moves from the outer to the inner domain.[16] Hence the first step in any hermeneutic enterprise is to understand the language of its text. But the language cannot convey the inner thoughts of the author in full fidelity because all linguistic expressions are infected with generality. This demands the second step in hermeneutics, which is to go beyond the public medium of language and capture the inner thoughts lying behind the linguistic expressions. These two steps are called the two moments of understanding (*Verstehen*) or interpretation.[17]

The first of these two moments is called the "grammatical" or "philological" phase; the second is called the "psychological" or "technical" phrase. These two moments require two different methods: the comparative and the divinatory methods. The former is the standard method used in any empirical or historical investigation, the method of comparing various objects for their similarity and difference. Hence it is also called the "objective" or "historical" method.[18] It is this method that establishes the understanding of linguistic expressions.

This objective or comparative method cannot be used in moving from the linguistic expressions of an author to his inner thoughts. Unlike linguistic expressions, the inner thoughts of other persons are not available for objective inspection and comparison. Even if we could compare the verbal expressions of an author with his inner thoughts, we could not establish a set of rules for the accurate construction of his inner thoughts on the basis of his verbal expressions. Because of the generality of verbal meaning, every linguistic expression can be used to describe a countless number of different inner thoughts. For example, the expression "I am sad" has a definite range of general meaning. Within that general range, however, it can be used to describe a potentially infinite number of different shades or states of sadness. In Hirsch's terminology, the meaning of a verbal expression may be said to be partially determinate and partially indeterminate. Schleiermacher is committed to the doctrine of partial indeterminacy of verbal meanings, in contrast to Husserl's commitment to the doctrine of total indeterminacy.

How can we recover the complete determinacy of an author's thought from the partial determinacy of his language? This question constitutes the heart of the psychological or technical phase of Schleiermacher's hermeneutic program. For every given verbal expression, there is a potentially infinite number of candidates that can be picked out as the inner content of that expression. What is the method to pick out the right one from this plethora of candidates? Schleiermacher calls it the divinatory method, that is, the method of divining the exact nature of inner thought lying behind the generality of linguistic expressions.[19]

The divinatory method is called subjective, because it is the method for penetrating the subjective domain of inner thoughts lying behind the objective domain of linguistic expressions.[20] It is subjective for another reason; it lacks the objective criteria and foundation of the comparative method. This negative characterization is not hard to understand, but its positive characterization is quite elusive. The divinatory method is said to be for the immediate apprehension of the individual by transforming oneself into another.[21] Schleiermacher does not explain what it means to transform oneself into another or how one can do it. If I could transform myself into you with the help of your verbal expressions, I would surely be able to know exactly what inner thoughts were meant to be conveyed by those expressions. Unfortunately, that is an impossible operation.

The transformation in Schleiermacher's divinatory method can be taken only figuratively; then it may mean the empathetic or intuitive spiritual communion between two persons. J. M. E. McTaggart is said to have enjoyed this sort of spiritual communion with one of his friends, but those who have the special gift of communicating in this mystical mode can dispense with verbal communications althogether. If the divinatory method is the method of intuitive communion, there is no reason for it to be attached to the grammatical method. But Schleiermacher is emphatic on the inseparability of the two methods or moments in his hermeneutic program.[22]

What Schleiermacher has in mind is perhaps the later hermeneutic method of the German *Geisteswissenschaften* school, the method of understanding (*Verstehen*) the thoughts and feelings of another person by imaginatively placing oneself in the position of another person. But this method is not meant to be a method of immediate apprehension or direct intuition; it is claimed to be as objective and as historical as Schleiermacher's comparative method. Since the act of divination or intuition is totally free of objective criteria, Schleiermacher admits that there can be no rules for guiding the mysterious passage from external expressions to inner thoughts.[23]

Schleiermacher's doctrine of divination may very well be a secular version of Martin Luther's biblical hermeneutics. In Luther's view, the Gospel consists of external words and invisible meanings.[24] The external words of the Bible are indistinguishable from any other linguistic signs, but the normal understanding of these words does not establish access to the true spiritual message contained in those words. Luther maintains that the invisible spiritual meanings of the Bible can be reached only when the external words of the Bible are read with the special aid of grace. Grace is the *intellectus* that penetrates the external words and perceives their spiritual meanings. The power of grace enables the children of grace to move beyond the domain of verbal expressions and establish an intuitive communion with the spiritual meanings of the Bible, the inner thoughts of its divine author.

Luther's biblical hermeneutics is meant to be a special program for understanding and interpreting the divine author and his writings. Schleiermacher's hermeneutic program appears to have come about as a generalization of this special program for the sake of understanding and interpreting human authors. In this generalization, unfortunately, Schleiermacher cannot retain the doctrine of grace, without which the divinatory method cannot perform the mysterious function of divination or intuition. If the function of divinatory intuition is inoperative, his hermeneutic program should be as ineffectual for understanding human authors as a pagan's attempt to understand the divine message without the aid of grace.

Public versus Private

I have explicated Hirsch's thesis on authorial intention as the ultimate determinant of verbal meaning in the context of Husserl's and Schleiermacher's theories of thought and language. The fundamental difference between these two versions of Hirsch's thesis concerns the question of publicly shared meanings. The Husserlian version of his thesis does not accept a public language, whereas the Schleiermacherian version of it does accept it.

It is impossible to implement the Husserlian version of Hirsch's proposal that the author's intended meaning be adopted as the ultimate criterion for determining the validity of all textual interpretations. Let us imagine two readers who are advancing two different readings of the same poem and who are happy to accept Hirsch's interpretive criterion. Let us further assume that both of them are convinced that their respective readings faithfully capture the author's intention. They have decided to ask the author himself to pronounce the verdict on their interpretations of his poem. There have been two objections voiced to this method of directly consulting the author: he is not usually available for this sort of consultation; and even when he is available, his memory may be too faulty for him to recall accurately the originally intended meaning of his own work. By happy circumstance, let us assume, the author whom our two readers are seeking for help is not only available but also blessed with perfect memory.

But this consultation cannot take place because our readers cannot avail themselves of a publicly shared language. Our readers can pose their questions by using a string of verbal signs. By our assumption, this string of words has no publicly shared meanings. Hence the author can never understand those questions the way they are understood by the readers posing them. Nor is there any assurance that the readers have understood those questions in the same way. Without the benefit of a publicly shared language, they cannot even come to recognize that they have produced different readings of the same poem. This recognition also requires the use of a publicly shared language. Without publicly shared meanings, it is impossible to escape the solipsistic world of private language. Anyone locked up in such a world can have neither agreement nor disagreement with anyone else.

I have based the Husserlian version of Hirsch's proposal exclusively on Husserl's theory of expressive signs, because the self-identity and permanence of meaning, the two essential features of Hirsch's interpretive criterion, belong to expressive signs alone. But every text presents itself as a string of indicative signs to everyone except its author. Hence interpretation may be understood as the operation of determining this indicative relation, that is, what inner thought is indicated by the author's text. But this indicative relation is impossible to determine. The indicative relation of smoke and fire, or a snake and its track, can be established by an empirical method, or what Schleiermacher called the "comparative" method, because the two terms of this relation can be empirically observed and compared. But there is no way to compare and inspect the author's language and the corresponding inner thought. Their indicative relation can be established only by Schleiermacher's divinatory method. But we have seen that this method requires the special aid of mystical intuition, a privilege denied to most of us mortals. Hence Hirsch's proposal again turns out to be infeasible for most of us.

The Schleiermacherian version of Hirsch's proposal is feasible, but its feasibility is only partial. The author's intended meaning can be captured only to the extent that it is expressed through a publicly shared language. Whatever lies beyond this public domain is accessible only to mystical intuition. Even if the author's intention can be caught through such a privileged access, it cannot be expressed through language. According to Schleiermacher, language is a medium of generality, while thought is the content of particularity. It is this disparity between the general and the particular that makes it impossible for the author's intention to be fully expressed through language. Insofar as the problem of expressing inner thought in all its particularity is concerned, the interpreter's language is not any better equipped than the author's. They equally belong to the domain of public language irrevocably infected with the generality of social conventions.

The arts of expression and interpretation appear to be possible only to the extent that language and thought are commensurate with each other. If their commensurateness is only partial, expression and interpretation can succeed only partially. The commensurateness of thought with language is the commensurateness of the intended with the expressed meaning. To be sure, the coincidence of these two meanings does not always obtain. There are abnormal situations in which the intended meaning fails to be fully expressed, because of some internal or external impediments, such as malfunction of speech organs or the constraints of force. Even without such impediments, a disparity between the intended and the expressed meanings can take place because some intended meanings are by their nature inexpressible through language. For example, if I try to describe the unique character of my sadness, I can never succeed. As Schleiermacher tells us, verbal expressions are too general to capture any experience or state of feeling in its uniqueness.

In normal speech contexts, however, the intended meanings are usually formulated through language such as "I am sad," "I am terribly sad," or even, "I am sadder than ever." That is, the intended meaning is formulated through the same language that is used for the expressed meaning. The intended meaning is the inner speech of the speaker; the expressed meaning is his outer speech. Since the same language is used for both the inner and the outer speech, the relation between the intended and the expressed meaning must be that of fundamental identity.

On some occasions, even Schleiermacher comes close to recognizing a fundamental identity between thought and language. He talks of the *Zusammengehörigkeit* of thought and language; he appears to mean that thought and language are the two aspects of one and the same thing.[25] He regards the unique style of an author as his way of expressing his unique thought.[26] On the basis of this fundamental identity between the intended and the expressed meanings, he defines the entire goal of hermeneutics as the fulfilled understanding of the author's style. If this is the case, the psychological phase of his hermeneutic program becomes gratuitous. His dualistic program, which had been dictated by his avowed disparity between thought and language, can be transformed into a monistic one. Within this monistic framework, no verbal expression can ever be indeterminate. Every expressed meaning must be as determinate as every intended meaning. Hence authorial intention becomes a gratuitous normative principle for textual interpretation.

Authorial intention has turned out to be either gratuitous or inaccessible in its presumed function as an interpretive norm. David Hoy highlights its inaccessibility by calling it "a regulative principle in a Kantian sense."[27] The author's intention may indeed be the ultimate objective that interpreters try to reach as closely as possible, but it cannot perform even this regulative function within Schleiermacher's dualistic framework. For this framework can provide no criterion for determining which of the meanings permitted by a text comes closest to its author's intended meaning, or which of them falls farthest from it.

Intention and Convention

The relation of thought and language is the fundamental premise for defining the nature of interpretation, and this relation can be that of identity or disparity. These two are respectively the premises for the two traditionally contending schools of interpretation, which Hirsch has labeled "intuitionism" and "positivism."[28] The intuitionism in hermeneutics presupposes an inevitable disparity between thought and language, message and medium. The words of a text can never fully express the intended meaning. They serve only as an occasion for instituting an intuitive communion with the author's intention, which transcends the linguistic medium. Positivism in hermeneutics repudiates the disparity between thought and language, and affirms the identity of thought and language. Every text or utterance is assumed to express fully the author's or speaker's intended meaning. Positivism allows no need for intuitive communion with the authorial intention.

In Hirsch's view, the traditional battle between intuitionists and positivists has now reappeared among the champions of speech-act theory.

We need only look at the arguments that are taking place within speech-act theory to see that the old polarity has simply reappeared in a new form. On the one side I find writers like John Searle stressing the conventionality and rule-governed character of speech-acts. On the other side I find the indom-

itable H. P. Grice stressing the dependence of meaning on subjective intention—the version of the intuitionist view.[29]

This is an erroneous characterization of the debates among the speech-
act theorists. All of them agree on the indispensability of both intention
and convention as two necessary constituents of speech acts.

To be sure, J. L. Austin and John Searle can be misunderstood to
disregard the speaker's intentions in their theories of speech acts, because
they say very little about those intentions. They do not say very much
about intentions, not because they regard them as dispensable in any
speech acts, but because they take them for granted as the essential
ingredients in those acts. They have every right to do so because the
very notion of a speech act entails its being an intended act. Given the
requisite intentions, Austin and Searle are trying to figure out what are
the necessary conventions for realizing them as speech acts.

Although H. P. Grice has placed his emphasis on the speaker's intentions, he does not ignore the conventions governing speech acts any
more than J. L. Austin ignores the speaker's intentions embodied in those
acts. Grice takes them for granted.

> Explicitly formulated linguistic (or quasi-linguistic) intentions are no doubt
> comparatively rare. In their absence we would seem to rely on very much
> the same kinds of criteria as we do in the case of nonlinguistic intentions
> where there is a general usage. An utterer is held to intend to convey what
> is normally conveyed (or normally intended to be conveyed), and we require
> a good reason for accepting that a particular use diverges from the general
> usage.[30]

What is intended by a speaker or an author can be known only by virtue
of what is normally conveyed by his or her expression, which is a matter
of general usage or convention. Grice's theory of intention presupposes
a theory of convention as firmly as Austin's theory of convention presupposes a theory of intention. I do not know of any speech-act theorists
ever committed to the notion of inner thought that transcends the public
medium of language. By Hirsch's definition, all of them are positivists;
they presuppose the fundamental identity of intention and convention.

Hirsch finally concludes that the two positions of intuitionism and
positivism are not only irreconcilable but also fundamentally untenable.

> The intuitionist is trapped by the fact that communicable language cannot
> possibly transcend sharable, and therefore public, conventions. If it could,

he would not need words at all. But the positivist, who stresses conventions and rules, cannot explain how these same rules can sponsor quite divergent meanings and interpretations. He cannot, for instance, determine through rules whether an utterance is ironic. Verbal understanding is not purely intuitive, then, but it cannot be purely rule-governed either, and it cannot be some arbitrary mixture of the two.[31]

If intuitionism and positivism are both wrong and if they cannot be combined into some "mixture," there is no way to postulate the relation between thought and language, the ultimate foundation of hermeneutics as a rational enterprise.

Although Hirsch rejects "some arbitrary mixture of the two," he may be endorsing their nonarbitrary mixture. But he offers no criterion for discriminating the nonarbitrary from the arbitrary mixture. Schleiermacher's dualistic hermeneutics is a mixture of intuitionism and positivism, but there is no way to tell whether this mixture is arbitrary or nonarbitrary. For all we know, it does not combine intuitionism and positivism into a single unity, but allows their duality. Positivism governs the grammatical stage, while intuitionism controls the psychological stage. This duality may mean that there can be no tertium quid between intuitionism and positivism.

If there is no tertium quid, every textual interpretation must be performed on one of the two premises: either that the expressed meaning is identical with the intended one, or that there is a disparity between the two meanings. As a matter of fact, these two premises seem to govern two different types of speech and expression, the normal and the abnormal. In normal speech contexts, the intended and the expressed meanings are presumed to be commensurate with each other. Every expression is assumed to mean whatever is meant to be expressed. This is to presuppose a fundamental identity of thought and language. But the same identity cannot be presupposed for abnormal speech contexts, where expressions cannot be presumed to express fully whatever is meant to be expressed.

Abnormal speech contexts can be further divided into the subnormal and the supernormal. The examples of subnormal speech are the cases of pathological malfunction which makes it impossible to give an adequate expression to inner thought. The examples of supernormal speech are the cases of supernatural revelation, for whose expression human language is woefully inadequate. In both types of abnormal speech, the intended and the expressed meanings are presumed to be incommensurate with each other.

All problems of interpretation can now be divided into two classes: abnormal and normal. The interpretation of abnormal speeches requires one hermeneutic device that is unnecessary for the interpretation of normal speeches. Since the former presupposes the disparity between thought and expression, it must postulate the nature of thought that fails to be expressed in overt speech, and the psychological mechanism that brings about this failure. This is done by Freud in his theory of libido and the superego's censorship. But a similar account of the disparity between thought and expression cannot be given for the interpretation of supernormal speeches. Hence their interpretation cannot become a rational discipline.

If normal speeches are constituted by the identity of thought and expression, they can never generate any problems of interpretation. In fact, this point appears to be fully borne out in our daily life. Despite all the talk about the danger of misunderstanding and the difficulty of understanding, we carry on our verbal acts without ever encountering any serious problems of interpretation. There may be some exceptions to this general rule of normal speeches, e.g., careless remarks, ambiguous assertions, or evasive statements. As far as the relation between thought and expression is concerned, these exceptions are similar to abnormal speeches, and may even be regarded as abnormal episodes in normal speech contexts.

Thus we are driven to the baffling question: Can any problems of interpretation ever arise in normal speeches? How can literary texts ever become problems for interpretation, if they are products of normal speech? Of course, it is possible to treat them as products of abnormal speech. Some pagan classics were interpreted by medieval exegetes as expressions of divine thought. It is equally possible to read the same classics as pathological revelations of repressed libido or collective subconsciousness. When Harold Bloom says that the poetry of every modern poet is usually the expression of his Oedipus complex, he is giving a pathological account of modern poetry.[32] Despite the increasing popularity of this pathological approach, we cannot reduce all interpretive problems in literature to the level of abnormal speeches. So our problem is how to account for the problems of interpretation in normal speeches, that is, without appealing to the disparity between intention and expression.

CHAPTER THREE
Context and Meaning

HIRSCH himself provides an eminent example of interpretive prob-
lems in normal speech contexts[1]—that is, the dispute between
Cleanth Brooks and F. W. Bateson in their interpretation of one of
Wordsworth's "Lucy" poems. Here is the poem in question.

> A slumber did my spirit seal;
>   I had no human fears:
> She seemed a thing that could not feel
>   The touch of earthly years.
>
> No motion has she now, no force;
>   She neither hears nor sees;
> Rolled round in earth's diurnal course,
>   With rocks, and stones, and trees.

In Cleanth Brooks' view, these few lines portray the lover's agonized
shock over the death of his loved one, the cruel event irrevocably transforming the once lively girl into a totally lifeless object to be whirled
around, together with other lifeless objects such as rocks and stones, in
the meaningless mechanical motions of this earthly globe. F. W. Bateson
gives these same lines a different reading: through her death, Lucy is
initiated into a far grander process of life and vitality, namely, the sublime
process of nature. In this Lucy poem, Brooks sees the mourning of
despair over the fragility of human life meaninglessly suspended in the
inert physical space, while Bateson finds confirmation of the inexhaustible cosmic life that permeates both animate and inanimate objects, the
human and the nonhuman worlds.

Hirsch regards this dispute as a typical case of textual indeterminacy
on the ground that the two readings, though incompatible, are equally

"permitted by the text."[2] But this is to overstate the case. It is not a textual dispute, pure and simple; it involves more than a text. The two readings of the same text involve two different linguistic contexts. Cleanth Brooks is reading the Lucy poem in the mechanistic context of contemporary physical science, in which the phenomena of life are regarded as accidental, momentary occurrences in the immense, desolate desert of inert matter and its senseless motion. F. W. Bateson is reading the same poem in the pantheistic context of nineteenth-century Romanticism, in which every object of the universe, animate or inanimate, is assumed to participate in the cosmic procession of universal spiritual force. Hence theirs is not a textual but a contextual dispute.

It is impossible to read a text without placing it in a linguistic context. We can assign a meaning to each word in a text and combine different words into meaningful configurations such as phrases and sentences. This operation of meaning-assignment is the first act of interpretation, which can be called "semantic operation." When we assign the meaning of one, two, three to the roman numerals I, II, III, or the meaning of addition and subtraction to the mathematical signs of $+$ and $-$, we are performing semantic operations. The decoding of a secret message or Rosetta Stone involves the same operation of assigning meanings to a string of meaningless verbal signs. When a language is considered as a systematic framework for this semantic operation, it can be called a semantic system or a code. The operation of coding and decoding a message always presupposes the existence of a code.

The Lucy poem may not present itself as a string of meaningless signs to most English-speaking people, but its reading still inevitably involves the semantic operation of meaning-assignment. This semantic operation produces its contextual indeterminacy, because it can be read in more than one semantic context. The fact that every word in the Lucy poem is still found in the active vocabulary of today's English does not guarantee that Wordsworth's English is the same semantic system as today's English. The words "trees" and "rocks" may refer to the same objects in both semantic systems, but they are given different meanings. In the semantic system of today's English, both trees and rocks are regarded as lifeless objects of inert matter. In the semantic system of Wordsworth's English, both of them were assumed to be physical manifestations of inexhaustible cosmic vitality.

The semantic character of every language is inseparably connected to its cultural context of beliefs and values, thoughts and emotions. Cleanth

Brooks illustrates this point with the problem of understanding Shakespeare.

> In order to understand Shakespeare, we simply have to understand what Shakespeare's words mean. And the implications of this latter point are immense; for they go far beyond the mere matter of restoring a few obsolete meanings. Tied in with language may be a way of apprehending reality, a philosophy, a whole world-view.[3]

The semantic character of Shakespeare's English embodies his way of apprehending reality, that is, his world view. Hence his English constitutes a semantic system quite different from ours.

At this point, it would be well to clarify the distinction between textual and contextual indeterminacy. When a text can be given more than one reading within a prescribed semantic context, it can be said to be textually indeterminate. However, when the indeterminacy of its meaning is dictated by the multiplicity of available semantic contexts, it should be called contextual indeterminacy. Likewise, the notion of semantic autonomy can be given two different meanings: textual and contextual. Textually construed, "semantic autonomy" has the same meaning as "textual autonomy"; namely, the notion that the meaning of a text can never be fixed by anything lying outside the text, because its meaning perpetually changes as a function of its autonomous development. But this is a dubious notion, for a text is no more than an inert material object inscribed with a set of linguistic signs, which can do nothing unless it is placed in a semantic system. In its own right, a text is like a fish out of water. It has no power; it is neither autonomous nor heteronomous.

"Semantic autonomy" can also mean the autonomy of a natural language as a semantic system. The semantic context of every natural language perpetually changes, together with the stream of life, and this perpetual change can dictate a corresponding change in the meaning of any text. The meaning of Shakespeare's works can transform itself in accordance with the semantic alteration of the English language. But this alteration cannot be called autonomous: it does not come from the text. It is heteronomous. It is dictated by the semantic autonomy of its language. Textual heteronomy is a by-product of linguistic autonomy. The changing semantic contexts can give us the impression that every text perpetually changes its meaning with its own inexhaustible power, but

the true source of this inexhaustible power and this perpetual change is
not the text itself but its readers and their changing semantic contexts.

Every natural language presents to the reader a range of possible semantic contexts for the interpretation of his text, thereby generating the
problem of contextual indeterminacy. The range of contextual indeterminacy is at the same time the range of contextual choice for the readers;
they have to choose appropriate contexts for the reading of their texts
from all the possible semantic contexts. For this reason, semantic autonomy that generates contextual indeterminacy is the semantic foundation of interpretive freedom or autonomy. Just as contextual indeterminacy has been mistaken for textual indeterminacy, so has the autonomy
of readers and their semantic contexts been misconstrued as the autonomy
of the text.

Semantic versus Pragmatic

The semantic operation of decoding the meaning of a text by placing
it in an appropriate semantic system may belong to the philological phase
of Schleiermacher's hermeneutics. But this semantic operation can still
leave its meaning indeterminate. Let us consider the sentence "My dog
may bite you." Its semantic meaning is fixed by the meaning of each
word and by the syntax of the sentence. But the same sentence can be
used for different purposes. By uttering this sentence, I can describe the
disposition of my dog, warn you about it, scare you away from my
house, or even tease you about your timidity. Depending on my purposes, I shall be performing different acts by using the same semantic
entity. As a constituent of these different acts, the same sentence can be
said to take on different pragmatic meanings (*pragma* is the Greek word
for *action*).

The meaning of a sign can be interpreted on two levels: semantic and
pragmatic. Its semantic meaning is the meaning it has on its own; it is
its dictionary meaning. Its pragmatic meaning is the meaning it gains
through its use; it inevitably involves the sign users, their intentions and
actions, and their situations and circumstances. By contrast, the semantic
meaning of a sign is totally independent of the contexts of its use, because
it is considered in abstraction from them. If we call "My dog may bite
you" an assertion or utterance, we are treating it as a pragmatic entity,
thereby giving it an implicit reference to a person and his action. It takes

a person to make an assertion or utterance, which is to perform a linguistic act. By calling the same linguistic entity a sentence, we can treat it as a purely semantic entity, without any reference to persons and their actions.

This distinction between semantic and pragmatic meaning underlies David Hoy's complaint that Hirsch "overlooks the difference between talking about meaning from the point of view of sentences and discussing it from the point of view of texts."[4] The meaning from the point of view of sentences may be called the sentence-meaning; it belongs to the semantic level. The meaning from the point of view of texts may be called the text-meaning; it belongs to the pragmatic level. A text can come into being only through a human action. But there is an inherent ambiguity in the expressions "sentence" and "sentence-meaning," because they can be used on not only the semantic but also the pragmatic level. A sentence in any text is still a sentence. The Lucy poem is composed of two sentences, and the meanings of those sentences are sentence-meanings. The customary device for avoiding this ambiguity is the distinction between a text-sentence as a pragmatic entity and a system-sentence as a semantic entity. Likewise, any sentence-meaning can be designated as the meaning of a text-sentence or that of a system-sentence. Again, the latter is a semantic entity, and the former a pragmatic one.

To read a text as a poem is to place it in a pragmatic context. On the semantic level, there can be no distinction between a poetic and a nonpoetic text. Even to treat a text as a text is also a pragmatic operation, because purely semantic entities have no textual reference. Hence every textual interpretation is a pragmatic act, which presupposes semantic entities. By the same token, every text production is a pragmatic event.

On the pragmatic level, authorial intention cannot be ignored, whereas it has no place on the semantic level. The nature of a pragmatic context appears to be determined by the intention of the pragmatic agent. If I say something to tease you, I constitute the pragmatic context of teasing you. The nature of this pragmatic context appears to be determined by my intention. Hence Hirsch's thesis on authorial intention should be restated in terms of pragmatic contexts: the meaning of a verbal expression can be made definite by determining its pragmatic context, and the character of a pragmatic context can be determined by discovering its speaker's or author's intention.

In this reformulation, Hirsch's thesis appears to gain considerable plausibility. The examples he uses to illustrate his thesis seem to fit this reformulation. The most interesting example is the story of how Daniel Defoe's pamphlet, *The Shortest Way with the Dissenters*, was received by his contemporaries.[5] On the surface, this pamphlet appeared to be a sincere recommendation to the activists of the Church of England on effective measures to be taken against the unruly dissenters; that is, to oppress, harass, banish, and execute them resolutely. *The Shortest Way* quickly became popular among the activists until they discovered the true identity of its author; he was not one of the activists, as they all had assumed, but one of the dissenters. With this discovery, *The Shortest Way* was reinterpreted as a clever satire on the repressive measures of the Church of England against the dissenters.

It may be said that *The Shortest Way* was initially misinterpreted by its readers because it was placed in a wrong pragmatic context, and that it was later given the right interpretation by being placed in the context of satire. It may further be said that the right pragmatic context for *The Shortest Way* was found only by discovering the true intention of its author. Even in this reformulation, Hirsch's thesis is not entirely valid. For the nature of pragmatic context is determined not by the speaker's or author's intention but by its expression.

The intentions buried deep in someone's heart can never contribute to the determination of any pragmatic contexts. However, the expression of an intention is the performance of an act. It is always the performance of an act that determines the nature of the context of the action. For example, if I have only the intention to kill someone, yet do nothing toward fulfilling it, I do not place myself in the context of murder. Only when I try to fulfill that intention through an act do I place myself in the context of murder. This is true of speech intentions also. It is not the speech intention itself, but the attempt to fulfill it, that constitutes the pragmatic context.

In certain cases, even the attempt to perform an act is not enough to constitute an adequate context of action. For example, Don Quixote had the intention of fighting a duel with a giant and tried his best to fulfill that intention, but did not succeed in placing himself in the context of a duel because the giant he assualted turned out to be a windmill. I may have the intent to kill someone and take the bold step of stabbing him with a knife, but the person I stab may turn out to be not a person but a fence post. In these two cases, even the performance of an act cannot constitute the purported context of action, because the performance is not backed up with an adequate situation or appropriate conditions.

The absence of appropriate conditions can impair the constitution of a pragmatic context. For example, I am one of a huge corporation's junior executives, who have been bombarded with orders from the senior officers day after day. In order to work out my frustration, let us suppose, I walk into the office of the corporation's president and solemnly issue a series of orders to him. I have every intent to reverse the roles between us, and I make every attempt to fulfill that intent. But for all my intent and attempt, I do not succeed in constituting the pragmatic context of ordering around the president of my corporation, because of the impediment of an inadequate situation.

Intention is only one of the many constituents in the constitution of a pragmatic context. By its nature, intention can never be discovered by direct inspection. What was discovered by the activists was not the intention, but the identity of the author of *The Shortest Way*. The intention of writing a satire was imputed to this author on the basis of his identity. The imputation of intentions is generally made on what Isabel Hungerland calls "the presumption of normality."[6] When the activists assumed that *The Shortest Way* was not a satire but a sincere piece written by one of their own spokesmen, they rested this assumption on the presumption of normality. In abnormal behavior, one of their own spokesmen could have written a scathing satire on their repressive measures. When they found out the true identity of the author, and reinterpreted *The Shortest Way* as a satire rather than a sincere piece, they were still operating on the presumption of normality. In abnormal behavior, a dissenter could very well have praised and supported the activists' repressive measures. But the most important presumption of normality made in this case was the presumption that *The Shortest Way* could be accepted as a piece of satire by the normal standard of that literary genre.

The normality of performance and that of situation are inseparable in any pragmatic context; one cannot be determined without determining the other at the same time. These two normalities jointly constitute what may be called the normality of pragmatic context. It is this normality of pragmatic context that serves as the fundamental premise in our inferential knowledge of the speaker's or author's intention. This normality establishes the connection between intention and performance, which enables us to infer the nature of intention on the basis of its performance.

The normality of pragmatic context is always culture-bound. What is and what is not normal, in the performance of pragmatic acts and their situations, are determined by the conventions of culture. What is accepted as normal in one culture can be regarded as abnormal in another, and vice versa. This is as true of historical variation as of cultural variation. Even within the same cultural tradition, what was regarded as normal at one historical period may be regarded as abnormal at another period. For these reasons, the recognition of pragmatic contexts always depends on our knowledge of cultural contexts. Since we can recognize the speaker's (or author's) intention through his pragmatic context, our recognition of this intention is always dependent on our knowledge of his cultural context.

The dependence of the speaker's (or author's) intention on his cultural context is not limited to the level of recognition, but extends to the level of constitution. When an agent of action intends to do something in a certain situation, he forms his intention and assesses the situation through the conceptual system that is operative in his cultural context. That our intentions are not only formed but also expressed through our shared cultural context makes our intentions and their expressions communicable and understandable to other members of our community. If our intentions were formed in each private consciousness and expressed without any reference to our shared cultural context, we would have no way to understand each other's intentions and behaviors. The shared cultural context makes possible the interaction of the members of its community. This is why Wilhelm Dilthey called it the "context of interaction" (*Wirkungszusammenhang*).[7]

Because the cultural context is the indispensable framework for the formation, expression, and recognition of our intentions, Dilthey calls it the "objective mind" (*objektive Geist*). His notion of objective mind is neither that of a metaphysical entity like Hegel's absolute mind (*absolute Geist*), nor that of a mystical entity like the *Volkesseele* of the German historical school. It is simply a system of conventions and norms, or a cultural context, shared by the members of a community, which may range from a village or a social club to a nation or the whole world. Hence Dilthey says that his objective mind is empirically given and is subject to empirical analysis.[8] He gives the objective mind its mental label only because it is the essential constituent in the formation and expression of the individual consciousness and its intentions.

The claim that consciousness and its intentions should be conceived in the context of the objective mind expresses a contextual view of intentionality, which goes hand in hand with a contextual view of language and meaning. Consciousness is always the consciousness of meaning, whether it be of perceptual or imaginary objects, of memory or anticipation, of feeling or thinking. Moreover, these meanings are perceived and conceived through the medium of language. Hence the theory of consciousness, the theory of meaning, and the theory of language are linked into one inseparable theoretical chain.

The difference between contextual and noncontextual theories of consciousness can be made manifest by contrasting Dilthey's conception of consciousness with that of Hirsch. Hirsch says, "There is no magic land of meanings outside human consciousness."[9] By "human consciousness" he obviously means the consciousness of each individual; he is claiming this individual consciousness as the only locus for meaning, language, and intentionality. He elaborates on this noncontextual view of consciousness as follows.

> I claim that these two moments—author's meaning and interpreters' meaning—exhaust the possibilities. For I hold that meaning exists only in consciousness, not in the verbal tokens themselves. Among my critics, there may be some slipping and sliding on the point, but I have not found any of them rejecting the view that meaning exists only in consciousness, nor any of them affirming the view that it exists in the physical tokens themselves. So far as I am aware, no empirical evidence supports the existence of meaning outside consciousness, and no, to me, known linguist or philosopher of language conceives of meaning as outside consciousness. But if meaning exists only in consciousness, then it exists only in the consciousness of (1) the author of a text and (2) the interpreters of a text. I have not been able to conceive of a third possibility, and am not aware that anyone else has.[10]

Hirsch does not seem to realize that the behaviorist theory of meaning and language is a notorious attempt to establish the locus of meaning outside individual consciousness. Dilthey's theory of the objective mind is another way of establishing the locus of meaning outside individual consciousness. In spite of these theories, Hirsch's claim of the individual consciousness as the sole locus of meaning appears to be an obvious truth of common sense. Any theory that attempts to establish any other locus of meaning than the individual consciousness appears to defy this obvious truth. But this obvious truth of common sense has been challenged for a good reason; it has no way to account for the possibility of communication between two individual consciousnesses.

If meanings are tightly locked up inside the consciousness of each individual, they cannot be communicated from one consciousness to another. In the first place, the meanings in one individual consciousness may be of a totally different kind from the meanings in another consciousness. In the second place, there may be no medium of expression and communication for those meanings. The second problem is encountered when we meet foreigners with whom we do not share a common language. The first problem is encountered when we try to commune with schizoids or with members of other species of animals. In the latter case, our problem is not so much the lack of a common language as the immeasurable disparity between our meanings and theirs.

Two individual consciousnesses must devise a medium of communication and interaction before they can exchange their meanings. Of course, this presupposes that the two consciousnesses have the same kind of meanings, because the medium of communication and interaction would be of no use or help if they were to have totally different kinds of meanings. But they cannot devise the medium in a joint effort. Such a joint effort will not be possible until the public medium of communication is made available. So one of them has to devise it all by himself and explain its meaning to the other, but the former can make its meaning known to the latter only by using another medium of expression and communication, whose meaning must also be made known to the other before it can be used. Thus, the noncontextual theory of consciousness and meaning inevitably falls into an infinite regress, if it is to account for the possibility of a publicly shared medium of expression and communication. This is the same kind of infinite regress that we have seen in connection with Husserl's theory of verbal meanings.

There are only two ways to avoid the infinite regress in question: the intuition of one consciousness by another, and the intervention of an agent of mediation between the individual consciousnesses. If two individual consciousnesses can even once intuit the meanings located in each other, they have a chance to set up a common medium of expression and communication. If the privilege of intuition is available at all times, they will never need any medium of expression and communication. Even the privilege of intuition, however, cannot dispense with the requirement that the meanings located in the two individual consciousnesses be homogeneous or similar. If the meanings in the two consciousnesses are completely dissimilar, their intuition may not amount to their comprehension.

I do not know of any theory of communication that is based on the doctrine of intuition between individual consciousnesses. Ironically, the behaviorist theory of meaning alone comes close to such a theory of communication. Insofar as my meanings are manifest in my behavior, you can be said to intuit my meanings because they are available for inspection and intuition. Hence true behaviorists are as unable as are intuitionists to recognize problems of expression and communication. Both theories can be said to eliminate or evade the problems of expression and communication.

There have been many theories of communication and interaction that employ an agent of mediation between individual consciousnesses. The most notable and notorious example is Leibniz's theory of preestablished harmony, according to which God, with his infinite power of creation, assures the similarity of ideas or meanings in all individual consciousnesses, and establishes the medium of expression and communication between those consciousnesses. Bishop Berkeley advocated a similar theory of communication and interaction. Kant's theory of transcendental consciousness was a metaphysical successor to Leibniz's theory of preestablished harmony; individual consciousnesses share the same ideas and communicate with each other because all participate in the transcendental consciousness. This doctrine of transcendental ego or consciousness was formulated within the confines of human finitude, but was later expanded into the absolute or infinite consciousness by Fichte and Hegel. This doctrine has been revived by Husserl.

Contextual Mediation

I have presented these fanciful theories of communication and interaction just to show how difficult it is to account for the possibility of communication and interaction within a noncontextual theory of consciousness. These fanciful theories were proposed and advocated not because their authors had a perverse compulsion to reject obvious truths and indulge themselves in farfetched theories, but because they found it easier to accept even these theories than the unaccountable mystery of communication and interaction between individual consciousnesses. Dilthey's theory of the objective mind is another such theory. But his objective mind is presented not as a metaphysical entity but as a functional one; it is defined as a system or context of interaction, that is, a system of conventions, through which members of a community interact. Dil-

they admits as many contexts of interaction for every individual as are
required for all his various activities, e.g., his activities in his family, in
his occupation, in his political world, in his religious organization. Dilthey says that the life of every individual is woven into a cluster of
interaction contexts.[11]

The objective mind is the totality of interaction contexts in any given
community: it contains "language, custom, every kind of life-form or
life-style as much as the family, the civic society, the state and the law."[12]
"From this world of objective mind," Dilthey says, "the self receives
nourishment from its early childhood."[13] This explains how the different
members of a community come to share the same set of conventions for
their context of interaction. By being initiated and nurtured in the same
objective mind, the members of its community can think and feel, act
and react, through a common set of conventions. That is, the meanings
or intentions in their individual consciousnesses can become sharable and
communicable. The objective mind is not only the medium for the
expression and communication of intentions but also the matrix for their
formation.

In this double capacity, the objective mind is the essential medium for
understanding the life of a person from the perspective of his own intentionality, that is, to know his thoughts and feelings, his actions and
reactions as they are perceived by himself. This way of knowing is called
Verstehen (understanding); it is diametrically opposed to the behaviorist
way of knowing another person. The behaviorist totally disregards the
consciousness of a person and his intentionality, and tries to know him
only through his observable behaviors. This is an attempt to apply the
method of natural science to human beings.

Although Dilthey did not know of behaviorism, he was convinced
that the method of the natural sciences was quite inadequate for understanding human beings. Hence he made an emphatic distinction between
Naturwissenschaften and *Geistenwissenschaften*.[14] The former studies the
natural world; the latter, the human world. Nature is the domain of
brute force, which can never be truly *understood*. *Naturwissenschaften* never
understands but only *explains* (*erklären*) natural phenomena by subsuming
them under general laws. "We explain nature; we understand human
life."[15]

Dilthey conceives understanding as a part of communication.[16] Communication is a joint act of exchange between two or more persons,
which consists of the act of expression and that of understanding. One

understands what is expressed by the other. What is expressed is called an "expression" (*Ausdruck*), which may range from a facial or verbal expression to political or religious behavior. Sometimes, expressions are referred to as "life-expressions" (*Lebens-äsßerungen*) or as "experience-expressions" (*Erlebnisausdrücke*).[17] To *understand* means to know the expressions from the perspective of the mind whose inner thoughts are manifested in those expressions, or to know the life-expressions as they are lived and the experience-expressions as they are experienced. That is to know from the perspective of the inside. The distinction between inside and outside, thought and expression, obtains only with mental beings. The mindless object has neither inside nor outside.

The distinction between the inside and the outside of the mental world always involves the relation of inner thought (intention) and its external expression. In the last chapter, we considered the two possible relations between them: their disparity, and their parity or identity. By assuming disparity between thought (its particularity) and language (its generality), Schleiermacher was forced to advocate the method of divination, the dubious method of divining the particularity of inner thoughts presumably hidden behind the generality of verbal expressions. His doctrine of divination has been charged with psychologism; he has been criticized for advocating the unscientific method of probing the psychological process in an author's mind.

In accepting the distinction between inner and outer, Dilthey does everything to avoid the trap of psychologism: "We must now determine what the inner (*Innere*) is. It is a common error to identify our knowledge of this inner side with the psychical course of life, namely, psychology."[18] He tries to overcome this common error by his doctrine of objectification, that is, inner thoughts are objectified in the medium of expression such as books and buildings, poems and paintings, laws and customs.[19] This doctrine of objectification is meant to be a rejection of Schleiermacher's dualistic conception of the expression and its content. Dilthey advocates a monistic conception: the expression and its content are not two but one.[20]

The basic level of understanding involves the simplest units of expression, which are called the elementary forms of understanding. On that level, Dilthey claims the immediate unity of the expression and what is expressed: "The way in which the two, e.g., the countenance and the terror, are not two distinct things but one (*Einheit*), is based on this fundamental relation between expression and its mental content."[21] Because the expression and its content are one and the same thing, he says, the latter cannot be known from the former through causal inference. For causal inference is admissible only for knowing the relation between two distinct entities which can be related as cause and effect.

Dilthey says that the elementary forms of understanding are like the letters of the alphabet; their combination produces the higher forms of understanding.[22] The function of these higher forms is to recognize the combination of elementary expressions in the entire context of life (das Ganze des Lebenszusammenhangs).[23] Unlike the elementary expressions, the contexts of life or action are not given but must be constructed except for the contexts of our own life or action. Consequently, to know the mental world of another person or culture involves the process of constructing a whole from parts rather than the process of inferring the inner from the outer.

Dilthey calls this method of constructing a whole from parts an inductive method. But it is not the method of simple induction that abstracts a general feature from a series of particular instances. It is the kind of inductive method that Kepler used in discovering the elliptical orbit of Mars. Scientific data for this discovery were the elaborate observations that Tycho Brahe had made of the planet. Kepler knew that those data failed to fit into not only Ptolemy's geocentric model, but also Copernicus' heliocentric one. He also knew that they did not make any better fit with Tycho's own hybrid model, according to which the planets are assumed to revolve around the sun while the sun is assumed to revolve around the earth. So Kepler had to construct his own model of Mars's elliptical orbit as the only hypothesis that could render a coherent account of Tycho's observations.[24]

Dilthey's method of inductive construction turns out to be only one phase in the circular process of understanding: the expressions can be understood only in the context of interaction to be constructed; but it can be constructed only on the basis of the expressions. Dilthey illustrates this circular process with the example of understanding a sentence: the meaning of a sentence can be understood by understanding the meaning of its component words and their combination, but the meanings of these words can, in turn, be understood by understanding the meaning of the sentence.[25] Dilthey calls this process the interaction between the whole and its parts in understanding. It has been known as the hermeneutic circle of the whole and parts: that is, the whole can be understood only through the understanding of its parts, but the parts can be understood only through the understanding of their whole.

Perhaps we should note that Dilthey's hermeneutic circle is his hermeneutic version of what has been known as the coherence theory of knowledge. This theory of knowledge has been proposed in opposition to the traditional conception of knowledge, the correspondence theory. The latter theory claims that what is known corresponds to what is the case, and that their correspondence can be established by observation. But this theory is applicable only to the things we can know through direct observation and inspection, but not to the things we come to know through inference or any other indirect method. For example, when I know by observation that it is cloudy, I know not only that it is cloudy but also that this corresponds to observable weather conditions. But when Kepler discovers that the orbit of Mars is an ellipse, he cannot establish by observation the correspondence of his theory with reality. Instead of observable correspondences, he must rely on the coherence of his theory with the observed data.

Coherence, however, is a reciprocal relation: a theory can be said to cohere with data, and data can be said to cohere with a theory. It is this reciprocal relation that makes the epistemological process involved a circular one. That is, a theory is constructed on the basis of data; data are explained within the framework of the theory.

It now remains for us to consider how Dilthey's method of inductive construction applies to the interpretation of *The Shortest Way*. We can begin with two different ways to express speech intentions: overt or covert. Overt expressions generally present no serious problems of interpretation. There is no real need to interpret them; they are simply understood. Such a direct understanding is impossible for covert expressions because the identity of their intended and expressed meanings is given only covertly.

P. F. Strawson gives two examples of covert expression: showing off and insinuating.[26] When I show off, I had better not overtly display my intention to do it, because such an overt display would have an adverse effect on my audience. When I want to insinuate something, I must also avoid an explicit exposure of my intention, because such an overt exposure is incompatible with the notion of insinuation. These covert expressions can generate contextual indeterminacy because they can be placed in more than one pragmatic context.

The Shortest Way was initially taken by the activists for an overt expression. On the discovery of the identity of its author, they recognized their mistake, and reclassified Defoe's work as a covert piece. By this reclassification, they could place it in the pragmatic context of satire, and thereby establish a coherence between Defoe's stand against the Church of England and his action as the author of *The Shortest Way*. The reinterpretation of his work was dictated by the principle of contextual coherence.

This should not give the impression that contextual operation is required only for the interpretation of covert expressions. By definition, overt expressions should be intelligible in and of themselves; their interpretation should require no contextual reference. But the judgment of whether an expression is overt or covert cannot be made on the basis of expression alone. It is a contextual judgment. Hence the understanding of even overt expressions ultimately involves contextual mediation.

CHAPTER FOUR
Semantics and Pragmatics

NOW that we have considered the problem of verbal meaning on semantic and pragmatic levels, we can see that the notion of using language in textual interpretation is an ambiguous one. This ambiguity is already contained in Schleiermacher's notion of the philological stage of his hermeneutics, for this stage can be construed as containing only the semantic level or both the semantic and the pragmatic ones. Dilthey resolves this ambiguity by situating his hermeneutics clearly on the pragmatic level.

To be sure, Dilthey gives no distinctly linguistic label to his notion of context; his context of interaction is called neither linguistic nor philological. But the notion of interaction context is inseparable from the use of language, because every context of action is constituted by the use of language. The use of language is not limited to our verbal utterances; its most fundamental use is to constitute our world, the context of our life and interaction. Hans-Georg Gadamer has tried to capture this pervasive use of language in the constitution of action context by stressing the linguistic character (*Sprachlichkeit*) of every interpretive context.[1]

The old notion of using language as a hermeneutic instrument is quite different from the relatively new notion of using the science of language as such an instrument. But this relatively new notion also harbors an ambiguity, because the scientific enterprise of investigating language can be conducted on two different levels, the semantic and the pragmatic. The science of language limited to semantic issues is semantics; it becomes pragmatics when it is extended to pragmatic issues. Hence the notion of using linguistics in hermeneutics can mean the notion of using semantics or pragmatics in it. But these two linguistic sciences can have quite different hermeneutic efficacies. As a preliminary to exploring their respective hermeneutic efficacies, let us consider some fundamental differences between semantics and pragmatics, especially their relations to syntax and phonology.

Semantics generally presupposes syntax and phonology. The meaning of a sentence, a clause, or a phrase cannot be determined without considering its word order. Likewise, the phonological values of a word or a sentence are equally essential for determining its meaning. Syntax and phonology are also presupposed in pragmatics, because the phonological values of words and their syntactic relations are indispensable for their use. For these reasons, syntax and phonology can be regarded as integral components of semantics and pragmatics.

Although both syntax and phonology are presupposed by semantics and pragmatics, they make different contributions. Let us consider the syntax of the sentence, "Lions eat rabbits." By changing its word order, we can produce another sentence, "Rabbits eat lions," which has a different meaning. By changing the syntax of the original sentence, we can also produce a sentence, "Lions rabbits eat," which has no meaning. These syntactic elements perform semantic functions, insofar as they control the meaning of those sentences.

Now consider the following two sentences, "A mighty fortress is our God" and "Our God is a mighty fortress." They have different syntaxes, that is, different word orders. But their syntactic difference performs no semantic function; the two sentences are semantically identical. By virtue of their different syntaxes, the two sentences can have different effect. Since the effect is the effect of their use, their syntactic difference belongs to their pragmatic functions.

The syntactic inquiry on the semantic level is limited to those grammatical problems that function as the essential determinants of semantic content. Hence it has been called "semantic syntax."[2] By contrast, the syntactic inquiry on the pragmatic level has to take into account the special problems of grammatical order that arise in various pragmatic contexts. Although the expression "pragmatic syntax" has not been used, this label can accurately designate the syntactic inquiry on the pragmatic level.

Some may object to the assertion that the syntax of "Our God is a mighty fortress" is different from that of "A mighty fortress is our God." In both sentences, the same phrase "our God" is the subject, the same verb "is" is the predicate, and the same phrase "a mighty fortress" is the complement of the verb. This is a semantic account of their syntaxes. This semantic account disregards the sequence of their subjects and predicates, which has pragmatic effect. Hence the objection can be met by using the distinction between semantic and pragmatic syntax. The two sentences have the same semantic syntax, but different pragmatic syntaxes.

The notion of pragmatic syntax is essential to understanding Stanley Fish's "affective stylistics."[3] He maintains that the order of sequence is central in determining the affective tone of our reading experience. Consider one of his favorite examples: "That Judas perished by hanging himself, there is no certainty in Scripture: though in one place it seems to affirm it, and by a doubtful word hath given occasion to translate it; yet in another place, in a more punctual description, it maketh it improbable, and seems to overthrow it." This involved sentence is from Thomas Browne's *Religio medici*. This sentence can be rewritten by changing the sequential order of its first two clauses: "There is no certainty in Scripture that Judas perished by hanging himself. . . ." Although these two sentences do not differ in syntax and semantics, Fish holds, they deliver two different reading experiences.

While the semantic identity of the two sentences is obvious, their syntactic identity is disputable. The second sentence is produced by changing the word order of the first sentence, and any change in word order is a change in syntax. Hence the two sentences must be different in syntax. But this syntactic change does not affect the semantic content of the original sentence; every word in the two sentences performs the same semantic function. Hence the two sentences can be said to have the same semantic syntax. But this does not alter the fact that the two sentences have different pragmatic syntaxes. It is these different pragmatic syntaxes that deliver two different reading experiences.

The original sentence begins with "That Judas perished by hanging himself," which is generally accepted as one of the emphatic certainties or biblically attested truths in all Christendom, and then runs into its denial. This sequence of experiencing first an assured certainty and then its denial is reversed in the other sentence, in which the announcement of denial precedes the presumed certainty itself. This difference in the order of sequence surely makes an important difference in our reading experience.

The impact or effect of talking or writing can be distinguished from its content. The former belongs to pragmatics; the latter, to semantics. In the distinction between what is to be said and how to say it, the former is a semantic question, while the latter is a pragmatic question.

The manner of talking or writing—how to say something—belongs to pragmatics, because the same semantic content can be given different powers or efficacies. For example, a poem and its paraphrase are semantically identical but pragmatically different.

Stylistics in general is concerned with the affective tone of the reading experience; as such, it belongs to pragmatics. Moreover, the pragmatic effect of talking and writing is often controlled by the order of sequence. Insofar as this order of sequence is determined by syntax, it belongs to the province of pragmatic syntax. By using the distinction between semantic and pragmatic syntax, Fish's thesis can be stated as follows: Although the semantic syntaxes of the two sentences are identical, their pragmatic syntaxes are different. This is just another way of saying that the two sentences are semantically identical but have different pragmatic effects because of their difference in pragmatic syntax.

Like syntax, phonology can also operate on semantic and pragmatic levels. The phonological values of a word, a phrase, or a sentence are obviously essential in determining its semantic identity. But they also perform pragmatic functions. In uttering such a simple sentence as "The cat is on the mat," for example, we can change the point of emphasis by changing its intonation. The point of emphasis belongs to pragmatics. The phonology that concerns pragmatic functions may be called pragmatic phonology, in distinction from semantic phonology, which is concerned with semantic functions. Prosody is a special branch of pragmatic phonology.

Semantic phonology is the foundation for pragmatic phonology; the former is presupposed for the operation of the latter. This is also true of the relation between semantic and pragmatic syntax. Without knowing the semantic syntax of the sentence "A mighty fortress is our God," it is impossible to recognize the effect of its pragmatic syntax. The presupposition of semantic syntax and phonology by pragmatic syntax and phonology is dictated by the fact that semantics is always presupposed by pragmatics. For the meaning of an expression is an indispensable condition for its use. Hence pragmatics is the most comprehensive science of language.

A pragmatic study of a language is so comprehensive that it practically requires the understanding of a whole culture. As we have seen, to understand the semantic context of a language is to understand its cultural context to the extent that the beliefs and values embodied in its semantic context constitute its cultural matrix. In addition to this matrix of beliefs and values, a culture as a concrete system of living includes the ways of acting and reacting on those beliefs and values. The pragmatic understanding of a language involves the understanding of those ways of acting and reacting. For example, to understand the language of banking on the pragmatic level is to understand the system of banking in which the language of banking is used. Likewise, to study the language of chess is to study the game of chess; to study the language of jokes and jests is to study the nature of those activities. This pragmatic conception of language is expressed in Wittgenstein's remark: "And to imagine a language means to imagine a form of life."[4]

Whereas the pragmatic study of language is comprehensive and concrete, its semantic study is relatively selective and abstract. It abstracts the signification function of language from the various contexts of its use. For this reason, semantics is much more amenable to generalization and systematization. In science, the level of abstraction dictates the level of generalization and systematization. Physics has become a far more general and systematic science than biology, because the former studies natural phenomena on a far more abstract level than the latter.

The generality of scientific concepts and propositions and their systematic unity are two standard criteria for determining the quality of a science. By these standards, semantics has fared far better as a scientific enterprise than has pragmatics. Linguistics has often been praised as the eminently successful attempt to elevate human studies to the truly scientific level. The target of this praise is not pragmatics but semantics, with its attendant syntax and phonology. Pragmatics still remains as informal and as unsystematic as most other social sciences.

The formality of semantics and the informality of pragmatics are already manifest in Aristotle's works in linguistics. His logical works can be classified as semantic treatises, because they are addressed to the semantic problem of linguistic meaning. His *Categoriae* deals with the questions concerning the meaning of categorial terms such as "substance," "attribute," and "relation." His *De interpretatione* deals with questions concerning the meaning-relation of different types of propositions such as affirmative and negative, universal and particular. The universal proposition "All Cretans are liars" implies the particular proposition "Some Cretans are liars" and the denial of the negative propositions "Some Cretans are not liars" and "No Cretans are liars." When one proposition implies another, their implication relation is their meaning-relation. The syllogistic rules are rules governing the meaning-relations of the premises and the conclusions, and the questions concerning these rules are treated in *Analytica priora* and *Analytica posteriora*.

Aristotle's logical works do not belong to what Rudolf Carnap calls descriptive semantics, which is an empirical discipline.[5] They are not concerned with the empirical question of how to discover the meaning each word has in any given language. This empirical question is usually handled by philologists and lexicologists. Aristotle's logical works belong to pure semantics; they are concerned with the universal rules governing the operation of semantic entities. The purity of pure semantics is obtained by abstracting the semantic study totally from the empirical content of semantic operations. This abstraction gives pure semantics an impressive degree of rigor and precision, and generality and systematic unity.

The same sense of rigor and precision, and generality and systematic unity cannot be found in Aristotle's works in pragmatics. Two of his works can be classified as treaties in pragmatics: his *Rhetorica* and his *De poetica*. The former investigates the use of language in persuasion; the latter, its use in poetry. The rules governing the use of language in persuasion and poetry are much more vague and complex than the rules governing the logical relations of semantic entities. Moreover, the former rules have a much more limited scope of application than the latter. The rules governing the use of language in persuasion may not apply to its use in poetry. But the logical rules of pure semantics apply to all pragmatic contexts. For example, the semantic validity of a syllogism remains the same whether the syllogism be used in poetry or persuasion, although it may have different pragmatic effect.

The formality of semantics and the informality of pragmatics have continued to be manifest down to the present day. What has emerged in our century as philosophy of language or linguistic philosophy has gone through two stages of development. During the first half of this century, its orientation was chiefly semantic. Only during the second half has linguistic philosophy made the pragmatic ascent. The speech-act theory is the salient product of this ascent, and it is a series of informal investigations of rules governing the use of language in various pragmatic contexts, such as making a promise or christening a ship.[6] The informal character of speech-act theory is in glaring contrast with the formal and the systematic character of linguistic philosophy in its semantic stage, as demonstrated in the works of Russell, Tarski, and Carnap.[7]

In the tradition of structural linguistics, the difference between semantics and pragmatics has been demonstrated in a different manner. It begins with Saussure's distinction between *langue* and *parole*.[8] This distinction is proposed to articulate two different ways to conceive language. A language can be viewed either as a system of linguistic rules and conventions, or as a collection of linguistic performances. One is to view the language as *langue,* and the other is to view it as *parole.* The relation of *langue* to *parole* is then explained by analogy to the relation of a symphony to its performance; the identity of a symphony is maintained throughout its different performances. Their relation is the relation of a type to its tokens, a universal to its instances.

These two views of language, Saussure holds, can generate two different approaches to the scientific study of language. One can lead to the science of *langue,* and the other to the science of *parole.* But these two approaches are not equally profitable. Since *parole* is only "the sum of particular acts," Saussure maintains, it cannot be studied scientifically.[9] But *langue* is the most suitable object for scientific analysis because it is "a self-contained whole and a principle of classification."[10] Of these two scientific approaches to the study of language, he concludes, "We must choose between two routes that cannot be followed simultaneously."[11] So he chooses the science of *langue* as "linguistics proper," and resolutely excludes the science of *parole* from his own investigation of language.

Saussure's view that the scientific study of language can be pursued either as the science of *langue* or as that of *parole* reflects his mistaken understanding of the relation of type to token and universal to particular in scientific inquiries. If he were to extend this view to natural science, he would have to say that there are two approaches to the scientific study of nature: the study of nature as a collection of natural phenomena and its study as a system of natural laws governing those phenomena. The former cannot be studied scientifically, and the latter alone can be the true object of natural science proper. That would surely be an absurd way to characterize natural science.

The two features of nature, its universality and its particularity, are inseparable in the scientific investigation of its phenomena. No doubt natural phenomena can be studied for the understanding of their particularity, but such a study has nothing to do with natural science. The study of particular phenomena can take on scientific significance only when it is used for the discovery and recognition of universals. Likewise it is impossible to make those universals the direct objects of scientific investigations. Since they have no independent existence, they can only be observed in and inferred from the domain of particular phenomena. Hence the study of universals and that of particulars are two sides of one and the same scientific procedure. For the same reason, there cannot be two scientific routes to the study of language. The science of *langue* and the science of *parole* are not two sciences but two inseparable features of one linguistics.[12]

The proper way to characterize the relation of *langue* and *parole* in linguistics is to regard *parole* as the empirical data for the articulation of *langue* as a system of conventions. Linguistics can be called the science of *langue* insofar as *langue* constitutes its scientific universals, while it can also be called the science of *parole* insofar as *parole* constitutes its scientific data. This is to regard the distinction between the science of *langue* and the science of *parole* as no more than perspectival; the same science of linguistics is being characterized from two different perspectives.

Even this perspectival distinction harbors one serious ambiguity; it can be accepted on either the semantic or the pragmatic level. As Saussure says, *langue* is language understood as a system of conventions. But every language can be regarded as a system of either semantic or pragmatic conventions. Hence the science of *langue* can be the study of either semantic or pragmatic conventions; it can be either semantics or pragmatics. The same ambiguity arises in the study of *parole*; it can be studied to provide empirical data for the articulation of either a semantic or a pragmatic system. Most likely, Saussure was not aware of this ambiguity because his central concern was always semantic.

There is no indication that Saussure even recognized the pragmatic dimension of language. All his linguistic concerns seem to be limited to the semantic level. His semantic conception of language is manifest in his description of *langue* as "a system of distinct signs corresponding to distinct ideas."[13] The relation of a sign to its idea is the semantic relation of a sign to its meaning. The same semantic conception of *langue* is operative in his characterization of *langue* as "a principle of classifications."[14] A semantic system is always a system of classification. The semantic relation of a sign to its objects can group those objects into a class and keep it apart from other classes designated by other signs.

This semantic bias in Saussure's conception of *langue* has leant a decidedly semantic orientation to the development of structural linguistics. Structural phonology, which has been the most eminent branch of structural linguistics, has been confined to the semantic level.[15] It has not dealt with the pragmatic issues of phonology. The structural study of semantics has also been attempted in the name of structural semantics.[16] The application of the structuralist approach to syntax has been conspicuously slow; Noam Chomsky's theory of deep structure (via Zellig Harris' works in syntax) may now be regarded as the result of its eventual application.[17] Chomsky's distinction between deep and surface structures is clearly made within the semantic level. Thus the development of structural linguistics as a whole has shown little interest in making the pragmatic ascent.

This confinement of linguistics within the boundary of semantics can produce no serious problems as long as the linguists are content with semantic inquiries. But they can precipitate a methodological crisis if they become involved in pragmatic issues, because their semantically confined linguistics is inadequate for handling pragmatic issues. Such a methodological crisis has been experienced by some progenies of structural linguistics in their eager attempts to demonstrate the efficacy of their science for pragmatic tasks.

Narrative Structures

A. J. Greimas tries to derive narrative categories by using the central principle of his structural semantics: all semantic terms are ordered in binary oppositions, for example, male vs. female, day vs. night, love vs. hate. By using this semantic principle, he divides the agents (*actants*) of stories into three binary pairs: Subject vs. Object, Sender (*Destinateur*) vs. Receiver (*Destinataire*), Helper (*Adjuvant*) vs. Opponent (*Opposant*).[18] According to him, these three pairs constitute three basic schemata of various narrative structures. For example, Wolfram von Eschenbach's story of Parsifal has a narrative structure that can be analyzed in terms of the Subject vs. Object schema: Parsifal is the Subject and the Holy Grail is the Object of quest. Since the narrative categories of Subject and Object can be derived from the syntactic categories of the subject of a sentence and the object of its verb, Greimas maintains, all narrative categories can be derived from syntactic ones, and all narrative structures can be accounted for by using those syntactically derived narrative categories.

This derivation claim involves some terminological ambiguity. The words "subject" and "object" can be used not only as syntactic but also as semantic terms. As syntactic terms, they describe the syntactic relation of words in a sentence. As semantic terms, they describe the semantic relation of words to their objects. In the sentence "Lions eat rabbits," the word "lions" is the syntactic subject, "eat" is its verb, and "rabbits" is the object of the verb. This is a syntactic account. In the same sentence, the word "lions" is the subject of an action, "eat" is an action verb, and "rabbits" is the object of an action verb. This is a semantic account.

In some cases, syntactic and semantic subjects may coincide, but this coincidence does not always obtain. Let us now rewrite the sentence "Lions eat rabbits" as "Rabbits are eaten by lions." The word "rabbits" has become the subject term of the new sentence, but not its semantic subject. On the semantic level, "rabbits" still remains the object of action. The semantic subject of the new sentence is the same as that of the original sentence, that is, "lions."[19] Syntactic categories are semantically neutral; a syntactic subject can designate not only a semantic subject but also a semantic object. For this reason, it is impossible to derive semantic categories from syntactic ones. Greimas' derivation claim gains a deceptive appearance of plausibility only from the terminological ambiguity of "subject" and "object."

Perhaps there is no need to take seriously Greimas' claim that his narrative categories of Subject and Object are derived from syntax. Since his intent is to construct a theory of narrative structure on the basis of structural semantics, it may be best to ignore all syntactic considerations insofar as they are irrelevant to semantic issues. We can simply accept Subject and Object as semantic categories established by structural semantics and then determine whether or not narrative categories can be derived from semantics.

As semantic categories, however, Subject and Object are again different from Subject and Object as narrative categories. By the Subject of a story, Greimas means its hero; this is a far richer notion than the notion of a semantic subject. Any agent of action can be called a semantic subject, if it is presented as the subject of an action verb in any sentence. The agent does not have to be a human being; even rabbits and lions can fulfill this semantic role. Whether a given agent (*actant*) should be regarded as the hero of a story or as a subsidiary character such as Helper or Opponent cannot be determined by semantic considerations alone, which are limted to the semantic character of each sentence.

Whereas sentences are semantic entities, stories are pragmatic ones. The composition of a story requires the use of sentences. Hence the role of an agent in a story is not a semantic but a pragmatic issue, which cannot be determined by semantic considerations alone.

The only thing that can be guaranteed by structural semantics is that the principle of binary opposition governs the semantic relations of narrative categories; for example, the meaning of Helper is opposed to that of Opponent, and that of Sender to that of Receiver. But this semantic relation is not limited to the words that are used as narrative categories. The same principle of binary opposition governs the meaning of any other words, for example, "saint" and "sinner," "good" and "evil," "hot" and "cold," "strong" and "weak," "here" and "there." Which of these countless words can function as narrative categories cannot be decided by semantic considerations. It can be decided only by considering the pragmatic roles they play in the constitution of a story.

Julia Kristeva has undertaken a far more ambitious project than Greimas. Greimas never showed the exhaustiveness of his narrative categories or of all the possible narrative schemata that can be derived from those categories. Hence his derivation attempt is more or less informal. Kristeva's ambition is to avoid this sort of unscientific informality and to achieve a systematic finality for her derivation. For this purpose, she uses the syntactic structure of a canonical (normal) sentence as the basis for her derivation of all possible narrative structures. She operates on the premise that all the possible narrative structures are implicitly contained in the various syntactic structures of a canonical sentence. The table of her derivation is given in figure 4.1.[20]

The diagram at the top of this table represents the grammatical structure of a normal sentence. The two long lines that join at the bottom of the diagram indicate the two major segments of a sentence, the subject and the predicate. The subject is indicated by the diagonal line on the left side, and the predicate by the diagonal line on the right side. These two segments of a sentence contain two linguistic elements, the *actant* and the *adjoncteur,* which may be translated as the agent and adjunctor. In the sentence "Odysseus was shrewd," for example, "Odysseus" is the agent and "was shrewd" is the adjunctor. However, the adjunctor can be used in two different ways, the predicative and the qualificative. In this sentence, it is used in its predicative mode. In the sentence "The shrewd Odysseus helped conquer Troy," it is used in its qualificative mode. The predicate adjunctor is symbolized as A^p; the qualificative adjunctor as A^q. The *actant* or agent is symbolized as Act (N), because it is generally represented by a noun or its equivalent.

In both its predicative and its qualificative mode, the adjunctor can be modified by adverbs; for example, "Odysseus was shrewd during the Trojan War" has the modifier "during the Trojan War." The modifier

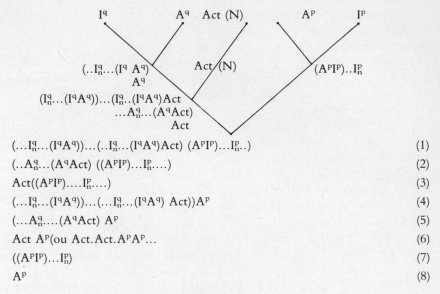

$$(...I_n^q...(I^qA^q))...(..I_n^q...(I^qA^q)Act)\ (A^PI^P)...I_n^P..) \tag{1}$$

$$(..A_n^q...(A^qAct)\ ((A^PI^P)...I_n^P....) \tag{2}$$

$$Act((A^PI^P)....I_n^P....) \tag{3}$$

$$(...I_n^q...(I^qA^q))...(...I_n^q...(I^qA^q)\ Act))A^P \tag{4}$$

$$(...A_n^q....(A^qAct)\ A^P \tag{5}$$

$$Act\ A^P(ou\ Act.Act.A^PA^P... \tag{6}$$

$$((A^PI^P)...I_n^P) \tag{7}$$

$$A^P \tag{8}$$

Figure 4.1

is called an "identificator." When the identificator operates on a predicative adjunctor, it is symbolized as I^P. When it operates on a qualificative adjunctor, it is symbolized as I^q. In the sentence "Odysseus, who was shrewd during the Trojan War, finally returned to Ithaca," the modifier "during the Trojan War" is a qualificative identificator that operates on the qualificative adjunctor "was shrewd." Altogether, according to Kristeva, five syntactic elements can explain the constitution of any canonical sentence: I^q (the qualificative identificator), A^q (the qualificative adjunctor), Act (N) (the agent or subject of the sentence), A^P (the predicative adjunctor), and I^P (the predicative identificator).

By using these five elements, we can tabulate the various grammatical forms that can be assumed by the subject and the predicate of a sentence. The subject can take the following three forms: (1) $(... I_n^q ... (I^qA^q))$ ... $(... I_n^q ... (I^qA^q)\ Act)$, (2) $(... A_n^q ... (A^q\ Act))$, and (3) (Act). For the sake of brevity, let us represent these three forms as S_1, S_2, and S_3. S_1 indicates the subject of a sentence that has qualificative adjunctors and their identificators or modifiers. The subscript n in $(... I_n^q ... (I^qA^q))$ means that it can be repeated any number of times, that is, the qualificative adjunctor can be joined to any number of qualificative identificators. S_2 indicates the subject of a sentence accompanied by any number of qualificative adjunctors, which are not modified by any identificators. S_3 indicates the subject of a sentence that has neither qualificative adjunctors nor their identificators.

The predicate can take the following two forms: (1) $((A^P I^P) \ldots I_n^P)$, and (2) (A^P). These two forms will be designated as P_1 and P_2. P_1 represents a predicate that is composed of any number of predicative adjunctors and their identificators. P_2 represents a predicate that has only one predicative adjunctor and no predicative identificator.

By combining these three subject forms and two predicate forms, Kristeva generates her eight types of narrative structure. The first three of these eight types are produced by combining S_1, S_2, and S_3 separately with P_1; the second three are produced by combining S_1, S_2, and S_3 again separately with P_2. The last two types are produced by using only either P_1 or P_2. Kristeva's eight types of narrative structure can be represented by the following formulas.

$$\text{Type 1} = S_1 \cdot P_1; \quad \text{Type 2} = S_2 \cdot P_1; \quad \text{Type 3} = S_3 \cdot P_1;$$
$$\text{Type 4} = S_1 \cdot P_2; \quad \text{Type 5} = S_2 \cdot P_2; \quad \text{Type 6} = S_3 \cdot P_2$$
$$\text{Type 7} = P_1; \quad \text{Type 8} = P_2$$

These eight types are explained as follows.[21]

Type 1 is the complete type of construction, which can be found in *Jehan de Saintré*. It consists of a series of qualifications (S_1) and a succession of exploits (P_1), each of these qualifications and exploits being chronologically, spatially, and modally defined.

Type 2 is the narrative structure in which the qualifications of the agent are not chronologically, spatially, or modally defined (that is, there is no identificator), but are given as immanent (S_2). This type is the same as Type 1 in having a series of agent's exploits (P_1). The difference between Type 1 and 2 lies in the manner of providing the qualifications or characterizations of the actant. They are given explicitly in Type 1, and implicitly in Type 2.

Type 3 has neither the explicit (as in Type 1) nor the implicit (as in Type 2) qualifications of the agent. It opens the story by narrating the exploits themselves (P_1), which is the common feature it shares with Type 1 and 2.

These three types of narrative structure correspond to the following three sentence structures.

1. Odysseus, who was shrewd and brave in destroying Troy, survived many trials and returned to Ithaca ten years after the Trojan War.

2. The shrewd and brave Odysseus survived many trials and returned to Ithaca ten years after the Trojan War.

3. Odysseus survived many trials and returned to Ithaca ten years after the Trojan War.

Kristeva is deriving the notion of agent from the notion of grammatical subject, the qualifications or characterizations of the agent from the qualifiers of a grammatical subject, and the exploits of the agent from predicates or predicative adjunctors. Her method of derivation is fundamentally the same as Greimas'; it is to derive narrative categories from syntactic ones. This derivation is scientifically illegitimate, because syntactic categories are narratively neutral as much as they are semantically neutral. For example, the subject of a sentence can be used in designating not only an agent, but also his action, his exploit, his goal, his sentiment, and many other things. As far as the description of his action or exploit is concerned, it requires a whole sentence or a series of sentences rather than a predicative adjunctor.

As Kristeva points out, Types 4 and 5 correspond to Types 1 and 2.

Type 4 consists of two parts: (1) a series of qualifications, which are chronologically, spatially, or modally defined (S_1); and (2) a single, unique trial (P_2), which ends the story.

Type 5 is the same as Type 4, but the qualifications of the agent are given implicitly as in Type 2 rather than explicitly as in Types 1 and 4.

These two types employ the same modes of qualifications or characterizations of the agent as Types 1 and 2 respectively, but the former differ from the latter in the manner of presenting the agent's exploits. Whereas Types 1 and 2 recount a series of chronologically, spatially, or modally defined exploits, Types 4 and 5 present only one unique exploit or trial. How can this difference be explained in Kristeva's derivation schema?

In her schema, the narrative category of trials and exploits is derived from the syntactic category of predicative adjunctors. Now the predicative adjunctors can appear in a sentence with or without modifiers; they can also appear singly or jointly. By combining these two modes of their appearance, we can produce four modes of combinations: (1) one predicative adjunctor with modifiers, (2) one predicative adjunctor without modifiers, (3) a series of predicative adjunctors with modifiers, and (4) a series of predicative adjunctors without modifiers. Kristeva has used mode (3) in deriving her Narrative Types 1, 2, and 3, and mode (2) in deriving her Narrative Types 4 and 5. She has evidently overlooked or ignored modes (1) and (4). She may have assumed that the predicative adjunctors cannot have any modifiers when they appear singly, and that they cannot avoid having modifiers when they appear jointly in a sentence. On this assumption, modes (1) and (4) become vacuous; but this assumption cannot be justified on syntactic grounds.

The omission of (1) and (4) from her table of derivation makes her table incomplete and unsystematic, or rather quite arbitrary. To make the matters still worse, even these four combinations do not exhaust all the possible modes in which predicative adjunctors can appear in a sentence. In modes (3) and (4) I assumed that, when more than one predicative adjunctor appear jointly in a sentence, either all or none of them have modifiers. This assumption rules out mode (5), which has the mixture of modified and unmodified predicative adjunctors. Since this mode can produce another form of a canonical sentence, to ignore it is to ignore another possible narrative type.

According to Kristeva's derivation table, Type 6 should correspond to Type 3 in the way Types 4 and 5 correspond to Types 1 and 2. Type 6 should be the same as Type 3 in having no qualifications of the agent, but they should differ in the narrative segment of trials and exploits. Whereas Type 3 has a series of defined trials and exploits $((A^P I^P) \ldots I^P_n \ldots)$, Type 6 should have only one undefined trial or exploit (A^P). But this expectation is thwarted by Kristeva's definition of Type 6.

Type 6 has the anecdotal narrative construction that presents one or more agents juxtaposed in the course of undergoing their trials.

Two items of this definition require explanation: how the notion of the anecdotal narrative construction has been derived from the syntactic structure of a canonical sentence; and how the notion of the plurality of agents has been derived from that syntactic structure. The introduction of these two narrative categories in Type 6 is an act of fiat. These two categories could also have been used in Types 1 through 5; to limit their use to Type 6 is another act of fiat.

Types 7 and 8 are derived from the sentential forms that have no subject, only a predicate. Since the category of agent is derived from the syntactic category of subject, these two narrative types can have no agent.

Type 7 is a narrative of a series of events (trials and exploits), which are not undertaken by any agents, or whose agents remain anonymous.

Type 8 is used for the exposition of maxims, or moral and philosophical propositions. Common examples of this type are ancient literary writings, such as the *Taote Ching*.

In Type 8, Kristeva no longer talks of exploits and trials. In all other types, she has claimed to derive the narrative category of exploits and trials from the syntactic category of predicative adjunctor. In Type 8, she is using the same category to derive moral maxims and philosophical propositions. This unexplained shift from exploits and trials to moral maxims and philosophical propositions is another act of Kristevian fiat.

Kristeva does not explain why moral maxims and philosophical propositions can be derived from the sentential structure with no subject. To be sure, some moral maxims can be expressed in the form of a subjectless sentence, for example, "Be true to yourself." But this grammatical fact cannot justify her derivation, because many other kinds of utterances, such as commands and requests, can also be expressed in the same form, and because many moral maxims are not expressed in that form. As a matter of fact, most moral maxims and philosophical propositions of the *Taote Ching* are stated in the normal form of the subject–predicate sentence.

In Type 7, Kristeva derives the narrative category of events from the syntactic category of predicative adjunctor. This derivation seems to be based on the assumption that trials and exploits can be regarded as events when their agents remain anonymous. However, the category of event is far more extensive than the category of trial or exploit; the former can include not only trials and exploits but also disasters, sufferings, exchanges, expeditions, or any other occurrences in human history. The category of event is one of the most universal categories. If it can be derived from the syntactic category of predicative adjunctor, there exists no category of historical and natural occurrence that cannot be so derived.

What, then, is the justification for deriving the narrative category of event from the syntactic category of predicative adjunctor? Kristeva may say that the description of events requires the use of predicative adjunctors. If this is a good enough reason for this derivation, then the narrative category of event can also be derived from the syntactic category of subject. For the description of events requires the use of subject as much as of predicate. In fact, an event is usually referred to by a noun phrase, which can either serve as the subject of a sentence ("The discovery of America was made by the Vikings") or function as a part of its predicate ("Their achievement was the discovery of America"). The syntactic categories of subject and predicate are equally indispensable for the description of an event, but their indispensability cannot justify the derivation of the category of event from any syntactic categories.

Throughout her derivation of narrative types, Kristeva assumes that the subject of a sentence precedes its predicate in a canonical sentence. Although this syntactic rule holds in most Indo-European languages, it does not always hold in other languages. In some languages, such as classical Hebrew and classical Arabic, the predicate verb of a sentence generally precedes its subject. If Kristeva were to use the syntactic structure of these languages for the derivation of her narrative types, she would have to revise them systematically. For example, Types 1 and 4 should read as Types 1' and 4'.

Type 1' is a complete type of construction. It consists of two segments. The first segment is a series of exploits, each of which is chronologically, spatially, or modally defined. The first segment is followed by the second segment, a series of qualifications or characterizations of the agent, each of which is also chronologically, spatially, or modally defined.

Type 4' also consists of two segments. The first segment, which opens the story, presents a single, unique trial. This is followed by the second segment, a series of the agent's qualifications or characterizations, each of which is chronologically, spatially, or modally defined.

Kristeva may not have been aware of the fact that the syntactic structure of some languages is quite different from that of most Indo-European languages. The structure of a canonical sentence, which has been used in her derivation of narrative types, is really the structure of a normal

French sentence. She may have assumed that the structure of a French sentence is derived from universal grammar. Nobody has been able to discover universal grammar, however; even Noam Chomsky has not been able to do much for it.

Once the diversity of syntax is admitted for different languages, Kristeva's derivation project can more clearly show its troublesome consequences. Her thesis that narrative types can be derived from syntactic structures implies that the former are determined by the latter. The narrative structures of French literature must be different from those of classical Hebrew to the extent that the French syntax is different from the classical Hebrew syntax. Moreover, the French syntax can also be different from the syntaxes of other Indo-European languages, because the similarity and differences of syntaxes largely depend on the different levels of abstraction and comparison. To the extent that the French syntax is different from the English syntax, the French narrative structures must differ from the English ones. In short, all narrative types are syntax-bound. This implausible thesis is entailed by Kristeva's derivation project.

The derivation attempts by Kristeva and Greimas involve three different linguistic levels: the syntactic, the semantic, and the narrative. The last of these three belongs to the pragmatic domain, which requires the use of syntactic and semantic elements. A story is constructed by using syntactic and semantic elements as its building blocks. To derive the narrative structures from either syntactic and semantic categories or structures is no more feasible than to infer the structure of a building from the shapes of its building materials.

Linguistic Poetics

The initial impetus for the linguistic reconstruction of narrative categories and structures had come from Roman Jakobson's "Linguistics and Poetics," a daring attempt to redefine poetics in terms of formal linguistics.[22] He opened this attempt by proposing a linguistic definition of poetic function.

> What is the empirical linguistic criterion of the poetic function? In particular, what is the indispensable feature inherent in any piece of poetry? To answer this question we must recall the two basic modes of arrangement used in

verbal behavior, *selection* and *combination*. If "child" is the topic of the message, the speaker selects one among the extant, more or less similar, nouns like child, kid, youngster, tot, all of them equivalent in a certain respect, and then, to comment on this topic, he may select one of the semantically cognate verbs—sleeps, dozes, nods, naps. Both chosen words combine in the speech chain. The selection is produced on the base of equivalence, similarity and dissimilarity, synonymity and antonymity, while the combination, the build up of the sequence, is based on contiguity. *The poetic function projects the principle of equivalence from the axis of selection into the axis of combination.* Equivalence is promoted to the constitutive device of the sequence.[23]

The meaning of this passage is tied up with three technical terms, "selection," "combination," and "equivalence." The first two of these three had been used by Jakobson to describe what he regards as the two fundamental features of every linguistic behavior.

Speech implies a selection of certain entities and their combination into linguistic units of a higher degree of complexity. At the lexical level this is readily apparent: the speaker selects words and combines them into sentences according to the syntactic system of the language he is using; sentences are in their turn combined into utterances.[24]

For example, we can say, "A child sleeps," by combining three words into a sentence. Before this combination, however, each of these three words must be selected, and this act of selection involves the relation of equivalence. The word "child" is selected from a group of words that are semantically equivalent to one another, e.g., "child," "kid," "tot," "youngster." This semantic equivalence is the foundation for the act of selection, according to Jakobson.

This brings us to the most opaque passage in Jakobson's linguistic definition of poetic function. This is his assertion that the poetic function promotes the principle of equivalence from the level of selection to that of combination.[25] As a preliminary to determining the meaning of this assertion, we have to find out how the principle of equivalence can operate on the level of combination. This point is illustrated as follows.

In poetry one syllable is equalized with any other syllable of the same sequence; word stress is assumed to equal word stress, as unstress equals unstress; prosodic long is matched with long, and short with short; word boundary equals word boundary, no boundary equals no boundary; syntactic pause equals syntactic pause, no pause equals no pause. Syllables are converted into units of measure, and so are morae or stresses.[26]

This passage seems to be concerned with phonological equivalence. The use of phonological equivalence in poetry is, Jakobson points out, quite different from the use of conceptual equation in metalanguage.

> It may be objected that metalanguage also makes a sequential use of equivalent units when combining synonymic expressions into an equational sentence: A = A (*"Mare is the female of the horse"*). Poetry and metalanguage, however, are in diametrical opposition to each other: in metalanguage the sequence is used to build an equation, whereas in poetry the equation is used to build a sequence.[27]

The sequence of words "Mare is the female of the horse" seems to connect two equivalent linguistic units, but Jakobson wants to say that equivalence is not a constitutive feature of that sentence. To be a constitutive feature of a sentence is apparently to function as the form of its expression rather than as its content. This difference between the form of an expression and its content seems to underlie his characterization of the contrast between metalanguage and poetry: "In metalanguage the sequence is used to build an equation [of contents], whereas in poetry the equation is used to build a sequence [of equivalent forms]."

To exploit the equivalence of linguistic forms of expression, whether the equivalence be syntactic, phonological, or morphological, appears to be what Jakobson means by "promoting the principle of equivalence from the level of selection to that of combination," which is sometimes called "the constitutive use of equivalence." He further illustrates the constitutive use of equivalence with the following two examples: "Without its two dactylic words the combination 'innocent bystander' would hardly have become a hackneyed phrase. The symmetry of three disyllabic verbs with an identical initial consonant and identical final vowel added splendor to the laconic victory message of Caesar: *'Veni, vidi, vici.'*"[28]

The two words "innocent" and "bystander" are equivalent in having three syllables each, and the poetic quality of the expression "innocent bystander" may indeed be attributable to this phonological equivalence. The phonological equivalence that operates in *"Veni, vidi, vici"* is a little more complex; the three words are equivalent in more than one regard. These three words are phonologically equivalent in having two syllables each, in starting with the same consonant, and in ending with the same vowel. What Jakobson tries to do with these two examples is to show that the musical character of poetic expressions can be explained in terms of equivalence as their constitutive principle. By "poetic function" he means no more than versification, as he candidly admits. He locates the essential feature of versification in what he calls "musical time": "Measure of sequence is a device which, outside of poetic function, finds no application in language. Only in poetry with its regular reiteration of equivalent units is the time of the speech flow experienced, as it is—to cite another semiotic pattern—with musical time."[29]

This notion of musical time is meant to be an elaboration of Gerald Hopkins' definition of verse as "speech wholly or partially repeating the same figure of sound."[30] By "the figure of sound" Hopkins meant the sound pattern, which generally obtains in versification. As examples of sound pattern, Jakobson mentions the accentual verse whose musical rhythm is established by the recurrent contrast between the stressed and the unstressed syllables, the quantitative (chronemic) verse whose musical time is constituted by the corresponding contrast between long and short syllables, and the tonemic verse whose sound pattern is articulated by repetitious contrast between different intonations or modulations.

The notion of phonological equivalence is surely indispensable in composing or recognizing a sound pattern; for example, the recognition of an iambic meter presupposes the recognition of the equivalence between one long syllable and other long syllables and between one short syllable and other short syllables, or between one stressed syllable and other stressed ones and between one unstressed syllable and other unstressed ones. However, the notion of equivalence alone does not fully account for the nature of sound patterns.

The notion of sound pattern is the notion of a pattern of structure for organizing the basic phonological elements into a unified whole, and the notion of equivalence governs only the notion of those basic elements. The notion of basic units in musical compositions is also governed by the notion of equivalence; for example, one C note is assumed to be equivalent to other C notes, and one quarter note is assumed to be equivalent to other quarter notes. But this equivalence between basic units alone does not explain the structure of musical compositions. Hence the notion of equivalence cannot be called the constitutive principle of verse, if the expression "constitutive" is meant to refer to structure rather than to basic elements.

Jakobson tries to define the notion of sound pattern with the principle of binary opposition, the central principle in his structural phonology: "The reiterative 'figure of sound,' . . . can be further specified. Such a figure always utilizes at least one (or more than one) binary contrast of a relatively high and relatively low prominence effected by the different sections of the phonemic sequence."[31] The notion of binary contrast or opposition is mathematically the simplest principle of organization, for it can operate with two basic units, e.g., long vs. short or high vs. low. A principle of organization even simpler than binary contrast is to reiterate one basic unit, but that would be too monotonous to constitute the musical texture of a verse. However, the simple structural principle of binary opposition cannot cope with the structure that involves more than two basic units; for example, the triadic structure of the dactylic words "innocent" and "bystander" or the structural relation of four lines in a quatrain.

These complex verse structures can be accounted for by introducing more complex structural principles than the binary principle. But the question whether any given sound pattern is musical or unmusical cannot be determined by any principles of phonology. Nor is there any phonological or other linguistic principle that can determine what poetic function is performed by any given sound pattern, musical or unmusical. To determine the phonological structure of a verse is one thing, and to determine its poetic function is an altogether different matter. The former alone belongs to phonology. The latter belongs to pragmatics because it involves the use of phonological elements for the poetic function.

The sound pattern of a verse is only one of the many aspects of its structure. Besides phonological elements, as Jakobson recognizes, the structure of a verse consists of may other linguistic elements, such as morphological, syntactic, and lexical ones. Every one of these linguistic elements presents exactly the same pragmatic issue as phonological elements. Their structure can be analyzed and described in terms of structural linguistics, but their poetic functions cannot be so analyzed and described. Their poetic functions are extralinguistic, if the science of linguistics is taken to be formal linguistics.

Whether a sound pattern is musical or unmusical is a question of value. Likewise, which poetic function is performed by a given sound pattern is also a question of value. One is the question of musical value, and the other is the question of poetic value. These questions of value do not arise on the semantic level or in the domain of formal linguistics, which is value-neutral. But they are inevitable on the pragmatic level, because the domain of values constitutes the domain of actions. Every action is a fulfillment of some purpose, and every purpose is a manifestation of some value. Where there is no value, no action can ever take place. In sober moments, even Jakobson defines the nature of poetic function in terms of value.

> How is poeticity manifested? In this: that the word is felt as word and not as simple substitute for the object named nor as explosion of emotion. In this, that the words and their syntax, their meaning (*signification*), their external and internal form, are not indifferent indices of reality, but possess their own weight and their own value.[32]

Poetic function is neither the cognitive function of representing an external object, nor the emotive function of expressing an internal feeling. Whereas these functions are instrumental and extrinsic, Jakobson is saying, the poetic function of words is intrinsic (they possess "their own weight and their own value"). But how can these weights and values be characterized except by saying that they are poetic (or aesthetic)? There seems to be no way to account for these intrinsic weights and values in purely linguistic terms, if linguistics is understood only as the science of Saussure's *langue*.

At the outset of his linguistic definition of poetic function, Jakobson tried to justify his enterprise with the following argument: "Poetics deals with problems of verbal structure, just as the analysis of painting is concerned with pictorial structure. Since linguistics is the global science of verbal structure, poetics may be regarded as an integral part of linguistics."[33] If poetic structure is nothing more than the verbal structure of a poem, then analysis of that verbal structure should be a legitimate province of structural linguistics, the global science of verbal structure. This is the fundamental premise for linguistic definition of poetic function. By elaborating on this premise, Roland Barthes tries to demonstrate the adequacy of structural linguistics for the study of all literary works.

> At every level, therefore, be it that of argument, the discourse or the words, the literary work offers structuralism the picture of a structure perfectly homological . . . with that of language itself. Structuralism has emerged from linguistics and in literature it finds an object which has itself emerged from language.[34]

In contrast to the self-containedness of literary language, Barthes claims, scientific languages have extralinguistic references, that is, they refer to objects lying outside themselves. Because of their extralinguistic dimension, he admits, they cannot be reduced to structural linguistics. But the language of literature, he holds, is free of extralinguistic references or "realistic illusion." Hence the language of literature can be exhaustively analyzed in terms of structural linguistics, and poetics can be made an integral feature of linguistics.

The assertion that the language of literature has no extralinguistic references is not easy to understand. Let us consider Byron's poem "Ocean"; surely it refers to an ocean or oceans. Without some knowledge or experience of an ocean, it would not be easy to understand or appreciate that poem. The references made by poetic language may not be to any particular objects, persons, or events because, as Aristotle says, poetry is mainly concerned with generalities even in its use of proper names. General references, however, are as extralinguistic as particular references; the former refer to classes of objects, while the latter refer to objects themselves.

The references made by the language of science can also be either general or particular. Scientific statements about the sun refer to a particular physical object; the scientific theories of atomic structure refer to a general entity. In this regard, the language of science is little different from the language of literature. Barthes may have in mind the language of fiction, that is, the language which refers only to fictional entities, as the paradigm for the language of literature. As we shall see in a later chapter, the reference to fictional entities cannot be regarded as no reference, because it still requires the semantic mechanism of referential framework.

Referential function is not the true extralinguistic obstacle to reducing the study of literary works to the science of linguistics, any more than it is the obstacle to reducing the language of natural science to the science of linguistics. The two words "the sun" refer to the same object, whether. they appear in a literary work or in a scientific treatise. Referential function is a part of referential semantics; it can be fully accounted for in terms of formal linguistics even on the semantic level. What cannot be so accounted for is the literary function of literary language and the scientific function of scientific language. These functions are truly extralinguistic, if the notion of language and its scientific study is confined to the semantic level.

On the pragmatic level, those functions can be regarded as linguistic because they are essential constituents in the use of literary and scientific languages. If linguistics is understood as pragmatics, the study of literary works is reducible to linguistics. But this reducibility is not a prerogative of the language of literature; it obtains, on the pragmatic level, equally for the language of natural science and for any other language. In this regard, the science of language is absolutely impartial, whether it operates on the semantic or on the pragmatic level.

Our consideration should not leave the misleading impression that structural linguistics cannot be used in poetics. Poetics is a branch of pragmatics, and pragmatics can always use structural linguistics as its instrument. But the use of structural linguistics for poetics is quite different from the reduction of poetics to structural linguistics. In the former case, poetics is the master and structural linguistics is its servant. In the latter case, structural linguistics is ultimately everything, both master and servant.

The use of formal linguistics in poetics is very much like the use of mathematics in physics. The physics that relies on extensive use of mathematics is called "mathematical physics." This label does not mean, however, that mathematical physics is an extension of mathematics, or that all the concepts and functions of physics can be defined in mathematical terms. Mathematics is only a servant, albeit indispensable, but not the master of physics. For the pragmatic concerns and values of the language of physics are emphatically extramathematical. The poetics that extensively employs structural linguistics may be called structuralist poetics or linguistic poetics, but structural linguistics can never be more than a servant of this new poetics.

CHAPTER FIVE
Pragmatic Ascent

IN the course of this investigation, I have introduced many constitutive elements of a pragmatic context that cannot be found in a semantic context. They are use and purpose, action and function, and above all the domain of values. It is now time to establish a formal definition of pragmatics. Its formal definition was first proposed by Charles Morris in his triadic division of semiotics into syntactics (syntax), semantics, and pragmatics. This triadic division was inspired by the triadic conception of sign that had come down from Charles Peirce, the father of semiotics. Whereas most natural phenomena assume two-term relations (cause and effect, or action and reaction), Peirce had observed, the unique character of semiosis is its three-term relation. A sign is not simply related to its object in a two-term relation; its signification function involves a third term, the interpreter or interpretant. In other words, a sign is "something which stands to somebody for something in some respect or capacity."[1]

Acting on Peirce's triadic conception of sign, Charles Morris recognized three elements of signification and called them the three correlates of semiosis: the sign vehicle, the designatum, and the interpreter.[2] In accordance with these three, he distinguished three dimensions of semiosis: the semantic, the pragmatic, and the syntactic. The semantic dimension is the relation of signs to their objects or designata, and the pragmatic dimension is the relation of signs to their interpreters. The semantic dimension is studied by semantics, and the pragmatic dimension by pragmatics. The syntactic dimension is quite different from these two; it is the formal relation of signs to one another. Morris called the study of this dimension syntactics.

A few years later, Rudolf Carnap proposed an alternative characterization of the three semiotic disciplines.[3] This is to regard them as three different levels of abstraction in the study of language. At the most concrete level, the study of language is pragmatics, which makes explicit reference to the speaker or, more generally stated, to the user of language. The study of language becomes semantics when it abstracts from the user of language and analyzes only the expressions and their designata. It finally becomes (logical) syntax when it abstracts even from the designata and analyzes only the relations between the expressions.

The most obvious difference between these two triadic divisions is that Carnap's is concerned with linguistic signs only, while Morris' is concerned with all types of signs, linguistic and nonlinguistic. But this difference is not significant. In the triadic division of semiotics, whatever can be said about linguistic signs can also be said about nonlinguistic signs, and vice versa. What then are the points of significant difference between Morris' and Carnap's proposals? They concern the nature of pragmatics and its relation to syntax and semantics.

Neither the nature of syntax nor that of semantics was a point of disagreement between Morris and Carnap, mainly because these two disciplines had been well established by the time of their proposals. Although the word "syntax" is a relatively unfamiliar term, it designates one of the oldest disciplines in the West, the study of the grammatical relationship of words in a sentence.[4] On the descriptive level, semantics is as old as the invention of dictionaries; lexicography and philology are special forms of empirical semantics. The natures of syntax and semantics had been further articulated by the emergence of formal and artificial languages. It generally requires two sets of rules to set up a formal or an artificial language: semantic and syntactic rules. Semantic rules assign a meaning to each sign or word in the language; syntactic rules determine the combination of different signs or words into a meaningful sentence.

But the notion of pragmatics as a semiotic discipline was a radically new idea. For both Morris and Carnap, pragmatics was a new science; hence they had to define it without being able to draw from any established scientific practices. Morris defined it as the study of signs in their relation to their interpreters. But the notion of sign interpreter was ambiguous. In its technical sense, it might mean no more than someone who performs the semantic operation of assigning meaning to signs. Since this semantic operation is already included in the semantic dimension of language, Morris' definition of pragmatics in terms of interpreters does not seem to make the domain of pragmatics any different from that of semantics. In the exposition of his definition, however, he uses the word "interpreter" much more broadly, thereby making its meaning equivalent to the notion of sign user.[5]

The notion of the language user is central in Carnap's conception of pragmatics. He allocates pragmatic investigations to three areas: the physiological processes in speech organs and the central nervous system; the psychological relations between speech behavior and other behavior; and ethnological and sociological conventions governing speech behavior.[6] But the investigation of sign users is not the same as the investigation of sign uses. Whatever takes place in any sign user may have no relevance to his or her use of signs. For example, the physiological process in speech organs and in the central nervous system may be relevant only to the investigation of how signs are produced, but not of how they are used. Although the use of signs is inseparable from their production, the two are not identical. The proper object of pragmatic investigations is not the sign user but the sign use.

Morris came to see the inadequacy of using the notion of interpreters or sign users in the definition of pragmatics. A few years later, when he gave his behavioral definition of semiotics, he redefined semantics as the study of "the signification of signs" and "the interpretant behavior without which there is no signification," and pragmatics as the study of "the origin, uses, and effects of signs within the total behavior of the interpreters of signs."[7] In this redefinition, Morris assigns the function of interpreters to semantics, insofar as it concerns the signification of signs. The function of interpreters is accepted in the pragmatic domain only if it involves the use of signs.

The reference to the interpreters of signs is no longer the unique feature in the definition of pragmatics; it is used in the behaviorial definitions of both semantics and pragmatics. It is also used in his behavioral definition of syntactics: it is the study of behaviors dealing with the rules for combining signs. Morris says, "The difference lies not in the presence or absence of behavior but in the sector of behavior under consideration."[8] But he does not explain the relation of the three sectors of semiotic behavior.

In his earlier definition of semiotics, Morris had described the relation of its three branches as follows.

> In a systematic presentation of semiotics, pragmatics presupposes both syntactics and semantics, as the latter in turn presupposes the former, for to discuss adequately the relation of signs to their interpreters requires knowledge of the relation of signs to one another and to those things to which they refer their interpreters.[9]

As Morris maintains, it is obviously impossible to study the pragmatic dimension of a language without first knowing its syntactic and semantic dimensions. But the converse does not seem to be true. It appears to be possible to study the syntactic or the semantic dimension of a language without knowing its pragmatic dimension. In what sense, then, does Morris claim that pragmatics is presupposed by syntactics and semantics? According to him, the study of syntactic and semantic rules involves implicit reference to the notion of interpreter, because those rules are rules governing the behavior of an interpreter.[10] But this implicit reference alone cannot justify Morris' claim that pragmatics is presupposed by syntactics and semantics, because the reference in question may involve no more than the syntactic and semantic functions of the interpreter. He has not shown that the study of syntactic and semantic rules involves the pragmatic functions of the interpreter.

The way pragmatics is presupposed by syntax and semantics may be different from the way syntax and semantics are presupposed by pragmatics. The word "presuppose" has become notoriously ambiguous and slippery ever since Kant made it a fashionable epistemological term. Morris appears to be using this one slippery word for describing the nature of two different relations. It may be this terminological ambiguity that Carnap tries to clear up by describing the relation of pragmatics to semantics and syntax with the notion of abstraction. According to his demarcation of three semiotic disciplines, semantics is an abstraction from pragmatics and syntax is a further abstraction from semantics, while pragmatics is the study of language on its most concrete level. For this reason, Carnap regards semantics and syntax as parts of pragmatics, and maintains that the three branches of semiotics "are not on the same level: *pragmatics is the basis for all of linguistics*"[11]

By restating Carnap's view in Morris' terminology, we can say that the syntactic dimension of semiosis is included in its semantic dimension as its constituent, and that its semantic dimension is included in its pragmatic dimension as its constituent. The three levels of abstraction in the study of language are obtained by reversing these three levels of inclusion. The three levels of abstraction are three levels of exclusion. Since the relations of inclusion and exclusion are asymmetrical, the mutual relations of syntax, semantics, and pragmatics are also asymmetrical.

This asymmetry in the mutual relations of syntax, semantics, and pragmatics is obscured by Morris' description. By using one and the same word "presuppose" in his description, he gives the misleading impression that those relations are symmetrical. He further reinforces this impression by labeling the three dimensions of semiosis as "coordinate," and maintaining that "the subsciences represent three irreducible and equally legitimate points of view corresponding to the three objective dimensions of semiosis."[12] These three subsciences are called by Morris the "mutually irreducible components" of semiotics.[13] This seems to imply that their demarcation is a matter of mutual exclusion; that is, whatever belongs to one of them is excluded from the other two. Mutual exclusion is a symmetrical relation.

Although Morris has not done well in articulating the mutual relations of the three semiotic disciplines, he makes a good start in defining the nature of sign use. It is defined in terms of purpose: "A sign S will be said to be *used* with respect to purpose y of an organism z if y is some goal of z and if z produces a sign which serves as means to the attainment of y."[14] This definition is explained with the example of a person writing a short story for the sake of making money. In this case, Morris says, the short story is *used* for the purpose of making money.

This example is not quite to the point, because it involves the use of signs only indirectly. What is directly used for making money is the short story, not the signs themselves. The use of signs takes place in the writing of the story. But to use something *in* an act is not the same as to use it *for* an act. The relation of means and end may be suitable for describing the latter use, but not for the former. What is needed for a better conception of pragmatics is a more adequate conceptual scheme for describing and analyzing the use of signs than the categorial relation of means to end. This need for conceptual refinement has called forth a few different attempts.

From Use to Act

Yehoshua Bar-Hillel has proposed that pragmatics be defined in terms of the use of indexical expressions.[15] These expressions are sometimes known as demonstratives; e.g., "this," "here," "now," "I," etc. Their references are fixed by the contexts of their use, that is, on the pragmatic level. On the semantic level, indexical expressions are devoid of references. For example, it is impossible to tell what is designated by the words "this" and "my" in the sentence "This is my dog," when the sentence is considered as a purely semantic entity. Hence, as Bar-Hillel maintains, the use of a sentence can be characterized as the use of its indexical expressions. The use of signs in general may be accounted for in terms of the use of indexicals. Hence the use of indexicals may be regarded as the most essential feature of pragmatics.

One drawback to characterizing the pragmatic function of language in terms of indexical functions is that many sentences or sign complexes do not contain indexical expressions. This defect may be mended by using P. F. Strawson's distinction between the meaning of an expression and its use.[16] For example, the expression "the king of France" can be used to refer to Louis XIV, Louis XV, or any other man who reigned over France. This referential meaning is not the meaning of that expression in its technical sense, because it is what is meant by someone's use of that expression. The meaning of that expression is what it means on its own, apart from the contexts of its referential use—that is, the idea of a man reigning over the country called France. Hence Strawson claims that the meaning of an expression should be distinguished from its use.

Strawson extends this distinction between meaning and use even to indexical expressions.[17] To know the meaning of an indexical sign is to know the general directions or conventions governing its use, which is quite different from knowing what is referred to by the use of that sign. This distinction between the meaning and the use of indexicals appears to be the very premise for Bar-Hillel's theory of indexicals and his conception of pragmatics. In fact, Bar-Hillel recognizes the coincidence of his views with Strawson's.[18] Therefore, the reference of an expression can be said to be always fixed by its use, whether the expression be indexical or not. Then the use of an expression can be equated with its referential function, and pragmatics can be defined as the study of referential function. This is a referential definition of pragmatics.

This referential definition seems to apply only to those expressions called nouns and noun phrases, but not to verbs, adjectives, or predicates in general. Richard Montague has tried to overcome this shortcoming in the referential definition of pragmatics by extending the notion of reference to verbs and predicates.[19] The predicate "is green" in the sentence "Grass is green" has no point of reference; its present tense refers to no particular moment of time. If the sentence is used by someone, however, its predicate gains the point of reference at the time of its use. Hence the use of predicates also involves a referential function.

The referential definition of pragmatics can also apply to sentences, if their meanings can be distinguished from their uses. Strawson has shown that this distinction can be made by using the notion of assertion and statement.[20] Let us consider the sentence "The present king of France is wise." It could have been *used* to describe Louis XIV or Louis XV. The use of this sentence could have produced a true assertion in one case and a false one in the other. The use of a sentence involves the operation of making an assertion and claiming its truth. By contrast, the meaning of a sentence does not; the meaning of "The present king of France is wise" can be known apart from its use and its truth value. The use of a sentence can also be accounted for in terms of reference; its use determines the reference of its subject and predicate.

This completes the referential definition of pragmatics. This definition establishes a new demarcation of pragmatics from semantics. Semantics can now be defined as the study of meaning in the Strawsonian sense, and pragmatics as the study of its use in the domain of reference. This demarcation can be further clarified by using Gottlob Frege's distinction between sense and reference.[21] According to him, what is generally associated with a sign or name is its reference. But he says that a sign has not only its reference but also its sense. For example, the two expressions "the morning star" and "the evening star" have different senses. The sense of "the morning star" is the conceptual or definitional sense contained in that expression: the idea of the star that shines brightly in the east immediately before sunrise. Likewise, the sense of "the evening star" is the corresponding conceptual or definitional sense: the idea of the star that shines brightly over the western horizon right after sunset. Although these two expressions have different senses, Frege holds, they refer to the same object, the planet Venus. Hence their reference or designatum should be distinguished from their senses.

Although Frege's distinction between sense and reference has been introduced to account for the meanings of proper names and definite descriptions, it can be regarded as an adaptation of the traditional distinction between two types of meaning in a general name or noun expression. For example, John Stuart Mill distinguished between the connotation and the denotation of a name, and this distinction was in turn a restatement of the distinction between comprehension and extension in the *Port Royal Logic*. During the nineteenth century, the term "comprehension" was replaced by "intension"; since then the neat, symmetrical pair of terms "intension" and "extension" has been more widely accepted than any other equivalent terms. For example, the intension (connotation) of "a bachelor" is the concept of an unmarried male of marriageable age; its extension (denotation) is all human beings to whom this concept can be applied.

Strawson's distinction between the meaning of an expression and its use can now be regarded as a restatement of the traditional distinction between intension and extension, or an adaptation of Frege's distinction between sense and reference. With this distinction, it can be maintained that the meaning of an expression is its sense or intension only, and that its reference or extension is established by the use of its meaning. The study of the former is semantics; the study of the latter is pragmatics. This may be called the Strawsonian demarcation of pragmatics from semantics. Although Strawson has made no overt attempt to make this demarcation, it is implicitly contained in his distinction between meaning and use.

The Strawsonian demarcation raises some troublesome questions. The first of them concerns the relation between intension and extension. The Strawsonian demarcation assumes that the extension of a sign comes into being only through the application of its intension to an object or objects. That is, it presupposes the primacy of intension over extension, which has been known as "essentialism." Edmund Husserl advocates this doctrine by distinguishing the meaning (*Bedeutung*) of a sign from its objective reference (*gegenständlicher Beziehung*) or correlate (*Gegenständlichkeit*).[22] He maintains that the objective reference of a sign is produced by the application of its meaning to objects, while its meaning is independent of all applications.

Essentialism has been opposed by nominalists. According to them, the primary meaning of a sign is its extension. Some nominalists deny the very existence of intension. Even when its existence is admitted, they maintain, the intension of a sign should be construed not as primitive but as derivative, derived from its extension. Thus nominalists have systematically reversed the claim of essentialists, and maintained the primacy of extension over intension.

The dispute between nominalists and essentialists is one of those typically interminable metaphysical controversies. The referential view of pragmatics is acceptable only to one of the two parties to this dispute. This is a serious drawback in that view. Now suppose that there is a definition of linguistics that is acceptable to only one of these two parties. This partisanship is an obvious defect. Frege wisely avoids this partisanship by giving equal weight to the sense and the reference of a sign in his theory of meaning. In his theory, intension and extension are equally primordial.

The referential view of pragmatics generates a few other problems besides that of metaphysical partisanship. Although we cannot consider all of them, we cannot disregard the problem of its consequence. By defining pragmatics in terms of extension and reference, we cannot open up a new domain of inquiry for pragmatics, that is, a domain untouched by the established sciences of semantics and syntax. Intension and extension have been the two subdivisions of meaning in semantics, and as such they have been the two focal points in semantic inquiries. The referential definition of pragmatics is to take one of these two focal points out of the domain of semantics and to relabel it as the domain of pragmatics. Instead of gaining a new scientific territory for linguistics, we are only subdividing the old one.

The referential definition of pragmatics is semantically biased.[23] As a matter of fact, it has been espoused mostly by semanticists. In their conception of pragmatics, the use of signs is confined to their semantic use. The real scope of sign use is much more extensive than that. Signs can be used on the syntactic level for their syntactic roles. Of course, they can also be used on the semantic level, but their semantic use need not be limited to a referential function. To use a sign to express a meaning is also a semantic use. The semantically unused signs are the uninterpreted signs—that is, those signs without sense or reference.[24]

Since any segment of semiotics can be said to involve some use of signs, the notion of sign use is a highly unreliable criterion for demarcating the domain of pragmatics. This criterion can allow any segment of semiotics to be relabeled as pragmatics. If the notion of sign use is to open up the domain of pragmatics beyond the established domains of syntax and semantics, it had better be different from the notions of syntactic and semantic use. For the sake of brevity, let us call such a notion of sign use the extrasemantic notion. Ludwig Wittgenstein advocates this extrasemantic notion of use in his definition of meaning as use.

In his *Tractatus*, Wittgenstein had conceived the meaning of every primitive sign as a name, which refers (*bedeuten*) to an object.[25] He had said, "The name means [*bedeutet*] the object. The object is its meaning."[26] An elementary proposition is a concatenation of names, which mirrors an atomic fact, which is a combination of objects.[27] The ultimate function of language is to represent reality through its propositions, which are constituted by its naming function. Since the naming function is the semantic function, Wittgenstein's early view of language is unequivocally semantic.

In his *Philosophical Investigations*, he rejects this semantic view of language. He examines thoroughly the nature of the naming function, and exposes its inadequacy as the central linguistic function.[28] He relocates this central function in the context of human life by using the notion of language games.[29] A language game is any institutionalized activity that involves the use of language. The naming function is only one of the various activities that can be performed in language games. Wittgenstein stresses that there are many other linguistic functions besides naming and referring, and that there are countless varieties of language games such as commanding and requesting, teasing and appeasing. To understand the meaning of a word is to understand its use in language games just as to know the meaning of a chess piece is to know its use in chess games. Hence his much-quoted definition of meaning: "the meaning of a word is its use in the language."[30]

The extrasemantic use of language is the pragmatic use. The countless varieties of pragmatic use generate a special type of complexity in pragmatics that can never be seen in semantics and syntax. J. L. Austin has tried to control this complexity by classifying and analyzing the various types of pragmatic use in his theory of speech acts. In the initial version of this theory, Austin isolates one special type of utterance from the usual ones. The latter are called descriptive or constative; they are either true or false. The former is called performative; it has no truth value. The examples of performatives are: "I do" as uttered in the course of the marriage ceremony, "I name this ship the *Queen Elizabeth*" as uttered in naming a ship, "I give and bequeath my watch to my brother" as occurring in a will, and "I bet you sixpence it will rain tomorrow." None of these utterances describes anything. All of them are used in performing certain acts, namely, the acts of getting married, christening a ship, making a will, and making a bet.[31]

Within performatives, Austin draws a further distinction: a performative utterance can be made either explicitly ("I promise that I shall be there") or implicitly ("I shall be there"). The implicit performative is also called the primary performative. The unique feature of explicit performatives is the use of the first-person subject and the performative verb in the present tense. The implicit performatives can be stated without using either of them ("Your book shall be returned next week" for "I promise to return your book next week"). Whatever is stated in an implicit performative can be restated in an explicit performative, and vice versa.

The distinction between constatives and performatives, Austin had thought, sets apart one special type of linguistic use from the general type, that is, the use of words in doing things from the use of words in saying things. Hence the title of his book: *How to Do Things with Words.* But he soon came to realize that saying something is also a kind of doing something. In short, constatives are just another kind of performatives. For example, the descriptive statement "The cat is on the mat" is the implicit form of the explicit performative "I tell you that the cat is on the mat." With this recognition, Austin had to revise his classification schema. This revised schema divides all speech acts into three classes: locutionary acts, illocutionary acts, and perlocutionary acts.[32]

To utter a word or a string of words is a locutionary act, insofar as it is considered only as the production of the word or the string of words. An illocutionary act is an act performed with the use of words beyond the act of locution, such as making a promise or describing the weather. If one says "I promise to keep you informed" for the sake not of making a promise but of uttering those words, one performs a locutionary act. If one makes the same utterance in making a promise, one performs an illocutionary act. An illocutionary act necessarily involves a locutionary act. A perlocutionary act is an act that aims at some effect beyond the acts of locution and illocution, for example, the act of persuading or frightening somebody. Like an illocutionary act, a perlocutionary act always involves a locutionary act.

The distinction between illocutionary and perlocutionary acts is not easy to understand. Let us compare the illocutionary act of making a promise and the perlocutionary act of persuading someone. By saying "I promise to keep you informed," I accomplish the act of making a promise. But I cannot achieve the effect of persuading someone in the same simple manner. I may be engaged in a speech act to persuade you, but you may remain unpersuaded. No doubt, I have performed a perlocutionary act in this case, as I have performed an illocutionary act in the other case. The outcome (or uptake) of an illocutionary act is contained in the act. In the perlocutionary act, the outcome or effect is not so contained. The outcome lies outside the speech act, because the two stand in the relation of cause and effect. Cause and effect are never contained within each other. An illocutionary act is said to have its force; a perlocutionary act is said to have its effect. The illocutionary force is contained in the speech act, but the perlocutionary effect is not.

The distinction between the illocutionary force and the perlocutionary effect reflects the difference between two types of relation an action can have with purposes. Let us take Charles Morris' example of writing a short story for making money. Writing a short story is a speech act. This act can be said to have two purposes: writing a short story and making money. The first of these two may be called the intrinsic purpose, and the second the extrinsic purpose. The purpose of writing a short story is an intrinsic element in the speech act of writing a short story. By contrast, the purpose of making money is extrinsic to that speech act. For this purpose, the act is only an instrument. But the same act is an end in itself, if it is viewed from the other purpose. An intrinsic purpose is realized *in* the performance of a speech act, and an extrinsic purpose *by* the performance of a speech act.

When a speech act is defined in terms of an intrinsic purpose, it is an illocutionary act. When it is defined in terms of an extrinsic purpose, it is a perlocutionary act. Writing a short story is an illocutionary act when its aim is taken to be the production of a short story. But it becomes a perlocutionary act when it is understood as a means for the purpose of making money. Even the illocutionary act of making a promise can function as a perlocutionary act, if the promise is made as a means to some further end. Since many speech acts can have both intrinsic and extrinsic ends, they can have both illocutionary forces and perlocutionary effects.

Speech acts can go wrong when they lack appropriate conditions. One cannot succeed in making a bet by simply uttering the words "I bet . . ."; one must have someone to accept the bet, something to bet on, and something to bet with. Austin calls these conditions felicity conditions. John Searle has divided them into three classes: preparatory (or prerequisite) conditions, sincerity conditions, and essential conditions.[33] Preparatory conditions are the right or the authority to perform certain types of speech acts, for example, the authority to perform a marriage ceremony or the right to sign a contract. Sincerity conditions concern the frame of mind. One may make a promise without the intention of keeping it or knowing that one cannot keep it. In that case, sincerity conditions are not fulfilled. Essential conditions concern the internal consistency of a speech act and its consistency with other acts. If any speech act violates logical laws, it fails to fulfill essential conditions— that is, it is logically inconsistent. If I tell you that the end of the world is coming tomorrow and yet behave as though the end of the world were infinitely remote, I do not fulfill essential conditions; that is, my acts are inconsistent with each other.

Meaning versus Significance

Our pragmatic ascent has not been easy, but it can provide a clearer overview of the various territories of linguistics, especially the demarcation between semantics and pragmatics. From this improved vantage point, we can now clarify Hirsch's distinction between verbal meaning and significance. He has introduced this distinction in order to articulate his theory of authorial intention. What is intended by authorial intention is the verbal meaning of a text and not its significance. Although the significance of a text may change, its verbal meaning must remain permanent because it is permanently fixed by its author's intention.

Hirsch's distinction between meaning and significance has been made difficult to grasp by his own explanations of this distinction. Those explanations give three different meanings to his distinction. The first one is most obvious; it separates out the two meanings generally contained in the word "meaning." These two meanings have been discriminated as "signification" and "significance" by Charles Morris.[34] The assertion "This message has no meaning" can mean either that the message has no significance, or that it has no signification. The demarcation of these two meanings of the word "meaning" constitutes the first sense of Hirsch's distinction between meaning and significance.

> The reader will have noticed that the two concepts which have presided over these chapters—meaning and significance—bear a close resemblance to the concepts of knowledge and value. Meaning is the stable object of knowledge in interpretation, without which wider humanistic knowledge would be impossible. The chief interest of significance, on the other hand, is in the unstable realm of value. The significance of meaning in a particular context determines its value in that context. For, significance names the relationship of textual meaning, and value is a relationship, not a substance. Value is value-for-people . . . and this value changes. A poem may have a very different value for me at age twenty and age forty. It may possess different values for people in different cultural contexts. A poem has no absolute value.[35]

Due to the ambiguity of the word "meaning," the assertion that the meaning of a literary work changes can refer to two different things, the change of its signification or its significance. One can avoid this ambiguity by using Hirsch's distinction, whether one does or does not subscribe to his thesis that the verbal meaning of a text is permanently fixed, whereas its significance perpetually changes. At this stage, his distinction is sensible and useful. But he wants to go beyond this sensible and useful proposal. He equates his distinction with Frege's distinction between sense and reference.[36] We have already seen that Frege's distinction corresponds to Husserl's distinction between meaning and its objective reference. According to Husserl, the meaning of an expression is permanently fixed, while its objective reference perpetually changes. This contrast between permanence and change is surely conducive to the exposition of Hirsch's thesis. It is evidently for this reason that Hirsch has equated his distinction between verbal meaning and significance with Husserl's and Frege's distinctions. This equation has produced the second sense of Hirsch's distinction.

The second sense is incompatible with the first sense. In the first sense, "significance" means importance; it belongs to the province of value. In the second sense, "significance" means reference, which is not a matter of value. Moreover, the second sense of Hirsch's distinction is not directly applicable to the domain of textual meaning and interpretation. As we have seen, Frege's and Husserl's distinctions are meant to be taken on the semantic level, which involves no speech act. The composition of a text or its interpretation is a speech act, which belongs to the pragmatic domain. If Hirsch seriously means to apply the semantic distinction between sense and reference to the domain of textual interpretation, he must show what meanings can be given to "sense" and "reference" on the pragmatic level. As we shall see in chapter 8, the pragmatic adaptation of these semantic categories is much more complicated than he seems to assume..

Hirsch also restates his distinction in the language of genre hermeneutics. This produces the third sense of the distinction between meaning and significance. The central principle of genre hermeneutics is that the meaning of a text can be correctly determined by assigning the work to the right genre. Following this principle, Hirsch calls the verbal meaning of a text its "intrinsic genre."[37] Every genre is governed by a set of norms, although those norms are subject to change. The same text—for example, Defoe's *The Shortest Way*—can produce different readings because it can be assigned to different genres. To read it as a sincere piece was to assign it to an extrinsic (wrong) genre; its intrinsic (right) genre was satire. To say that the meaning of a text is fixed by authorial intention now means that its intrinsic genre is permanently determined by its author's intention. The intrinsic genre is called the "willed type," because it is a type determined by the author's will.[38]

The notion of genre in interpretation belongs to pragmatics, because speech acts can be divided into different kinds or genres. Since each pragmatic genre is governed by its own set of norms, a mistake in genre assignment can produce a distortion of textual meaning. But a correct genre assignment cannot settle all the questions that may arise in textual interpretation. In fact, most of those questions appear after a correct genre assignment; for example, most questions on Dante's *Commedia* or Milton's *Paradise Lost* go well beyond the level of genre assignment.

A correct genre assignment is indeed a necessary but not a sufficient condition for determining textual meaning. Hence to equate textual meaning with intrinsic genre is an overstatement. To give some plausibility to this overstatement, Hirsch tries to make the notion of intrinsic genre much more particular than the standard notion of genre.[39] For example, the intrinsic genre of *Paradise Lost* can be specified by enumerating all the particular features of Milton's epic. To this unique class no other epic besides Milton's can be assigned. Whereas the standard notion of genre is the notion of general class, Hirsch's notion of intrinsic genre is the notion of unique class, which can have only one object for its membership. Such a unique class is called a "unit class" by Alfred Whitehead and Bertrand Russell.[40]

The nature of a unit class can be specified only by knowing the nature of its member. The nature of *Paradise Lost* as a unit class can be specified only by knowing *Paradise Lost* as an individual poem. Hence the assignment of a poem to its unit class cannot serve a preliminary function in determining its meaning the way its assignment to a general class can. For the assignment of a poem to its unit class or intrinsic genre can be made only after the determination of its meaning.

Hirsch's identification of textual meaning with intrinsic genre has evidently been intended as a methodological proposal for determining the author's intended meaning. But this proposal turns out to be vacuous, because his intrinsic genre can be specified only after textual meaning is known. Nevertheless Hirsch is on the right track in proposing the use of genre for determining textual meaning. But the use of genre, as we shall see in the next chapter, involves much more extensive operations than the determination of authorial will or intention. For the nature of a genre can shape the type of authorial intention as much as the shape of authorial will can change the nature of a genre.

CHAPTER SIX
Pragmatic Norms

THE speech-act theory is the only noteworthy development that has taken place in pragmatics since its formal definition as a science by Charles Morris and Rudolf Carnap. Some attempts have been made to determine its applicability to literature, because the production of literary works and their interpretation can be regarded as speech acts. But the initial obstacle to its application to literary analysis was foreseen by J. L. Austin himself. He had observed that the normal conditions for speech acts do not obtain in the use of literary language: "The normal conditions of reference may be suspended or no attempt made at a standard per-locutionary act, no attempt to make you do anything, as Walt Whitman does not seriously incite the eagle of liberty to soar."[1] Since the normal conditions for speech acts do not obtain in literature, Austin relegated it to the abnormal or parasitic use of language.

Speech Act in Literature

Undaunted by Austin's discouraging observation, Richard Ohmann has taken upon himself the task of applying the speech-act theory to literature. At the outset he reaffirms Austin's claim that the felicity conditions for normal speech acts are not fulfilled in literature. Of a declarative sentence in a lyric poem, for example, it is pointless to ask whether or not the statement is made under appropriate circumstances, whether or not the objects referred to really exist, or whether or not the poet believes what he says. Since the appropriate conditions of a normal speech act do not obtain in the case of literary utterances, Ohmann cannot recognize the normal illocutionary forces in those utterances.

A literary work is a discourse whose sentences lack the illocutionary forces that would normally attach to them. Its illocutionary force is mimetic. By "mimetic" I mean purportedly imitative. Specifically, a literary work purportedly imitates (or reports) a series of speech acts, which in fact have no other existence. By so doing, it leads the reader to imagine a speaker, a situation, a set of ancillary events, and so on.[2]

Whereas normal speech acts take place in the real world, literary speech acts are situated in the world of mimesis. Richard Ohmann reinstates Aristotle's theory of mimesis to account for the deviation of literary speech acts from the standard norms. Because of this deviation, Ohmann calls them "quasi-speech-acts." Whereas normal speech acts are performed in the context of carrying on the world's business—requesting and responding, agreeing and disagreeing, warning and urging—the quasi-speech-acts of literature are conducted in the unreal or imaginary world of pretense or mimesis.[3] This may be called Ohmann's quasi-speech-act theory of literature.

Against this theory of literary speech acts, Mary Pratt has advanced a double-pronged objection: this theory is overly dependent on the fictive or mimetic character of literary discourses; and the fictive dimension of speech acts is not limited to literature, but can be found in the so-called normal speech acts.[4] The first of these two points seems to be sound and obvious. Not all works of literature are written in the fictive or imaginary mode, nor is fictiveness a necessary condition for literary writings. In support of the second point, Mary Pratt adduces the following examples.

The "scenarios" in the Oval Office, the hypothetical situations used in mathematical problems and philosophical arguments, assumptions made "for the sake of discussion," speculation about "what he'll do next" or "what might have happened if only. . . ." are all fictional, as indeed are imaginings, plannings, dreams, wishings, and fantasizings of almost any kind. It is "suspended illocutionary force" in Ohmann's sense that distinguishes teasing from insulting, irony from deceit, devil's advocating from real advocating, and hypotheses from claims.[5]

Mary Pratt is right in stressing the obvious fact that imaginary or fictive talk is extensively used in our normal conversations taking place in the context of the real world. By forgetting this fact, logical positivists had assumed that they could completely eliminate the use of imaginary or hypothetical talks in scientific discourses, which were allegedly concerned only with the reality of this world. But it was soon realized that the fictive or imaginary talks were as indispensable to our normal speech acts as the factual or real ones. These two modes of speaking constitute as it were the two legs of one speaking body. It is this realization that has led to the semantics of possible worlds and counterfactual statements.[6] This new semantics has been applied to literature. For example, Teun van Dijk says that the persons and events referred to in literary texts are located in the "speaker-hearer possible worlds," that is, the possible worlds established and shared by the speaker and the hearer.[7]

In using the possible-worlds semantics, we have to be careful about its terminological distinctions. The domain of possible worlds does not exclude the actual world; our actual world is only one of the countless possible worlds.[8] Any world that is possible in actuality or in imagination is a possible world. While some possible worlds are actual, others are imaginary or counterfactual. But a possible world is not always a mimetic world. The relation of mimesis is a relation of resemblance. When a copy resembles its original, the former can be regarded as a mimesis of the latter. But not every relation of resemblance is a relation of mimesis. Identical twins may resemble each other, but they do not necessarily imitate each other. The relation of mimesis is an ontological relation between an original and its copy. Hence a mimetic world is a possible world that derives its genesis from an imitation of an actual world.

A writer can situate his literary work in the real world or in a possible world that is mimetic or fictive. In the latter case, he can either construct a possible world on his own or adopt one from some other source. The possible world thus constructed or adopted may show a close or remote resemblance to the actual world. The creation of a possible world is the speech act of an author, but this speech act should be distinguished from the speech acts taking place within the possible world thus created. For this distinction, we can use Teun van Dijk's labels: "macro-speech-acts" and "micro-speech-acts."[9] Shakespeare's act of creating his play *Hamlet* is a macro-speech-act, while Hamlet's speeches in that play are micro-speech-acts.

In writing a fiction, a writer can adopt the conventions of the real world as the conventions governing the micro-speech-acts within his fictive literary world. In that event, the nature of speech acts in the fictive world cannot be any different from that of the speech acts taking place in the real world. This is another way of saying that the people in a fictional world talk fundamentally the same way as the people of the real world do. Mary Pratt tries to substantiate this fundamental identity or similarity between the norms and rules governing the ordinary speech acts and those governing the poetic speech acts. In her view, any attempt to assert a fundamental or essential difference between the two is to commit what she calls the "poetic language fallacy," namely, the fallacy that the poetic language is fundamentally unlike the ordinary language.[10]

In some fictions, however, it may be impossible to adopt the speech conventions of the actual world because these conventions are incompatible with the psychological and physical properties of the people inhabiting those fictive worlds. Even if those imaginary people are neither psychologically nor physically different from real people, a fiction writer still has the choice of adopting a set of speech conventions different from the conventions of the actual world. The creation of new conventions is as much of a writer's prerogative as the creation of persons and events. Hence the micro-speech-acts of a literary work can be governed by a set of norms and rules fundamentally different from those governing normal speech acts. There is no a priori reason to ensure the identity of literary speech acts with normal speech acts any more than to ensure their difference, insofar as these literary speech acts are understood to be the micro-speech-acts.

The norms and rules governing the Newspeak in George Orwell's *1984* may indeed be different from the norms and rules prevailing in our society. But they may be very much like those obtaining in some other societies. The norms and rules governing speech acts can vary not only from one society to another, but from one literary work to another. Hence it is hard to control the entire dispute on the question of whether literary speech acts are fundamentally the same as or different from normal speech acts. But we may settle the questions of their reference and truth conditions, because they are much simpler questions than have been thought.

Whereas what is said in a normal speech act is meant to be true or to be taken as true, it has been argued, what is said in a literary speech act is meant neither to be true nor to be taken as true. Likewise, whereas what is said in a normal speech act refers to an object existing in the real world, what is said in a literary speech act does not refer to any object. This account of the difference between factual and fictive speech acts rests on the assumption that reference can be made only in the real world and that truth conditions can be given only in the real world. This assumption has been contested by the advocates of possible-world semantics.

In the fictive world, references are made and truth conditions are given in fundamentally the same way as they are made and given in the actual world. In the play *Hamlet*, the prince of Denmark has to refer to his father in talking and thinking about his father. Semantically, the reference of his talk to his father is not any different from the reference of your talk to your father in the actual world. No doubt, your father exists in the actual world, while Hamlet's father exists only in the fictive world. But this fact makes no difference in the semantic mechanism of reference. In fact, it is impossible to construct the micro-speech-acts in a fictive world without the semantic mechanism of reference.

In the fictive world, the truth conditions function exactly the same way as in the real world. Without presupposing truth conditions, Sherlock Holmes cannot discriminate true statements from false ones. In that event, he cannot undertake any detective work. In a fictive world, a statement can be verified or falsified. Processes of verification and falsification in the fictive world cannot be any different from those operative in the actual world. Like reference, truth conditions are essential constituents of micro-speech-acts in every possible world.

The so-called abnormality of literary speech acts has been artificially produced by restricting the domain of reference and truth conditions to the actual world. The other felicity conditions of speech acts can also obtain in the fictive worlds. For example, when a fictive person makes a promise, he can fulfill the sincerity condition. If a wedding takes place in a fiction, the marriage shall be null and void unless the ceremony is backed up with requisite conditions. This is another way of saying that the pragmatic rules in any fictive world need not be different from those operating in the actual world.

The macro-speech-acts of literature require a different account from that of micro-speech-acts. Conan Doyle's act of creating Sherlock Holmes is quite different from Sherlock Holmes's speech acts in his fictive world. Sherlock Holmes's statements can be given reference and truth conditions in the world of Conan Doyle's fiction, but Doyle's statements that create this world of fiction cannot be given reference and truth conditions in that world. Nor can they be given in the actual world; Doyle's statements do not refer to anything in this actual world. Thus, it seems to be impossible to account for the nature of macro-speech-acts with the semantics of either the actual or the possible worlds. Then how can we explain the nature of the literary speech act that produces a poem, a play, or a novel? Samuel Levin tries to answer this question by adapting John Ross's theory of implicit performatives.[11]

John Ross's theory has been developed as an expansion of J. L. Austin's observation that performatives can be stated either explicitly or implicitly. If I say to you, "I warn you that my dog is vicious," I make an explicit warning or perform an explicit speech act of warning you. By contrast, if I say to you, "My dog is vicious," I may make an implicit warning or perform an implicit act of warning you, although my statement may appear to be only a descriptive one. That is, the statement "My dog is vicious" implicitly has the same illocutionary force as "I warn you that my dog is vicious," or "My dog is vicious; therefore I ask you to watch out." The explicit performatives have linguistic devices that express their illocutionary forces, but the implicit performatives do not have such devices.

John Ross maintains that all declarative statements are implicit performatives whose illocutionary forces can be spelled out in higher sentences.[12] For example, the illocutionary force of the statement "My dog is vicious" can be spelled out in a higher sentence accompanying it such as "I tell you (that) my dog is vicious," or "I warn you (that). . . ." When the higher sentence is written out, it shows the deep structure of the original statement, which can now be regarded as a surface structure. Hence all declarative statements can be regarded as surface structures whose implicit illocutionary forces can be perspicuously shown by the deep structures of their higher sentences.

In Samuel Levin's view, a poem or a novel behaves like a declarative statement; it has no explicit device for stating its illocutionary force. What is explicitly expressed in a literary work is only its locutionary content. If we do not know the distinction between the deep and the surface structures, we are likely to miss the illocutionary force of a literary work. This failure to identify and recognize the illocutionary forces in literary works can, he proposes, be remedied by explicating the deep structure of literary speech acts in higher sentences. For this explication, he assumes that every poem or novel is presented within the frame of the following higher sentence.

(1) I imagine myself in and invite you to conceive a world in which . . .

The deep structure of every poem or novel contains (1) as its topmost sentence, which expresses its implicit illocutionary force; and this topmost sentence is deleted in its surface structure, which functions as its form of presentation to its readers. For example, Yeats's "Byzantium" is to be understood implicitly as beginning "I imagine myself in and invite you to conceive a world in which (I say to you) 'The unpurged images of day recede.'"[13]

Samuel Levin goes on to say that (1) contains two performative expressions: *I imagine myself in (a world)* and *I invite you to conceive a world*. Of course, it is these performatives that express the illocutionary forces of a literary work. The second of these is clearly a performative; one clearly performs the act of inviting someone by telling him or her, "I invite you to. . . ." But it is not easy to see that the first of the two expressions is also a performative. When someone says, "I imagine myself in (a world)," he may be only reporting what he is doing. In that event, the expression of its illocutionary force requires another higher sentence, "I tell you (that) I imagine myself in (a world). . . ."

In maintaining that *I imagine myself in (a world)* is also performative, Samuel Levin uses George Lakoff's distinction between two meanings of *I*: the *I* as the participant and the *I* as the observer.

> Lakoff considers a sentence like *I dreamed that I was playing the piano*. This sentence has two different readings. In one, which he calls the 'participant' reading, the *I* who is dreaming is essentially the same *I* who is playing the piano. In the second reading, the 'observer' reading, the *I* who is dreaming sees himself, from a displacement, as sitting at the piano and playing it. Compare, where the ambiguity is split, the two sentences: *I imagined playing the piano* and *I imagined myself playing the piano*. In the first sentence the *I* of the complement sentence has been deleted; the result is the participant reading. In the second, the *I* of the complement has been raised to the matrix sentence, then reflexivized, and this yields the observer reading: *I imagined myself playing the piano*. Lakoff points out that verbs like *dream* and *imagine*, so-called world creating verbs, implicate more than one universe of discourse or possible world, the world in which I am dreaming and the world of my dream.[14]

Lakoff's main point is to show that such verbs as *dream* and *imagine* can implicate more than one universe of discourse or possible world. When I report my dream to someone, I make the report to someone living in the real world about the dream that took place in a possible world. Hence my report refers not only to the real world in which the report is made, but also to the dream world that is situated within the real world. However, this referential complexity of a world within a

world does not make the word *dream* a performative verb. By saying
"I dream . . ." I do not perform the act of dreaming any more than I
can perform the act of building a house by saying "I build a house."

The utterance "I imagine myself in (a world)" can be a report, but
not a performative. The act of uttering those words is not the same as
the act of imagination. Whereas I cannot invite someone without saying
"I invite you to . . . ," I can imagine a world without saying "I imagine
myself in a world. . . ." To utter the words "I invite you to . . ." makes
the speech act an act of invitation. The utterance of those words is an
essential constituent of the speech act; it constitutes the illocutionary
force of the act. But to utter the words "I imagine myself in a world
. . ." does not make the speech act an act of imagination; the utterance
of those words is not an essential constituent of the act of imagination.

Yet Samuel Levin goes on to explain his position as follows.

> In the higher sentence that we are positing for poems then, the *I* refers to
> the poet, in this world, but the *myself* which the poet imagines is in another
> world, the world created by the poet's imagination. In that world it is no
> longer the poet who moves, but a projection of himself, his persona. The
> second *I* in our higher sentence, the one who is doing the saying, is thus
> the *I* of the persona. The verb *imagine*, furthermore, is in this context a
> performative verb: the act of imagining has been performed; it is not merely
> being reported.

This passage is not altogether clear. What is clearly stated is that the
higher sentence of a poetic speech act involves two *I*'s and two worlds;
that is, the poet as a real person (the *I*) composing a poem in this real
world, and his persona (the *myself*) projected into the imaginary world
created by the poet. What is unclear is the reason why Levin asserts that
the second *I*, the persona of the poet, rather than the poet himself, is
"the one who is doing the saying." All along we had been given the
impression that Levin's aim was to clarify the nature of the poet's speech
act rather than his persona's and that the higher sentence was implicitly
spoken by the poet rather than by his persona.

The claim that the higher sentence is spoken by the persona is uncon-
vincing. Whoever speaks the sentence "I imagine myself in a world
. . ." must be the same person who creates a world through his imagination. But a persona cannot create or imagine a world; at best it can
be given a pretense of doing it. It is plausible for the poet to have his

persona move around in the world of his imaginative creation, but implausible for him to have the persona create a world by himself. A persona
is not an agent, but a product of imagination and creation.

This brings us to the most troublesome question. Whose speech acts
are we talking about, the acts of the poet or the acts of his persona? A
poem or a novel is often presented as an utterance of the poet's or the
novelist's persona rather than of the poet or the novelist himself. The
nature of speech acts performed by these personas is fundamentally the
same as that of speech acts performed by the characters in a poem or a
novel. These two types of speech acts are alike situated in the textual
world; they can be explicated by textual analyses.

Personas and fictive characters may involve the possible worlds of
different levels. While the poet's or the novelist's persona may be situated
in a possible world created by the poet or the novelist, the characters
may be projected into a possible world supposedly portrayed by his
persona. Nonetheless, all of them are contained in the textual world
constructed by the poet or the novelist. If this act of constructing a textual
world is to be called the macro-speech-act, the acts of the persona should
be regarded as micro-speech-acts along with the acts of the characters.

What then is the nature of the macro-speech-act of composing a poem
or constructing a novel? Do we really need Levin's higher sentence to
explain it? His account of poetic illocutionary forces seems to complicate
the issue by conflating two features of literary writings: the composition
of literary works and their presentation to the readers. These are two
different types of acts, which can be performed at different times and
even by different persons. A poem or a novel must be composed by a
poet or a novelist, but it can be presented to the public by his agent
rather than himself. To be sure, these two acts can be performed con-
currently, as in the case of an impromptu composition in front of an
audience. But their simultaneous performance need not erase the distinction in question.

When a poet or a novelist presents his poem or his novel to his audience
or public, his act of presentation can be explained by Levin's higher
sentence or some similar devices. His act of presentation amounts to
saying "I invite you to the following world which I have imaginatively
constructed," or "I want to show you what I have created," or even,
"I request you to buy a copy of my work." In the case of a simultaneous
creation and presentation, the writer's act my be explained by one of the

following sentences: "I want you to listen to what I am going to tell you," or "I request your attention because I want to present an impromptu composition of mine."

These requests for attention and response can be made by someone other than the poet or the novelist, that is, by someone who wants to recite a poem or a story that he has heard from someone else. His speech act can be explained by a higher sentence such as "I want you to listen to a story that I heard from my mother," or "I want to share a story with you, although its origin is unknown." This fact alone clearly establishes the conceptual demarcation between the act of presentation and the act of creation. As far as the act of presentation is concerned, it always takes place in the context of verbal exchange between two persons or more than two persons. Hence it can be accommodated within the general theory of speech acts, which has been developed mainly to account for the normal activities of verbal exchange or conversation in our private and public lives.

The act of creation is quite different from the act of presentation; the former does not require the context of interpersonal verbal exchange. The act of composing a poem or a novel is fundamentally the same as the act of composing a sonata or constructing a gadget. Unlike the acts of presentation, all these acts of creation or production can be performed by solitary individuals. When one makes a gadget or a sonata, one may anticipate to present it to the public or sell it to a buyer. Hence one may be forced to take into account the prevailing taste of the public or even the idiosyncratic biases of potential clients. Despite these social or cultural constraints on his works, the creator can and usually does perform the act of creation or production in solitude.

Does the act of composing a poem or a novel contain any implicit illocutionary forces that can be spelled out by the use of higher sentences or any other linguistic devices? This question may be answered by asking a similar question: Does the act of composing a sonata or constructing a gadget contain any implicit illocutionary forces? I am inclined to give a negative reply to this question. No act of creation per se is an act of illocution, while the act of presentation is always such an act. Here lies the fundamental difference between these two types of acts.

The act of creation may involve a verbal medium as in the case of composing a poem or a eulogy, but the use of language as medium does not endow the act of creation with any illocutionary forces. In J. L. Austin's words, an illocutionary act is to perform an act with words, but not every act that involves the use of words is an illocutionary act. Illocutionary acts are those acts that involve the use of words in the context of interpersonal interaction; to perform a performative act is to do things with words *to another person* or *other persons*. Hence his theory of illocutionary acts and forces does not apply to the things that I do with words to myself or by myself, for example, talking to myself or writing a reminder for myself.

It is quite conceivable to extend the notion of illocutionary acts and forces to the domain of solitary discourses. Then we can say that one performs the illocutionary act of warning oneself, chastising oneself, or advising oneself. These acts may even be called the solitary illocutionary acts in distinction from the communal ones. But even such an extension of the notion of illocutionary acts cannot readily make that notion applicable to the acts of creation. One may conduct a continuous conversation with oneself in the course of composing a poem or a sonata, but these solitary illocutionary acts do not form any essential constituents of the act of creation. They are only means for performing the act of creation.

The act of creation or production may involve the cooperation of several individuals, and their cooperation may require a series of continuous illocutionary acts. These illocutionary acts may determine what they are going to make and how they are going to make it. Nevertheless, these acts can give no illocutionary forces to the act of creation or its product, for they are only means for performing that act or for producing that product.

Because of this fundamental difference between the act of creation and the act of presentation, we may call them two different types of pragmatic acts. Both of them can be regarded as pragmatic acts because they alike involve the use of words. But one of them has illocutionary forces and the other does not. They can be said to be performed in two different types of pragmatic contexts: the context of creation and the context of presentation. The latter is an illocutionary context, but the former is not.

Some acts of literary creation may seem to involve an illocutionary context. For example, when Swift writes a satire about his countrymen, he may seem to be engaged in the illocutionary act of ridiculing them. But even there the distinction between the act of creation and the act of presentation should be retained. While he is writing a satire, he does not perform any illocutionary acts—that is, he is not telling anyone anything. Only when he presents his satire to the public does he perform an illocutionary act. The force of this illocutionary act can be expressed by such higher sentences as "I invite you to this beautiful picture of your true selves," or "Enjoy this piece, if you want to know what you really are like." The act of presentation can also be regarded as a perlocutionary act if it is viewed in terms of its effect. But these acts of illocution and perlocution should not be confused with the speech act of creation.[15]

Not every pragmatic act is illocutionary or perlocutionary. Illocutions and perlocutions belong to only one of many pragmatic genres, the one sometimes known as interlocution or conversation. Speech acts in literature have no reason to conform to the norms of this genre. Every pragmatic genre is governed by its own norms. To label literary speech acts as abnormal on the ground that they do not conform to the norms of interlocution is a genre mistake, the mistake of subsuming one pragmatic genre under the norms of another pragmatic genre.

Universal versus Regional Pragmatics

If the speech-act theory is concerned with only one pragmatic genre, it belongs to a regional pragmatics. Is it possible to construct a universal pragmatics, the pragmatic science that can set out the norms of all pragmatic genres? If there is such a universal science, its principles can be readily applied to literature as well as to any other genre. But not many attempts have been made to construct universal pragmatics. Even Aristotle limits his pragmatic investigations to two regional pragmatics, rhetoric and poetics, whereas he is mainly concerned with universal rather than regional semantics in his logical treatises.

Neither Charles Morris nor Rudolf Carnap has done anything serious for universal pragmatics beyond proposing their definitions of pragmatics. Looking back over Carnap's long linguistic career, Morris pointed out his "general tendency to regard pragmatics as an empirical discipline, and not to recognize the possibility of a pure pragmatics coordinate with pure semantics and pure syntactics."[16] By "pure pragmatics" Morris seems to mean the study of universal pragmatic principles that are valid in all pragmatic regions. In response to Morris' observation, Carnap says, "Today I would agree with Morris that there is an urgent need to develop pure pragmatics, which would supply a framework for descriptive pragmatics. It seems that this idea is now in many minds, and is ready for realization."[17]

The works that Carnap had anticipated for the realization of pure pragmatics have largely turned out to be those that implement the referential view of pragmatics. Since referential pragmatics cannot handle the pragmatic norms that go beyond the domain of reference, it is not much more useful than the old pure semantics. There is only one person who has made the daring attempt to construct a universal pragmatics truly in the pragmatic domain. Jürgen Habermas makes this attempt in his essay "What Is Universal Pragmatics?" He opens it by declaring, "The task of universal pragmatics is to identify and reconstruct universal conditions of possible understanding."[18] He maintains that the fundamental norm of communication is to reach understanding between the parties involved, and that any other social action is derivative from this fundamental act of communicative understanding.

Habermas then asserts that every communicative action involves four universal validity claims. That is, anyone engaged in a communicative action claims to be:[19] *uttering* something understandably; giving [the hearer] *something* to understand; making *himself* thereby understandable; and coming to an understanding *with another person*. These four validity claims are regarded as the essential conditions for a normal state of linguistic communication. Habermas then goes into a long discussion on the various aspects of linguistics and the various ways of studying language. Perhaps the most important point in this discussion is that universal pragmatics must use the notion of communicative competence, the ability to use language in social communication, in place of Chomsky's notion of linguistic competence, the ability to construct sentences. He states this preference on the ground that Chomsky's notion is monological, whereas the notion of communicative competence is dialogical.[20]

Habermas defines communicative competence in terms of its component competencies: the ability to choose a propositional sentence to represent something in the world; the ability to express intentions through language; and the ability to perform speech acts in conformity with recognized norms.[21] These three abilities are called the universal-pragmatic aspects. The analysis of these aspects involves two areas called "Theoretical Level" and "Object Domain."[22] The analysis of the first universal-pragmatic aspect involves the theory of elementary propositions and the object domain of reference and predication. The analysis of the second universal-pragmatic aspect involves the theory of first-person sentences and the domain of intentions and their expressions. The analysis of the third universal-pragmatic aspect involves the theory of illocutionary acts and the domain of interpersonal relations. The analysis of these three aspects evidently constitutes the heart of Habermas' universal pragmatics.

Now Habermas goes into a discussion of the speech act theory, which is presumably meant to be his analysis of the third universal-pragmatic aspect. He says nothing further about the analysis of the first and second aspects. Evidently he presumes that the analysis of these two aspects has been accomplished. The analysis of the first aspect is the analysis of an elementary proposition, whose meaning is determined by the referential function of its subject and by the predicative function of its predicate. These two functions have been analyzed in formal semantics and syntax. The analysis of the second aspect can be presumed to have been accomplished by sociolinguistics. This linguistic science has placed special emphasis on the commmunicative use of language, such as the use of personal pronouns in social interaction. Habermas has probably picked up the notion of communicative competence from sociolinguistics. Some aspects of sociolinguistics belong to semantics—such as the semantics of pronouns—while other aspects belong to pragmatics, such as the social norms governing the different modes of addressing the elderly and the young, or the male and the female in some societies.[23]

Habermas' discussion of the speech-act theory is partly an exposition and partly a critique. The upshot of his critique is to propose his triadic schema of classification in place of Austin's and Searle's classifications. According to this new schema, there are three types of speech action: constatives, regulatives (commands and requests), and avowals (of speaker's intentions and attitudes). These three kinds of speech action take three different modes of communication: cognitive, interactive, and expressive. They also involve three different types of themes: propositional content, interpersonal relation, and speaker's intention; and three different validity claims: truth, rightness and appropriateness, and truthfulness.

As Habermas clearly implies, his triadic classification of speech acts and their contents does not change the fundamental character of the speech-act theory. His vaunted attempt to construct a universal pragmatics amounts to no more than accepting the speech-act theory, with the proviso that it has to be accompanied by the first two universal-pragmatic aspects. Since these two aspects are the semantic requirements presupposed for the performance of any speech acts, they are obviously acceptable to anyone espousing the speech-act theory. As we have already seen, semantics is presupposed for pragmatics. Austin and Searle did not even mention those two aspects, probably because they had regarded them as too-obvious preconditions for any speech acts. To call them the first two universal-pragmatic aspects or preconditions of speech acts does not alter the boundary of pragmatic investigations. The domain of Habermas' universal pragmatics remains identical with that of speech-act theory, that is, the province of interlocution.

Since many of our speech acts locate themselves outside the province of interlocution, it is a terminological mistake to label Habermas' pragmatics as a universal pragmatics. Of course, this label can be justified if he can demonstrate his assumption that the communicative use of language is its most fundamental use, and that all other uses of language are derived from this most fundamental one. But he has made no attempt at this demonstration, and there seems to be no reason to believe that it is a plausible assumption. It appears to be clearly implausible to derive the literary or religious function of language from its function in interlocution. Hence Habermas' universal pragmatics is just another regional pragmatics.

In general, the central function of a regional pragmatics is to determine the pragmatic norms of a given speech region. Since Habermas' investigation of interpersonal communication does little in performing this function, his investigation is of little use even as a project for a regional pragmatics. The determination of pragmatic rules for any region of language use is not easy, because those rules are by their very nature vague and informal. By comparison with this difficult task, Habermas' work in classification and reclassification is relatively superficial and perfunctory. The question of whether the avowals ("I confess to you . . .") should be placed in the same class with or in a different class from the regulatives ("I ask you to . . .") is a matter of classificatory preference; to settle this question is no more than a preliminary step toward determining the pragmatic norms involved in those speech acts. This preliminary maneuver of classification is often mistaken for the ultimate task of systematization in Teutonic scholasticism and eclecticism.

The difficulty of specifying the vague and informal pragmatic rules can readily be seen in H. P. Grice's attempt to articulate the rules governing conversations under the following four headings:[24]

(1) *Quantity:* Make your contribution neither more nor less informative than is required for the current purposes of the exchange.
(2) *Quality:* Try to make your contribution a truthful one.

(3) *Relation:* Be relevant.
(4) *Manner:* Be perspicuous in your expression.

These four rules are called conversational maxims. Since they are maxims, they can be obeyed or violated. But their violation can be either real or apparent. In response to the question whether Austin is smaller or bigger than Boston, let us suppose someone tells you not only that Austin is smaller than Boston, but also that Austin is also smaller than New York and Chicago, that Austin is hot in summer, that Austin is located in Texas, and a few other things. His volubility, Grice would say, really violates the maxim of making one's contribution to a conversation neither more nor less than is required for the purpose of the conversational exchange.

Grice explains the apparent violation of those maxims with the use of tautologies and metaphors. Tautologies such as "War is war" and "Women are women" can violate those maxims, taken literally, because they are noninformative. But they are informative on the level of what Grice calls conversational implicatures; that is, the informative content of those tautologies implied through the contexts of conversation. Likewise, metaphors such as "You are the cream in my coffee" violate conversational maxims, taken literally, because they are false on the literal level. But their truthfulness can be perceived on the level of conversational implicatures. According to Grice, every conversation takes place on two levels of communication: what is said and what is implied. The question of whether or not the conversational maxims are violated can be determined by examining their application to both levels.

Grice's four maxims appear to be no more than four different ways to say that statements made in conversational exchanges should be appropriate to the purpose of exchanges, that is, appropriate in informational quantity and quality, in the manner of exchange, and for the subject matter of conversation. Hence Grice himself regards those four maxims as expressions of one Cooperative Principle. But there is one problem for such a principle; it can hold only when the two parties to the exchange subscribe to the same set of purposes. Let us reconsider the case of our voluble respondent. He clearly violates Grice's maxim, if his purpose is to answer your question whether Austin is smaller or bigger than Boston. Now suppose that this is not his purpose, and that his purpose is to harass you. For that purpose, his response to your question is perfectly adequate, although it is inadequate for the purpose of answering your question.

Our respondent seems to be bound by Grice's maxim only on the condition that his sole purpose is to answer your question. Under most normal conditions, it may be a matter of decency and politeness that he should try to answer your question in an appropriate manner. But there can be no linguistic rules or pragmatic maxims that can prescribe a form of behavior for every occasion. For a further complication of the problem, Grice's rules cannot be regarded even as maxims of politeness and decency. As Robin Lakoff has pointed out, the maxim of saying only truthful things is sometimes violated for the sake of politeness and considerateness.[25] A. P. Martinich has proposed to amend Grice's maxim of quality so as to read "Be authentic: that is, do not knowingly participate in a speech act for which the conditions of successful and nondefective performance are not satisfied."[26] Although this amendment produces a laudable maxim, it completely shifts the locus of Grice's maxim from the quality of information exchanged in a conversation to the attitude of its participants.

Grice's conversational maxims hold only on the condition that the sole purpose of conversation is restricted to the exchange of information. From this restriction logically follow his four maxims, his four different ways of claiming that every utterance in conversations ought to be appropriate for the exchange of information. If the exchange of information is the sole purpose of conversations, they should be conducted in an appropriate manner for that purpose. But many of our conversations are meant fo fulfill purposes other than that of exchanging information. We often talk not to inform others, but to tease or amuse them, to provoke or appease them, to edify or mystify them, or even just to break the silence. Hence Grice's Cooperative Principle cannot be regarded as the universal pragmatic principle governing the use of language in conversations.

Perhaps the only thing that can be proposed as a universal pragmatic principle is: "Be appropriate in what you say and how you say it." For this reason probably, the notion of appropriateness (*prepon, decorum*) was the central category in Roman rhetoric. It had already been used as a pragmatic device by Aristotle, although his use had limited it to the domain of diction. He said that diction should be appropriate, and defined the appropriateness of diction as its correspondence to its subject.

"Correspondence to subject" means that we must neither speak casually about weighty matters, nor solemnly about trivial ones; nor must we add ornamental epithets to commonplace nouns, or the effect will be comic, as in the works of Cleophon, who can use phrases as absurd as "O queenly fig-tree." (*Rhetoric* 1408a12–16)

The notion of appropriateness need not be confined to diction, because it can be applied to any relation of means and end. Hence the Stoics transformed it into an ethical category and translated the Greek word *prepon* as the Latin word *decorum*. The magnitude of this word as a Stoic ethical category can be seen in Cicero's statement: "Such is its essential nature, that it [*decorum*] is inseparable from moral goodness; what is appropriate is morally right, and what is morally right is appropriate" (*De officiis 1:93–94*). In rhetoric, Cicero regarded the notion of *decorum* as the universal rule (*Orator* 71). *Decorum* becomes the fundamental principle with Horace and the source of all true rules for art with Quintilian.[27]

Most of the things that have been said in pragmatics can be restated in terms of appropriateness. Austin's felicity conditions are sometimes called the appropriateness conditions. Grice's conversational maxims can be improved by being restated in terms of appropriateness.

(1) *Quantity:* Make the amount of information exchanged appropriate to the occasion.
(2) *Quality:* Make the truth of your contribution or its lack of it appropriate to the occasion.
(3) *Relation:* Make your contribution appropriate to the subject matter under discussion.
(4) *Manner:* Use appropriate modes of expression.

The category of appropriateness is also extensively used by sociolinguistics in dealing with pragmatic conventions of social communication, for example, the appropriate social forms of address between the young and the old. Since the question of appropriateness is usually determined in reference to contexts, it is sometimes called "context grammar."[28]

The category of appropriateness is uniquely pragmatic; it cannot be used in any other branches of linguistics. Syntax, phonology, and semantics all have their norms and rules, and their violation can produce abnormal linguistic phenomena. But none of them can be said to be appropriate or inappropriate in their own right; their normality and abnormality do not directly translate themselves into their pragmatic appropriateness and inappropriateness. A grammatically normal sentence cannot be appropriate for a pragmatic function that calls forth the use of a grammatically abnormal sentence. The questions of appropriateness and inappropriateness arise only in pragmatic contexts, and can be settled only in reference to pragmatic norms and functions.

We have said that the category of appropriateness is relational, that is, it applies to the relation of means and end. But this relation does not exhaust the category of appropriateness. When we say that discourtesy is inappropriate in the behavior of the young toward the old, we are not placing the behavior of the young in a means–end relation. Nonetheless the use of this category is still relational; it involves interpersonal relations. In the domain of interpersonal relations, appropriateness is not only a means but also an end in itself. For this reason the Stoics assigned ethical significance to the category of appropriateness. Thus this category can carry two different types of value: the intrinsic and the extrinsic.

This duality of appropriateness reflects the duality of human actions: some actions are performed for their own sake, while others are performed for the sake of something else. When we want to stress the instrumental dimension of the category of appropriateness, we can replace it with any terms of instrumental value such as "useful," "effective," or "serviceable." In the contexts of instrumental value, appropriate speech acts are those that are useful, effective, or serviceable for some purpose. What is referred to by these various words is the general notion of instrumental efficacy, and Austin's notion of perlocutionary effects belongs to this general notion.

When we want to stress the intrinsic dimension of the category of appropriateness, we can replace it with any terms of intrinsic value such as "excellent," "marvelous," or "outstanding." The intrinsic value of a speech act can either reside in the act itself or derive from its product. The speech act of telling a joke can be regarded as an excellent one, either because it has produced an excellent joke, or because it has delivered a joke in an excellent manner. One is an act of creation, and the other an act of performance. In the former case, the category of excellence does not apply directly to the act; the direct object of its application is the speech product rather than the speech act.

The pragmatic norms governing speech products are different from those governing speech acts. Whereas speech acts can have no independent existence, speech products can exist as independent entities. The former exist only as actions and attributes of some persons, but the latter have their own substantial being. Hence speech products can be analyzed and appreciated in their own right. This underlies the fundamental methodological difference between Aristotle's *Poetics* and his *Rhetoric*. In his

Poetics, poetic products are analyzed as independent entities; they are shown to have their own structures and to perform their own functions. In his *Rhetoric*, persuasive speeches are investigated only as constituents of persuasive acts. For this reason, his *Rhetoric* presents nothing equivalent to his analysis of tragedy and the *Oedipus Tyrannus* as an organic unity.

Because of the ontological difference between speech acts and speech products, the pragmatics of the former should be distinguished from the pragmatics of the latter. This distinction has generally been overlooked by those who have tried to apply the speech-act theory to literature. The difficulties encountered in their applications largely arise from the fact that the pragmatic norms for understanding and evaluating speech acts are inappropriate to understanding and evaluating speech products. What is really needed for the pragmatics of literature is the pragmatics of speech products.

CHAPTER SEVEN
Pragmatic Functions

THE pragmatics of speech products is the study of speech products, their traits and their functions. Insofar as pragmatics is a science, the study of these traits and functions must be conducted on a general level. The objects of its scientific generalization must be not the individual speech products but rather their classes or genres. Thus described, the pragmatics of speech products shows itself as one of the oldest disciplines, genre criticism. It is one of Aristotle's enduring legacies.

Aristotle's *Poetics* was the first treatise in genre criticism; it was a systematic investigation of poetry as a general genre and tragedy as a special one. All subsequent works on poetry and tragedy belong to these two branches of genre criticism. There is no reason to limit genre criticism to the study of these two genres; such other genres as comedy, novel, satire, and lyric have produced their own genre studies. In our own century, genre criticism has gained special impetus from Robert Hutchins' and Mortimer Adler's attempts to revive Aristotelianism at the University of Chicago, and the Chicago school of genre criticism has emerged and thrived as a product of this revivalism.

The central task of genre criticism is to determine and articulate the nature of a given genre, and one of the standard methods for performing this task is to study the genre traits. For example, the genre criticism of tragedy is the study of those traits that constitute the essence of tragedy. Since the notions of genre and its essence are unmistakably Aristotelian, genre studies have always had a tendency to accept the Aristotelian essentialism, namely, the notion that the generic essences are universal and eternal. Although this essentialism has been invalidated by Charles Darwin's theory of evolution in natural science, it is still accepted, consciously and unconsciously, in many quarters of human studies. In literary criticism, it has been espoused by not only the committed

Aristotelians, but also by those conscious neither of embracing Aristotelianism nor of practicing genre criticism.

Most of the New Critics have, though unconsciously, acted on genre essentialism. In exalting the paradox and irony of a poem as its most significant features, for example, Cleanth Brooks is informally accepting paradox and irony as the universal genre traits of poetry.[1] As such, they are assumed to constitute the universal essence of poetry as a genre. In my *Cultural Thematics*, I have shown that these generic traits constitute not the universal essence of poems in every culture and historical epoch, but the provincial nature of modern European poetry.[2]

I have also shown that these generic traits of modern European poetry reflect the historical nature of the modern European sensibility, which is fundamentally paradoxical. Modern European sensibility developed in the transition from the medieval concern with the other world to the Renaissance concern with this world. But this transition was not an easy one to make, for it was as difficult to abandon and forget the old religious concerns that had governed European life for over a millennium, as to remain faithful to them in the face of the rising concerns with the secular world. This difficulty induced an acute sense of ambivalence and ambiguity into the Renaissance ethos. Many Renaissance figures tried to resolve this ambivalence by their bold attempt to realize the medieval religious ideals in the secular world. They hoped that this would enable them to remain faithful to both their old and their new concerns, because they were not abandoning their old concerns but rather transferring them to a new domain of realization.

However, the attempt to realize the old religious ideals in the secular world involved an inherent contradiction. The medieval religious ideals had been developed as the ideals of infinite perfection, which could be realized even in the eternal kingdom of God only with the aid of his infinite power. These ideals could not easily be accommodated within the mutable kingdom of finite human beings. Thus the bold Renaissance attempt resulted in a series of irresolvable dialectical conflicts between the finite and the infinite, the eternal and the temporal, the human and the divine. This inevitable conflict between old ideals and their new realm of realization produced the unique Renaissance spiritual epidemic called *paradoxia epidemica*.[3] Thus the Renaissance ethos and sensibility came to be permeated by a pervasive sense of paradox.

This is a brief account of how the modern European sensibility has been permeated by the sense of ambivalence, ambiguity, and paradox since the Renaissance. Modern European poetry has reflected the same sense of ambivalence, ambiguity, and paradox because it is a product of modern European sensibility. That is, the New Critics' favorite criteria for poetic excellence are derived from those provincial genre traits of modern European poetry. They have mistaken a provincial set of generic traits for a universal set, because they have developed their canon of poetic analysis on the limited basis of modern European poetry without knowing its limitations.

The provinciality of the New Critics' allegedly universal poetic criteria becomes obvious as soon as these criteria are extended beyond the province of modern European poetry. For example, the sense of paradox and irony seldom stands out as the central characteristic of medieval or ancient poetry. Since the generic traits of the New Critics just do not apply to poetic works produced outside the province of the modern European tradition, the practice of New Criticism has been limited to the confines of that province.

To mistake provincial traits for universal ones has been one of the unhealthy tendencies in intrinsic criticism. Since intrinsic criticism concentrates its effort on the intrinsic nature of literary works, it has tended to dissociate the study of those works from their pragmatic contexts. Once those works are dissociated from their historically given contextual nexuses, they can easily be mistaken for timeless monuments. The study of these timeless monuments and their timeless essences has been regarded as the ultimate aim of intrinsic criticism. But the sense of timeless traits and essences only reflects the lack of historical sensitivity, and this lack is a serious obstacle to the pragmatic investigations of speech products. For the essence of every speech product lies in its historicity; its pragmatic norm is historically given and its pragmatic function is historically determined. Perhaps the historicity of genre and their traits can best be elucidated by demonstrating the continuous changes that have taken place in the pragmatic function of poetry and literature.

Poetic Function

Since the Renaissance, the central function of poetry has been taken to be aesthetic, that is, the function of producing and providing aesthetic delight. This aesthetic view of poetry is so deeply ingrained in our own sensibility that we usually assume that its aesthetic function is transcultural and transhistorical. A broader historical perspective will show that this aesthetic view is another provincial trait that has been mistaken for a transcultural universal.

In ancient Greece, the central function of poetry was to aid the perpetuation of its tradition and cultural heritage. The Homeric epics served the same sacred function for ancient Greeks that the Old Testament did for the Jews and the Bible for the Christians. They were sacred texts that passed on from generation to generation the wisdom of their sages and the annals of their heroes, which constituted the chief instrument in molding their civic virtues, temperaments, and sentiments.[4] For this reason, the bards were their sages, prophets, and teachers until the emergence of Greek sophists and philosophers, who for the first time challenged the bards' immense authority. Homer had been revered as the universal fountain of all knowledge; his authority had been as awesome as that of Apollo and his Delphic oracles. Although the pre-Socratic philosophers were already trying to replace the poets as the agents of discovering and dispensing truth and knowledge, some of them even wrote in poetic styles, because they still regarded the language of poetry as the only worthy medium for the exposition of truth and knowledge, the noblest gifts from immortals to mortals.[5]

In *The Frogs*, Aristophanes stages a debate between Aeschylus and Euripides on the social function of poets. In this debate, Aeschylus says to Euripides, "Come, tell me what are the points for which a noble poet our praise obtains." Euripides replies to Aeschylus, "For his ready wit, and his counsels sage, and because the citizen folk he trains/ To be better townsmen and worthier men." Their discussion of poets' social function is finally summed up by Aeschylus.

Aye, such are the poet's appropriate works: and just consider
      how all along
From the very first they have wrought you good, the noble bards,
      the masters of song.
First, Orpheus taught you religious rites, and from bloody
      murder to stay your hands:
Musaeus healing and oracle lore; and Hesiod all the culture of lands,
The time to gather, the time to plough. And gat not Homer
      his glory divine
By singing of valour, and honour, and right, and the sheen
      of the battle-extended line,
The ranging of troops and the arming of men?[6]

When Plato examines, in his *Republic*, the role of poetry in the education of youth and especially in the molding of character, he is not
introducing a new approach toward poetry. Instead, he is just examining
its traditional role. Even his criticism of poets is not new. The Greek
sophists had already challenged the authority and capacity of the poets
to perform the awesome social functions that had been long assigned to
them. Plato continues the sophists' challenge to the poets' authority in
claiming that poets are not true knowers even though they can sometimes
say marvelous things through divine inspiration. In most cases, however,
Plato is convinced that poets are ignorant persons who say many scandalous things about mortals and immortals alike. Consequently, he ban-
ishes the poets from his ideal state, and thereby divests them of their
traditional social roles.

Although Plato's banishment of poets from his ideal state was a radical
measure, his debunking of their authority as the true source of knowledge
and wisdom was more or less an announcement of the *fait accompli* in
Plato's Athens, where the bards' traditional role as the ultimate source
of knowledge and wisdom had been taken over by the sophists and the
philosophers. This *fait accompli* indicates the immense transformation of
Greek culture from the Homeric epoch to the Platonic epoch. As many
have recently noted, this was the transformation of an oral into a written
tradition. Behind this formal change lies the substantive one: the knowledge and wisdom that had been a matter of tradition and heritage were
turned into an affair of inquiry and criticism. The bards and rhapsodists
had performed the function of transmitting the old traditional heritage
from one generation to another; the sophists and philosphers now set
out to perform the new function of critical inquiry. Thus the problem
of poets was produced by the transformation of Greek culture and
society.

Even the discomfort and offense Plato feels toward the so-called scandalous tales of Homeric epics may indicate the vast cultural transformation of ancient Greece between the time of those epics and the time
of Plato's Athens. It is highly probable that the Homeric Greeks found
nothing offensive or scandalous in the Homeric episodes of the mortals
and the immortals. On the contrary, it is most likely that those stories
portrayed for them truly edifying actions and events. By the time of
Plato's Athens, Greek culture had so changed that the Homeric heroes
and heroines could no longer be accepted as ideal models for human
conduct. If so, the cultural transformation of ancient Greece had per-

formed a serious transvaluation of the values and ideals embodied in Homeric epics.

It has often been said that Aristotle in his *Poetics* meant to defend poetry against Plato's attack. But this traditional understanding of Aristotle's position on poetry is only partly true. He never disputed Plato's repudiation of the poets' traditional authority as the ultimate source of knowledge and wisdom. He had no disagreement with Plato over the fact that the poets could no longer be accepted as the revered authorities of knowledge and wisdom, nor their poems as sacred utterances for edification and instruction. But Aristotle offered a different resolution for the problem of poets and their works.

In place of Plato's radical measure of banishing the poets from the state altogether, Aristotle recommended the moderate measure of allowing them to practice their craft mainly for the sake of the pleasure that could be derived from their works. Aristotle's was a functional resolution of the problem of poets: that is, he resolved the problem by radically reducing the traditionally extensive social functions to the restricted function of providing harmless pleasure. Even this functional resolution may have been no more than a formal announcement of what was already taking place in his Athens.

These two resolutions of the problem of poetry reflect the different assessments Plato and Aristotle had made of poets and their powers. In Plato's view, the power of poets and their works was just too great to be safely tolerated within the state. Almost every time Plato talks of poets, he betrays, one way or another, his pervasive concern with their mysterious power. In the *Apology* (22B), he has Socrates say, "Then I knew that not by wisdom do poets write poetry, but by a sort of genius and inspiration." In the *Ion*, Socrates uses the metaphor of magnet to describe the divine power from which poetic inspirations emanate.

> This is not an art in you . . . but a divine power, which moves you like the stone Euripides calls a magnet. . . . For this stone not only attracts iron rings, but also imparts to them the power of attracting other rings; so that it can form a chain of iron and rings, suspended one from another, all of which derive their power of attraction from the original stone. In the same manner the Muse inspires men herself, and then through these inspired persons the inspiration spreads to others, thereby establishing a chain of inspiration. For all good poets, epic as well as lyric, compose their beautiful poems not from art, but through inspiration and possession. (*Ion* 533D–E)

Socrates goes on to say that the chain of poetic inspiration cannot easily be contained within the poets and rhapsodes. Through poetic recitations and theatric performances, it reaches out for the audience. Just as an inspired and possessed poet is not truly himself, so the members of his audience cease to be themselves when they are possessed by the emanating power of poetic inspiration. Hence Plato gives the label of divine madness to the manifestation of poetic inspiration. Since this divine madness and frenzy adversely affect the character of persons, he does not allow the citizens of his ideal state to have even the pleasure of witnessing the performances of poets and story-tellers visiting from other states unless they are of the austere kind (*Republic* 398A).

Far from sharing Plato's view of poetry as a gift of divine inspiration rather than a human art, Aristotle defines poetry as an art of imitation (*Poetics* 1447a1–17). Since the impulse to imitate is one of the strongest human instincts, he holds, the art of imitation provides one of the most fundamental pleasures in human life. In addition to this pleasure of imitation, poetry can also produce some therapeutic benefit, the catharsis of fear and pity. For these reasons, Aristotle readily accepts the art of poetry as an essential feature of a well-ordered state and its experience as a wholesome dimension of human life. His attitude toward poetry seems never to be influenced by Plato's deepseated anxiety and ambivalence.

This difference between Plato and Aristotle in attitude toward poetry may be compared to the difference in people's attitudes toward wild beasts and their domestic counterparts. Most civilized societies of antiquity regarded the legacy of oral tradition as a flock of wild beasts still roaming about their enlightened cities; that is, as objects of attraction and aversion, fascination and suspicion. In those societies, the legacy of oral tradition was represented by the bards, seers, and magicians. Plato tries to keep poetry safely outside the walls of his ideal state, because he still regards it as a wild beast. But Aristotle gladly accepts it as a source of delight and benefit, because he believes that its wildness has been domesticated.

In the modern world of literary criticism, Aristotle has been hailed as the father of intrinsic criticism. His treatment of poetry has been regarded as one of the first attempts to assess the value of poetry for its intrinsic function of providing aesthetic pleasure. In the meantime, Plato's treatment of poetry has been denounced as an extrinsic criticism, an attempt to assess the value of poetry for such extrinsic functions as molding the character of youth, pronouncing inspired words of wisdom, or establishing the ideals for human conduct.

What is the intrinsic function of poetry, and what are its extrinsic functions? It is impossible to provide transcultural answers to these questions, because the functions of poetry are always culture-bound. Over a long period of time, as we have seen, the so-called extrinsic functions of poetry had been considered intrinsic by the ancient Greeks. Those functions are now considered as extrinsic to poetry in our culture, but this is no more than our provincial view, which should not be mistaken for a universal truth.

Insofar as the Homeric Greeks normally expected their bards to pronounce original words of wisdom, to mold the character of their youth, and to set the standards for their conduct, and insofar as their bards regarded the performance of these functions as primary, these expectations and intentions constituted the pragmatic context for their poetry. It is this pragmatic context that determines what is intrinsic and what is extrinsic to their poetry. Since every pragmatic context is embedded in a cultural context, the distinction between the intrinsic and the extrinsic functions of any speech product can be decided only in reference to the relevant cultural context.

Aristotle's view of poetry is still quite different from our modern intrinsic view. The essential feature of the latter view is the primacy of the aesthetic value and function; that is, the primary function of poetry is to provide aesthetic pleasure. This modern notion is not in the center of Aristotle's theory of poetry. Even the word "aesthetic" was not known to him. Aristotle gives two reasons for the pleasure of poetry (*Poetics* 1448b4–23): imitation, and the sense of harmony and rhythm. In his view, the instinct of imitation is most natural to human nature (a human being is more imitative than any other kind of animal), and the exercise of this instinct is always a source of great pleasure. Even when the real scene or event is painful, he observes, its imitation (or representation) is delightful to us. To provide this pleasure of imitation is the central function of poetry. The pleasure derived from the sense of harmony and rhythm may be given the modern label of aesthetic pleasure, but it is only secondary to the pleasure of imitation.

Aristotle recognizes six components of tragedy: plot, characters, diction, thought, spectacle, and melody (*Poetics* 1450a1–14). None of these is an aesthetic quality or attribute. In his discussion of plot, Aristotle considers the question of beauty as no more than "a matter of size and order" (*Poetics* 1450b37). As such, beauty has no special connection with poetry; it is a universal property that can be found in all objects, whether they be objects of art or of nature. When he talks of the proper pleasure produced by a well-constructed story, he attributes it to the organic unity of the story, which is presumably derived from its imitation of "the organic unity of a living creature" (*Poetics* 1459a21).

Aristotle's claim that poetic pleasure is mainly mimetic (or imitative) implies that he assigns to poetry an ontological status lower than that of reality. This is to restate Plato's claim that poems and other artifacts are only copies of real things. Even the central term in Aristotle's *Poetics*, *mimesis* (imitation), is derived from Plato's usage. In describing the nature of poetry and other arts, their production and function, Plato uses the word *mimesis* and its cognates: *mimetike* (mimetic art), *mimetes* (imitator), *mimesasthai* (imitate), *mimoumenon* (imitated), and *mimetikos* (imitative) (*Republic* 598B, 597E, 604E, 605A). Of course, Plato and Aristotle do not share the same notion of what counts as reality, and yet they agree on the unreality of artifacts or rather their quasi-reality.

In Aristotle's ontology, substances alone are truly real. The paradigm of Aristotelian substances is a living organism. In his view, the hallmark of being truly real or being a substance is "to be one," that is, to have an organic unity or indivisibility. Because man-made products do not have organic unities, Aristotle regards them as only quasi-real. True substances can never be made by human hands; they can come into being only through natural birth. For the same reason, all works of art are only quasi-real; their unity and reality are only imitative.

To be sure, Aristotle often uses artifacts as standard examples of substances, mainly because the distinction of form and matter can be much more easily illustrated in their case than in the case of natural objects. However, this advantage becomes a serious disadvantage when he tries to stress the inseparability of form and matter in substances. Whereas form and matter are truly inseparable in natural objects, they are not so in artifacts. The unity of form and matter in artifacts is not as perfect as in natural objects. Hence Aristotle holds that the word "unity" is not any more univocal than the words "substance" and "being" (*Metaphysics* 1053b24). He expresses the same point by claiming that none of these words denotes a genus, for a generic term is univocal. The nonunivocality of these ontological categories means that Aristotle's ontology admits different degrees of being one and being a substance, that is, different degrees of being and reality.

In Aristotle's view, another hallmark of true substances is the indestructibility of their forms, because no true form is ever made or begotten. Since the forms of man-made objects do not enjoy this privilege of indestructibility, Aristotle questions the true substantiality of those objects: "Perhaps, indeed, neither these things themselves [artifacts],nor any of other things which are not formed by nature, are substances at all; for one might say that the nature in natural objects is the only substance to be found in destructible things" (*Metaphysics* 1043b22–23).

Since mimetic objects are ontologically inferior to real objects, Aristotle subordinates the mimetic function of poetry to the ethical and political functions of the real world, whenever the former comes into conflict with the latter. He maintains that the following are two of the plots to be avoided in a tragedy: a good man falling from happiness to misery, and a bad man rising from misery to happiness (*Poetics* 1452b33–40).These two plots are so offensive to our ethical sense that they cannot produce the normal mimetic pleasure of poetry.

Aristotle also recognizes the didactic function of poetry in his *Nicomachean Ethics* and *Politics*. On this point, he is also in agreement with Plato. To be sure, the didactic function does not have the same exalted prestige as the function of pronouncing the inspired words of wisdom and truth. However, if Aristotle were asked to assess the comparative merit of the didactic and the mimetic functions of poetry, he would undoubtedly rank the former higher than the latter. For the didactic function belongs to the world of reality, while the mimetic function belongs to the world of its copies. In Aristotle's world, the mimetic function is indeed the most natural function of poetry, but not its highest function.

None of these Aristotelian notions about poetry is acceptable to the modern intrinsic approach. Since the Renaissance, however, the champions of modern intrinsic criticism have done their best to transform Aristotle's doctrines into their own views. In his commentary on Aristotle's *Poetics*, for example, the sixteenth-century Aristotelian Lodovico Castelvetro maintains that the sole end of poetry is to provide pleasure and that poetry has nothing to do with the question of utility, which belongs to the end of government.[7]

This is one of the first emphatic statements of the primacy of poetry's aesthetic function. Even Dante would have taken it as a gross misunderstanding of his poetry, had someone told him that the primary function of his *Commedia* was to provide aesthetic pleasure. Like Plato and

Aristotle, Dante would have assumed that the didactic function of instructing his fellow Christians on the nature of the other world was far weightier than the aesthetic function, and that whatever beauty or aesthetic pleasure might be found in his *Commedia* was meant to be used as an effective aid to this didactic function.

In the modern West, this ancient and medieval notion of the didactic function came to be regarded as too debasing for decent poetry. In our century, it has been condemned as didactic heresy. Thus emerged the doctrine of aesthetic autonomy, that is, the aesthetic function of poetry could not be subject to any other function. This doctrine was finally formalized by Kant in his *Critique of Judgment*.

In the meantime, the doctrine of aesthetic autonomy was given its ontological support in the transformation of Aristotle's notions of *poesis* (making) and *mimesis*. As we have seen, these functions had been relegated to the lowly domain of quasi-reality, because no man-made products could have the organic unity of real substances. Only nature and her species were assumed to be capable of generating true substances, because they were not subject to the human process of making and unmaking. Hence Aristotle believed that nature and her species were not only truly real but also eternal (or uncreated), whereas artifacts could be neither truly real nor eternal.

During the Middle Ages, however, the ontological status of artifacts was dramatically elevated through the Christian dogma of creation. In opposition to Aristotle's doctrine of the eternity of nature, Christianity taught that nature has been made by God. God came to be conceived as the Great Artisan, whose function was emulated by poets and other artists. Since the Middle Ages, this analogy of artistic function to the divine creative function has helped exalt the role of artists and their products. The mimetic function of poets and other artists has been transformed from the lowly trade of making unreal copies of real things into the noble profession of making ideal things which are even better or more perfect than real things. This is the modern doctrine of artistic creation or ideal imitation, which goes together with the doctrine of aesthetic autonomy.

These two doctrines constitute the heart of the modern intrinsic approach to poetry. Since both doctrines were diametrically opposed to Aristotle's own views, his *Poetics* in its original form could not be directly exalted as the ultimate authority for modern intrinsic criticism. This is why battalions of critics and aestheticians have had, over several cen-

turies, to make a concerted effort to transform (in the name of interpretation and reinterpretation) the basic concepts of Aristotle's *Poetics* so
as to conform with their own views. Of course, this transformation has
been achieved at the cost of relocating his immortal poetic manual from
its original to our modern context.

Aesthetic Function

To secure the autonomy of aesthetic function was by no means easy.
It took a sustained struggle against the supremacy of religious values and
functions. During the Middle Ages, the religious end had been the highest
end, ruling over all other human ends and values—not only aesthetic but
even ethical and intellectual values. Under the supremacy of religion,
there could be no other goals that human beings should seek for their
own sake. All nonreligious values were ultimately subservient to religious values. This subservience had imposed heteronomy on all nonreligious activities. Consequently the heteronomy of aesthetic function
had been the firmly established norm during the Middle Ages.

This view can be better appreciated by contrasting it with that of the
ancient Greeks, who regarded knowledge as one of the highest human
values and its pursuit for its own sake as one of the noblest activities.
This pagan view of knowledge was an offense to the medieval Christian
sense of values. Denouncing the pagan view of knowledge, St. Bernard
of Clairvaux says, "For there are some who desire knowledge for its
own sake; and that is shameful curiosity" (*Sermones in cantico canticorum*
12.3).

The absolute subservience of all nonreligious values to religious ones
was, for the first time, considerably weakened by St. Thomas Aquinas,
who recognized to some extent the intrinsic merit of nonreligious values.
To give a measure of autonomy to nonreligious values (natural ends)
was one of his main purposes in demarcating the natural and the supernatural orders. In making this move, he was heavily influenced by Aristotle's secular ethos. For this reason, he was regarded by his conservative contemporaries as subversive of the supremacy of religious values
and supernatural ends, but subsequently came to be adopted by the
modern Catholic Church as her official theologian by the time she could
no longer demand the total subordination of secular values to the supremacy of sacred ones.

Among other things, the secularization of the West during the Renaissance initiated the liberation of nonreligious values from the domination of religious values and established their autonomy in place of their heteronomy. This autonomy was the basis for developing the modern intrinsic conception of poetry and other arts. The new champions of aesthetic autonomy seized on Aristotle's *Poetics* as their Bible, because it appeared to be the only systematic exposition of the intrinsic value of poetry and other arts. All they had to do was to close their eyes to the lowly station Aristotle had given them by calling their functions mimetic; even better, they could elevate the function of the arts by transforming Aristotle's notion of *poesis* (making) from its original notion of copying into the magic notion of creation.

The long struggle for aesthetic autonomy took many centuries, and the eighteenth-century Enlightenment roughly marked its successful conclusion. With the *philosophes* and philosophers of that century, the autonomy of ethical, political, and aesthetic values was conclusively established. With the thinkers of the seventeenth century, however, the autonomy was still ambiguous and precarious. For example, Leibniz and Spinoza could not fully separate ethics and politics from religion and theology, although they had secularized the latter by transforming them from matters of dogma into matters of rational inquiry. The celebrated doctrine of the divine right of kings was still an attempt to justify the secular power of a king by invoking the power of religious authorities. Milton's *Paradise Lost* stands as an eloquent testimony that poetry was still used in the service of higher values. The Baroque of the seventeenth century was a period of transition and ambivalence, whose spirit has been poignantly captured in the fascinating ambiguity of seventeenth-century metaphysical poetry.

The Romantics of the late eighteenth and the early nineteenth centuries transformed the autonomy of aesthetic values and functions into their supremacy. Literature and other arts were now expected to provide the highest values and perform the highest functions in human life. Kant's third *Critique* played a pivotal role in the transition from the period of aesthetic autonomy to that of aesthetic supremacy. In the introduction to this *Critique*, Kant contemplates an awesome mission which nobody had ever thought of assigning to aesthetic experience, that is, the mission of healing the fissure created by his division of moral kingdom from the domain of nature. In his first *Critique* he had shown that the kingdom of nature is governed by the laws of natural necessity; in his second

Critique he had argued that the domain of moral experience is governed by the laws of moral freedom. He now recognizes a great gulf between these two realms and the need to bridge it.

> Albeit, then, between the realm of the natural concept, as the sensible, and the realm of the concept of freedom, as the supersensible, there is a great gulf fixed, so that it is not possible to pass from the former to the latter (by means of the theoretical employment of reason), just as if they were so many separate worlds, the first of which is powerless to exercise influence on the second: still the latter is *meant* to actualize in the sensible world the end proposed by its laws; and nature must consequently also be capable of being regarded in such a way that in the conformity to law of its form it at least harmonizes with the possibility of the ends to be effectuated in it according to the laws of freedom.[8]

Kant now claims that the function of bridging this fissure can be discharged by the faculty of judgment, the faculty of aesthetic experience. According to him, the domain of nature belongs to the faculty of knowledge, while the domain of morality belongs to the faculty of desire. The faculty of judgment, which governs the domain of aesthetic experience, lies between the faculties of knowledge and desire. Through this strategic location, Kant maintains, the faculty of aesthetic experience can perform the critical function of mediating between the domain of necessity and the domain of freedom. Although he never explained how this mediation could really be accomplished, his idea of aesthetic mediation came to captivate the imagination of many Romantics burdened with the problem of healing the spiritual fissure of the Enlightenment.

In his *Letters on the Aesthetic Education of Man*, Schiller expanded Kant's pregnant idea in proposing aesthetic experience as the universal magic for healing all the systematic fissures inherited from the Enlightenment: form vs. matter, reason vs. sense, the spiritual vs. the physical, freedom vs. slavery. This was nothing short of the function of salvation, which used to belong to religion. Literature and other arts thus came to play the role of surrogate religion for the godless world. Schopenhauer also espoused the same quasi-religious view of the aesthetic function in claiming that only aesthetic experience has the power to redeem human beings from the loathsome ocean of suffering and frustration and that one can free oneself from the shackles of subjective desires and feelings and attain the harmony of objectivity only by contemplating the beautiful.

Coleridge's theory that art reconciles the subjective and the objective, the internal and the external, was a British version of this quasi-religious conception of literature and other arts. Keats echoed a similar sentiment in the conclusion of his "Ode on a Grecian Urn."

> When old age shall this generation waste,
> Thou shalt remain, in midst of other woe
> Than ours, a friend to man, to whom thou say'st,
> "Beauty is truth, truth beauty,"—that is all
> Ye know on earth, and all ye need to know.

Old age and other woes used to be the central human problems, which could be resolved only by religion; Keats is now invoking the power of art to resolve these problems of human fragility and mortality.

With the supremacy of aesthetic function, ironically, poetry has regained the awesome position it had once occupied in the Homeric age. In those days, however, poetry had exercised her revered authority by virtue not of her beauty but of her alleged superhuman power to deliver truth and wisdom. Plato and Aristotle brought poetry down from her exalted position to a humble station in the shabby world of copies and imitations because she had been shown to produce only beauty and delight, and never truth and wisdom. With the Romantics, she is now given the supremacy of all values by virtue of her beauty alone, which is declared to be the only truth and all the truth that needs to be known on earth.

Wagner finally adorned this new quasi-religion with the traditional religious rituals in his program of music-drama. His Bayreuth Theater was a shrine to the religion of art; the Bayreuth festivals were its rites of devotion and jubilation. The Bayreuth syndrome was by no means a Wagnerian idiosyncrasy, but a crystallization of widespread sentiment prevailing in almost every theater and concert hall in Europe. It is this quasi-religious aesthetic sentiment that was ridiculed by Kierkegaard's observation: "Most people, nowadays, look for edification in theater and entertainment in church." Most people were more elegantly attired in theaters and concert halls than in churches and temples; they maintained a more solemn atmosphere in the former than in the latter. In fact, they had every reason to be and do so, because they were really seeking in music and drama the meaning of their existence, which they could no longer find in their Bibles and sermons.

Kierkegaard's sustained attack on aestheticism and the aesthetic mode of existence makes its most profound sense in the context of this aesthetic supremacy. He regarded the aesthetic mode of existence as the most serious offense against both ethics and religion. He also believed that this aesthetic supremacy was founded on the degenerate sense of ethical and religious values. Hence his criticism and satire of aestheticism were presented together with his attack and satire of the degenerate ethical and religious sensitivities.

Even Kierkegaard's vicious attack on the Hegelian system was ultimately an attack on aestheticism. Hegel's dialectical logic was meant to be a logical system for articulating all types of conflict and their reconciliation. Before Hegel, many had been obsessed with Kant's idea of using aesthetic experience as the magic healer of the fissure in human experience. But their proposals and expositions had all been vague; nobody seemed to have a clear notion of how aesthetic experience was supposed to perform this healing function. Hegel's ambition was to convert these vague talks into a system of articulate conceptions. In his system, conflict is recognized as the universal principle of world history; the historical progress is seen as a series of inevitable conflicts and their eventual reconciliations. His dialectical logic is meant to demonstrate the logical necessity that generates and reconciles every type of conflict (the contradiction of thesis and antithesis and its resolution in synthesis). Since his logic of dialectical synthesis was a magic schema of universal reconciliation, it made the most soothing appeal to his conflict-ridden contemporaries.

Hegel's system had too many dubious joints and loose ends, and most of his so-called dialectical demonstrations were pompous tricks of equivocation in oracular language. Those who accepted his system seldom had the intellectual acumen to see through his dialectical trickery. They devoutly embraced it mainly for an aesthetic reason, to satisfy their pantheistic longing for universal reconciliation. This aesthetic motivation was operative not only in Hegel's followers but in their master himself. In Hegel and the Hegelians, the aesthetic motivation produced perhaps the most scandalous self-deception of the intellect.

Hegel claimed that his philosophy of absolute idealism fulfilled the truth of art and religion. Although this claim was offensive to some and incredible to many others, it turned out to be true in an ironic sense. Since the aesthetic motivation was the central force for the dialectical movement of his absolute idealism, his philosophy was the surrogate for art, which was exalted to the old position of traditional religion and was serving the pantheistic function of universal reconciliation. Hence his absolute idealism was at once art and religion for the devout Hegelians—devout enough to accept his dialectical dogmas at their face value. Contrary to Hegel's claim that art and religion were sublated in his philosophy of absolute idealism, philosophy was, in his hand, subverted and converted into art that was replacing religion. In appearance, art was being subordinated to philosophy; in reality, art was reigning over philosophy and replacing religion.

This was the extent of aesthetic supremacy, which could not have been dreamed of in the days of aesthetic autonomy. The doctrine of aesthetic autonomy is the claim that the aesthetic domain of human experience must be governed by its own autonomous ideals and values rather than by nonaesthetic ideals and values. In the days of aesthetic supremacy, however, aesthetic ideals and values were exalted as the highest principles of human existence that must govern not only its aesthetic but also its nonaesthetic dimensions.

Kierkegaard was one of the few sober souls who refused to be mesmerized by Hegel's philosophical aestheticism. Many conflicts in human existence can, he argued, never be resolved in a Hegelian synthesis, because they are conflicts of incompatibles such as the temporal vs. the eternal, the finite vs. the infinite, the secular vs. the sacred. The only way to cope with these conflicts is to make an existential choice between two incompatibles. Hence Hegel's dubious logic of dialectical synthesis (both/and) should, Kierkegaard concluded, be replaced by the austere logic of existential choice (either/or).

If Kierkegaard is right, Kant's dream of healing the fissure of human existence through aesthetic mediation turns out to be only a dream. In this incurable fissure of human existence does Kierkegard locate its ultimate problem, that is, the despair of being human, and labels it as the sickness unto death. He analyzes the nature of this sickness as the irreconcilable conflict of the temporal and the eternal, the finite and the infinite. Only in the power of faith does he recognize the possibility of overcoming this sickness. For the knight of faith, the synthesis of the incompatibles can be achieved by the grace of God.[9] This synthesis is the miracle of all miracles and the marvel of all marvels, which can never be understood in human terms.

This marvelous miracle, Kierkegaard maintains, is exemplified in Abraham's sacrifice of his son Isaac. In order to demonstrate the gravity of this biblical event, he invites us to situate ourselves in Abraham's position and consider what we could have done in response to God's cruel command that the budding life of his only son, the joy and hope of his old age, be sacrificed on Mount Moriah. Humanly speaking, he holds, all of the alternatives open to anyone in Abraham's position are bound to lead to one of two dreadful consequences: either he must lose his son for the sake of his God, or he must renounce his God to retain his son.

Even if God gives the son back to his father after the trial, Kierkegaard claims, the father can never truly regain his son. Once the father has shown his willingness to take the brutal measure of sacrificing his son for God, he can never again look at his son as the source of his joy and pride. So the son is irrevocably lost to the father, as soon as he accepts God's command. The father can save and cherish his son only by defying and denouncing God. Whether the father defies his God or renounces his son, he cannot avoid "fear and trembling." But no trace of fear or trembling can be found in the behavior of Abraham, Kierkegaard claims; the knight of faith is sure of every step he takes from his home to the top of Mount Moriah. Throughout his journey, he never suffers from dread and anxiety, because he is absolutely sure of retaining both his son and his God. It is this absolute sense of assurance and his total freedom from dread that render his act of faith incomprehensible in human terms.

In Kierkegaard's recounting of Abraham's story, Isaac stands for the temporal world, or rather whatever is cherished in it. Hence Abraham's sacrifice of Isaac may be taken as an act of renunciation, that is, the act of giving up the finite and the temporal (his son) for the sake of gaining the infinite and the eternal (his God). If Abraham's act is taken in this sense, Kierkegaard argues, there can be nothing truly marvelous or incomprehensible in it. Nor can there be any way to account for Abraham's freedom from dread, the most salient differentia that sets apart his greatness from the greatness still possible within human power, for example, the greatness of those tragic heroes who have made tremendous sacrifices for some great causes.

The marvelous incomprehensibility of Abraham's faith, in Kierkegaard's view, lies in the very fact that it enables him to retain both the finite and the infinite, the temporal and the eternal, without any conflict or compromise. Humanly speaking, Kierkegaard stresses, this is an impossible feat, because these two spheres of human existence are incompatible. The acceptance of one always dictates the terrible consequence of renouncing the other. But Abraham accomplishes this impossible feat of overcoming their incompatibility through the power of his faith. By virtue of this feat, he has been revered as the father of faith.

If we correctly understand the superhuman character of Abraham's faith, Kierkegaard contends, we must admit that God alone has the power of healing the conflict between the finite and the infinite, the temporal and the eternal. This is the deadly conflict that manifests itself as the perpetual despair of being trapped in the Kantian fissure between freedom and necessity; that is, as the sickness unto death, which is Kierkegaard's redefinition of what has been known as sin or perdition in our religious tradition. Thus he tried to return the function of ultimate reconciliation and redemption from the aesthetic to the religious domain, by demonstrating its superhuman character.

Kierkegaard's condemnation of aestheticism as a surrogate of religion was not heeded by many. This surrogate flourished with its own clergy and laity. While the audience of theater and concert hall constituted the laity of this new religion, the poets and other artists played the role of its priests and prophets. To the latter, the religion of art became a sacred vocation, which demanded their total dedication. The devout sense of dedication to this new vocation is piously enunciated by Rainer Maria Rilke: "I feel that this is my belief: Whoever does not consecrate his whole being to art with all his wishes and values can never reach the highest goal." Of course, the highest goal is the aesthetic end that can be achieved only through artistic creation.

Proust perhaps brought the quasi-religious conception of literature to its greatest fulfillment. The Proustian remembrance that brings together all the scattered fragments of human life into an ecstatic unity is what Schiller and Schopenhauer would have regarded as the ecstasy of aesthetic contemplation. It is solely for this moment of aesthetic ecstasy that Proust appears to have struggled throughout his life. Art could no longer be regarded as only one among many features of life. It had become its ultimate end, which alone gave meaning and unity to human existence. In the age of aesthetic supremacy, the Proustian aesthetic vision served the ultimate function analogous to the function that the beatific vision was presumed to serve in the days of religious supremacy. Even the once-radical motto, "Art for art's sake," does not full capture the gravity of this ultimate function; on its face value, it accurately describes the nature of the aesthetic function in the days of aesthetic autonomy. In the age of aesthetic supremacy, not only art but everything else was perceived as existing for the sake of art, for its power and its glory.

The supremacy of art and literature finally turns into their tyranny, which exacts every possible sacrifice from human existence in the form of devotion and dedication. Tolstoy describes this tyranny.

> In every large town enormous buildings are erected for museums, academies, conservatories, dramatic schools, and for performances and concerts. Hundreds of thousands of workmen—carpenters, masons, painters, joiners, paperhangers, tailors, hairdressers, jewelers, molders, typesetters—spend their whole lives in hard labor to satisfy the demands of art, so that hardly any other department of human activity, except perhaps the military, consumes so much energy as this.
>
> Not only is enormous labor spent on this activity, but in it, as in war, the very lives of men are sacrificed. Hundreds of thousands of people devote their lives from childhood to learning to twirl their legs rapidly (dancers), or to touch notes and strings very rapidly (musicians), or to draw with paint and represent what they see (artists), or to turn every phrase inside out and find a rhyme to every word. And these people, often very kind and clever, and capable of all sorts of useful labor, grow savage over their specialized and stupefying occupations, and become one-sided and self-complacent specialists, dull to all the serious phenomena of life and skilful only at rapidly twisting their legs, their tongues, or their fingers.[10]

Tolstoy feels revulsion against the tyranny of art. The revolt against this tyranny constitutes the very essence of the anti-art movement that has dominated literature and other arts during this century. The function of art in this new context of the anti-art movement is to awaken human beings from the opiate of aesthetic contemplation and return them to the reality of their own existence, thereby terminating the tyranny of art and restoring the integrity of human life. Hence the works of this new art must be boring rather than engaging, disturbing rather than comforting, unintelligible rather than intelligible, and insignificant rather than significant. In short, they must be meaningless rather than meaningful. This is the main reason for the meaninglessness of contemporary literature, art and music. They are meant to disengage human beings from the Circean magic of art and help them overcome their alienation from their own life.

Henceforward, beauty and truth must be sought not by running away from the reality of life to the artificial world of art, but by returning to the real world of human existence. "The world of beauty must be established not in the special world of art, but in the everyday world of our life." This is the positive dimension of the anti-art movement, which has been manifested in environmental art, industrial art, documentary theater, nonfiction fiction, etc. All these arts and attempts have one thing in common, namely, the returning of art to life as its servant. This new function of art has been dictated by the unique historical character of our postmodern cultural context.

CHAPTER EIGHT
Thematic Projection

THE social function of literature is not its only pragmatic function. Equally important is its thematic function, which is the function of expressing some thematic ideas. These two functions are, in fact, inseparable. The social functions of education and entertainment, satire and exposé, must presuppose some thematic content. Now we shall see that the nature of thematic function is as emphatically context-bound as that of social function.

Heroes versus Saints

For Aristotle's Athens, the most important genre was tragedy. The tragic dimension of human existence was the most important theme for him and his Athenians. The bulk of his *Poetics* is devoted to the analysis of a tragic drama, that is, how the theme of a tragic hero is represented on the stage. With the advent of Christianity, however, this thematic function had to lose its preeminence, because the Christin dogma of Providence could not allow any room for the tragic fate of humanity. If the whole world was really ruled by the omniscient and omnipotent God, there could be no real possibility of the victory of evil over good, which was an essential condition for the tragic ethos of ancient Greece. Thus the tragic hero of antiquity came to be replaced by the Christian saint and martyr, and its tragic drama by the Christian morality play.

Only after a long period of secularization, which had considerably weakened the Christian faith in Providence, did European literature regain its tragic themes during the sixteenth and the seventeenth centuries. But the character of these new tragic themes was quite different from that of the Greco-Roman themes. This thematic difference is incisively captured by W. H. Auden's characterization of Greek tragedies as the tragedies of necessity and Elizabethan tragedies as the tragedies of possibility. The difference between the Greek and the modern European conceptions of tragic fate reflects the difference between the corresponding conceptions of nature. In the Greek view, nature is what is; in the modern European view, nature is what is made. In Greek tragedies, the fate of a tragic hero is part and parcel of nature as what is, the domain of necessity. In Elizabethan tragedies, the fate of a tragic hero is also part and parcel of nature, the nature of the tragic hero, his action, and his circumstances. But the nature of these things is the nature not of what is but of what is to be made through the contrivance and ingenuity of the tragic hero himself.

The necessity of nature that governs the fate of Greek tragedies takes on many different forms. Agamemnon kills his daughter Iphigenia for the necessity of undertaking the Achaean expedition against Troy; his wife Clytemnestra kills Agamemnon for the necessity of avenging his murder of their daughter; their son Orestes kills Clytemnestra for the necessity of avenging her murder of Agamemnon. The tragic fate of Oedipus is governed by the necessity of a preordained fate; that of Antigone is dictated by the necessity of ethical duty for her dead brother. The tragedy of Hippolytus and Phaedra portrays the cruel necessity of unnatural passions.

In the Elizabethan dramas, the actions of tragic heroes spring from their own ambitions and volitions rather than from the necessity of external forces. Out of his own ambition and decision, Macbeth kills Duncan and usurps his throne. The witches in this play do not simply foretell the fate of Macbeth already preordained by some external authority, as the Delphic oracle does in Sophocles' *Oedipus Tyrannus*. The prophecy of those witches is one with Macbeth's own dreams; their prophecy can even be regarded as a projection of his ambitions and aspirations. In contrast to this, the fate decreed by the Delphic oracle in Sophocles' play is something everybody concerned dreads and tries to forestall.

When old King Lear initiates a tragic course of events by handing over his kingdom to Goneril and Regan and casting off Cordelia, he does so out of his own desire and choice rather than by any force of necessity. Furthermore, Cordelia's behavior is governed by the old principles of duty and necessity, while that of Goneril and Regan is guided by the new principles of desire and love. Since the old king himself is a devotee of these new principles, he is gravely offended by Cordelia's conduct.

Thus the entire play is controlled by the new forces of desire and volition, which supersede the old forces of duty and necessity.

Quite often, the desires and ambitions of Elizabethan tragic heroes are instigated or manipulated by some other persons. For example, Macbeth's ambition is fanned by his wife's instigation; Othello's jealous determination to kill Desdemona is manipulated by Iago's cunning. But this fact does not alter the fundamental feature of Elizabethan tragedies: tragic fate is woven out of human desire and cunning, ambition and manipulation. Since desire and ambition, decision and manipulation, constitute the basic fabric of Elizabethan tragic fate, the category of possibility is the most essential condition for Elizabethan tragedies. Desires and decisions, ambitions and manipulations, become the central existential issues only when the domain of necessity as the matrix of human life is replaced by the domain of possibility.

The role of these new tragic heroes, who weave the fabric of their fate from their own ambitions and aspirations, is only one dimension of what has been known as the Renaissance man. In my *Cultural Thematics*, I have shown that this new breed of man emerged as a way of imitating God in power and glory. During the Middle Ages, the imitation of Christ had been the governing ideal for all Christians, and this had been the imitation of God in weakness and suffering. The new imitation of God in power and glory had come about as a thematic reversal of the old imitation. Molded through this new imitation, the Renaissance man cannot allow anything outside himself to dictate his fate. I have called this new breed of man "a sovereign individual" because he exercises sovereignty over his own destiny.[1]

The concept of sovereign individual is the concept of man that is presupposed in Hobbes's and Locke's theories of social contract. Every man is said to be free and equal because he is "absolute lord of his own person and possessions, equal to the greatest, and subject to nobody" (*Second Treatise of Civil Government* ch. 9). The rise and fall of such an individual cannot take place merely as the outcome of external forces, but can be achieved only through the inner working of his own desires and decisions. This new conception of human will and fate even becomes the foundation for Calvin's doctrine of predestination. Although every soul is predestined to be saved or condemned, he holds, its predestination is fulfilled through the operation of its own will.

To impute personal desires and volitions to Greek tragic heroes as the primary force of their fateful actions would be reading our own modern

ethos into Greek tragedies. It would be anachronistic to regard Clytemnestra's murder of Agamemnon and Antigone's defiance of Creon's de-
cree as motivated principally by their personal feelings and desires. In
imputing to Oedipus the subconscious desire to kill his father and marry
his mother, Freud is reading the ancient Greek play in the context of the
modern European ethos. He is internalizing external forces. Although
this internalization can transform Oedipus into a type of tragic figure
indistinguishable from that of King Lear and Macbeth, it goes directly
against the central theme of Sophocles' immortal work, namely, the
inexorability of external forces.

What Freud shares with Shakespeare is the dread of internal necessity,
the necessity of the forces working within the human soul. By contrast,
the Greek tragedians were mainly concerned with the necessity of external forces. In their works, even the operation of uncontrollable passions was attributed to external agencies. In Euripides' play, for example,
Phaedra's abnormal passion for her stepson Hippolytus is presented as
the manifestation of an Olympian force rather than of her own desires
and longings. Hence it may be more accurate to characterize modern
European tragedies as the tragedies of inner necessity rather than as the
tragedies of possibility. The possibilities that confront the modern tragic
heroes are like the witches waylaying Macbeth in the heath: they only
constitute the occasion for the externalization of his inner necessity.

During the Middle Ages, the epic themes were also incompatible with
the Christian ethos. Although they are not necessarily tragic, they concern heroic actions and emotions. The ethos of heroic actions and emotions was alien to the medieval theme of imitating Christ in weakness
and suffering. The ultimate aim in the imitation of Christ was to recognize the totally powerless and helpless character of human beings. The
recognition and acceptance of this human condition was called the virtue
of humility, the foundation of all other Christian virtues.

This virtue of humility was the spiritual foundation for Christian saint-
hood and martyrdom. To be a Christian martyr was not to wage a heroic
battle against Satanic forces, but to accept all the sufferings and perse-
cutions in humility. To be a Christian saint was not to display the power
of sanctity, but to become a humble receptacle for the infusion of divine
grace. These Christian ideals were diametrically opposed to the pagan
ideal of being a great hero. Whereas the Christian ideals were rooted in
the sense of humility, the pagan ideal thrived on the sense of pride, the
awareness of one's power and excellence. Since the sense of pride was

contrary to the sense of humility, pride was condemned as the root of all sins by medieval Christians, whereas it had been praised as the root of all virtues by ancient ages. Consequently any heroic conception of man was unthinkable and unpardonable during the Middle Ages. Therefore the revival of epic themes also had to wait for the emergence of the sovereign individual during the Renaissance.

Dante's *Commedia* may appear to be one exception to this general tendency, because it is usually regarded as a great medieval Christian epic. But it is not easy to locate epic themes in the *Commedia*. To begin with, Dante does not even call his work an epic; he simply lables it a comedy, that is, not a tragedy. Next, the narrative structure of the *Commedia* fundamentally deviates from that of ancient Greek and Roman epics. Dante's epic does not have the type of epic hero whose greatness generally constitutes the thematic content of a classical epic. To explain away this anomaly, Dante scholars and critics have exalted Dante the traveler as his own epic hero, who allegorically represents all Christians in their momentous struggle against sin and condemnation and for their purgation and salvation.

Dante the traveler, unfortunately, makes a shabby epic hero, because his chief function is to see and report, the function of a traveling reporter. There are a few things he does on his own during his journey, but all of them are no more than the normal actions and reactions one can expect from any alert and attentive observer. Dante discharges even this function of a traveling reporter under the tutelage of his divinely appointed guides. True to his Christian mold, Dante the traveler is just too powerless and too helpless a creature to perform a heroic action or assume a heroic stature.

Throughout his journey, Dante the traveler remains a pathetically helpless creature to be rescued, escorted, comforted, instructed, chastised, and edified by his three guides, whom he reverently accepts and follows as his teachers and masters. He represents the medieval ideal of a Christian, who cannot take a single step in the right direction without divine assistance. The anomaly of his role as an epic hero can perhaps best be elucidated by comparing his relation to his three guides with the relation of Aeneas to Venus and that of Odysseus to Athena. In the *Odyssey* Athena guides the epic journey of Odysseus; in the *Aeneid* Venus the mother of Aeneas performs the corresponding role for her son.

In Vergil's epic, Venus comes to the aid of her son Aeneas at the tragic end of the Trojan war. While Troy is burning, Aeneas finds Helen hiding in Vesta's shrine and is about to wreak his vengeance on her. Then and there his divine mother Venus appears and instructs him that the real cause of the Trojan war has been neither Helen's beauty nor Paris' misconduct, but the Olympian immortals themselves. She counsels him to take immediate flight from Troy to the land of his future home, and promises to be with him throughout his journey (*Aeneid* 2.567–620). Aeneas begins his epic voyage under the exhortation and guidance of Venus, just as Dante's journey is initiated under Vergil's exhortation and guidance.

Although Aeneas firmly believes and proudly proclaims that his journey is guided by his divine mother ("matre dea monstrante viam," *Aeneid* 1.382), Venus plays primarily the role of his patron and protectress rather than that of his guide and escort. For example, she pleads the cause of her son to Jupiter in the heavenly council of the immortals (1.229–96; 10.17–61), protects him against Juno's fury and trickery (4.90–128), solicits Neptune's aid for his safety on the ocean (5.779–815), and cajoles Vulcan into making celestial armor for him (8.370–453). In performing these acts, she always stays in the background, remote from the scenes of Aeneas' epic actions.

On a few occasions, Venus fulfills her function as Aeneas's patron and protectress in the midst of the epic scenes. For example, she protects Aeneas and his troops by enveloping them in a thick mantle of cloud during their trip from the Libyan coast to Dido's palace, and secures his safety there by making Dido fall in love with him (1.411–14, 657–722). Before the outbreak of the war between Aeneas' Trojans and Turnus' Rutulians, she sends her son an omen of the impending war in fulfillment of her promise (8.520–40), and brings the celestial armor to him (8.610–25). During the final battle against the Rutulians, Aeneas is treacherously wounded by an arrow and his physician Iapyx can neither cure the wound nor relieve the pain. Shaken with a mother's anguish over her son's agony, Venus comes invisibly to the aid of the physician and miraculously cures Aeneas' wound by secretly dissolving some magic herb in the river water to be used for washing his wound (12.411–29). During Aeneas' single combat with Turnus, she intervenes twice to neutralize the unfair effect of intervention by Juturna on behalf of her mortal brother Turnus (12.468–573, 766–90). Even in these events, Venus does nothing overt enough to detract from the heroic actions of her son.

Only once during Aeneas' epic journey does Venus function in what can be truly regarded as the role of guide or escort. This singular occasion arises on the hero's escape from a shipwreck near the Libyan coast. She appears to her bewildered son, explains to him the nature of the land and its people, and tells him to go to the palace of Dido (1.305–401). Even on this occasion, she does not present herself as an immortal purporting to instruct a mortal; she comes on the scene only as an innocent Tyrian huntress pretending to be in search of her sister lost in the forest. Not Venus but Aeneas opens their conversation, throughout which she maintains the posture of a stranger toward him. Only after her departure does Aeneas realize that the stranger was his own divine mother and laments, "Thou also cruel! Why mockest thou thy son so often with vain phantoms? Why am I not allowed to clasp hand in hand and hear and utter words unfeigned?" (1.407–09)[2]

Throughout the *Aeneid*, except for one or two special occasions, Venus is kept in the background and is not allowed to interfere directly with her son's decisions and actions. Their contact is infrequent; their communication is usually indirect. This poetic device helps ensure the autonomy of Aeneas as the epic hero by forcing him to be on his own most of the time. In contrast to Aeneas' remote relation with Venus, Dante the traveler maintains direct contact with his guides and receives continuous guidance from them throughout his journey. This is dictated by his incapacity to stand and act as an autonomous agent. Because of his dependence on his guides, Dante always stands in subservience to them. He oftens refers to his guide Vergil as his lord and master ("tu duca, tu signore, e tu maestro," *Inferno* 2.140). When Dante meets Beatrice and Bernard of Clairvaux, he shows an even greater sense of reverence and dependence than he has shown toward Vergil. Throughout his journey, he is assisted and instructed like a helpless pupil by his three guides.

The role of Venus in the *Aeneid* was evidently modeled after that of Athena in the *Odyssey*, but there is a noteworthy divergence between the two. Since the *Odyssey* was the model for the composition of the *Aeneid*, it may be instructive to compare the role of Athena as the guide and protectress of Odysseus and Telemachus with that of Venus on the one hand and with that of Dante's three guides on the other.

In the *Odyssey*, Athena deals differently with Odysseus and with his son. In the first two books of this Homeric epic, she appears to the young Telemachus first in the guise of an outsider Mentes and then in that of a native Ithacan Mentor, and tries to help him cope with the unruly behavior of Penelope's suitors. As Mentor, she gives him not only fatherly counsel but also practical help in procuring a ship and its crew, and then guiding his voyage to Nestor's palace at Pylos. In these episodes, she behaves like Dante's guides. However, she terminates this role on their arrival at Pylos and leaves Telemachus to his own devices, thereby providing him with a chance to grow up into a mature, autonomous hero. By the time Telemachus has to return to Ithaca, Athena appears to him directly, advises him to return at once and to avoid the suitors' ambush (*Odyssey* 15.9–42). But she does not supervise his return trip.

On behalf of Odysseus, Athena plays the role of the invisible protectress in the same way that Venus does on behalf of Aeneas. Athena pleads in the council of Olympians for the release of Odysseus from Calypso's island and secures Zeus's consent for his return to Ithaca (*Odyssey* 1.44–95). With Athena's invisible help, Odysseus escapes from Poseidon's storm and lands on the Phaeacian shore (5.424–93). Appearing in a dream, Athena induces the Phaeacian princess Nausicaa to go out to the river mouth and wash her apparel there (6.20–40). By this device, Nausicaa and her maids run into the naked and tired Odysseus, give him food and clothing, and escort him to the outskirts of her father's city, where Nausicaa leaves him to make the trip on his own to the palace (6.110–315). In response to his prayer (6.323–27), Athena appears to him in the guise of a young maiden carrying a pitcher and leads him to the palace (7.18–77). During this trip, she protects him by shrouding him under a wondrous mist (7.14–17). This episode was evidently the model for Venus' protection and guidance of Aeneas from the Libyan coast to the palace of Dido.

After this episode, however, Athena does not appear to Odysseus until he lands on the shore of Ithaca in book 13. This may give the impression that she stays as remote from him as Venus does from Aeneas. But this is only the appearance, which covers a fundamental difference between the roles of the two goddesses. The Phaeacians deliver Odysseus to the shore of Ithaca while he is asleep. When he wakes up, he is anxious to know where he is. At that moment Athena appears to him as a young herdsman of sheep, to whom Odysseus introduces himself as a Cretan trying to escape from a righteous murder and weaves a tall tale to back up this false identity (13.256–86). Athena responds to this crafty move by shedding her disguise and praising his craftiness. She tells him:

> But come, let us no longer talk of this, being both well versed in craft, since thou art far the best of all men in counsel and in speech, and I among all the gods am famed for wisdom and craft. Yet thou didst not know Pallas

Athene, daughter of Zeus, even me, who ever stand by thy side, and guard thee in all toils. (13.296–301)[3]

This is the first time Athena reveals her identity to Odysseus, but this revelation establishes the mutual identity between the two. She tells him that he is the mortal counterpart of the immortal Athena, or rather that he perfectly personifies Athena's unique characteristics. From this mutual identity follows the truth of her claim that Athena always stands by Odysseus and guards him in all his toils. Through that identity, she remains intimately present with him throughout his epic voyage.

This intimate presence of Athena with Odysseus is expressed in two ways: in the external circumstances and in the internal dispositions. The Athena-like dispositions are manifested in the shrewd plans and ingenious schemes that Odysseus devises in confrontation with critical situations. The Athena-given circumstances are marked with some emblems of the goddess such as her shrine, grove, or an olive tree. For example, when the hero escapes from Poseidon's storm and lands sick and naked on the Phaeacian shore, he faces the dilemma of spending the night in the dark forest's undergrowth at the risk of becoming the wild beasts' easy prey or remaining on the shore and succumbing to the night's damp air and the hoarfrost of the morning. At that critical moment, he finds a twin olive bush whose dense foliage protects him from the cold wind and the wild beasts during the night (5.465–93). When Nausicaa leaves him alone at the outskirt of her city, she tells him to wait at a grove of poplar trees sacred to Athena, where Athena responds to his supplication and comes to his aid (6.291, 321–31). While he is imprisoned in the Cyclops' cave and is seeking an appropriate instrument for fighting the giant, he finds a club made from an olive tree, with which he eventually blinds the Cyclops and escapes (9.317–400). When he has to prove his own identity to his wife, he appeals to the old trunk of an olive tree, which served as the center in the design of their bedroom and marriage bed (23.181–204). These two modes of Athena's presence with Odysseus are usually conjoined. This conjoint operation of Athena's internal and external presences is perhaps best represented in the episode where Odysseus and Athena sit down under a sacred olive tree and together devise the tactical plans to subdue the suitors (13.371–440).

Athena's relation to Odysseus makes a striking contrast to Venus' relation to Aeneas. The former is the relation of immediate presence and mutual identity; the latter is the relation of remote presence and separate identity, that is, the identity of two distinctly separate personalities. For example, Aeneas does not share his central virtue, piety, with Venus through their mutual identity, as Odysseus and Telemachus share shrewdness with Athena. This difference between the two sets of hero–patron relationships is perhaps most dramatically exemplified in the final battles in the two epics. Whereas Odysseus and Athena jointly plan and prepare for Odysseus' confrontation with the suitors, Aeneas does not receive such divine assistance from Venus in preparation for the battle with the Rutulians. During Odysseus' battle with the suitors, Athena remains visible in the guise of a swallow, and actively assists him not only in the execution of the battle but in its peaceful conclusion (22.236–309; 24.542–48). During Aeneas' war in Italy, Venus remains invisible to everybody concerned, and performs a relatively marginal role in the execution of the war and its conclusion.

These two different relations between the human hero and the divine patron produce two different kinds of epic heroes. Odysseus' heroic stature is derived from his mutual identity with Athena; he performs his functions as an epic hero through the shrewdness and resourcefulness he shares with her. Aeneas' heroic stature is established by his separate identity from that of Venus, which establishes his independence as an agent of action.

Dante's relation to his three guides is a mixture of the Odysseus–Athena and the Aeneas–Venus relationships. His three guides are immediately present to him even more emphatically than Athena is to Odysseus. But Dante does not enjoy the sort of intimate identity with them that we have seen between Odysseus and Athena. On the contrary, his separate identity from his guides is more emphatically pronounced than that of Aeneas from Venus. In short, Dante's guides are immediately present to him throughout his journey, and yet their immediate presence does not override their separate identity from him.

The dual relationship of immediate presence and separate identity between Dante and his three guides makes it impossible for him to attain the great stature of a Homeric or Vergilian hero. The immediate presence of Dante's guides to him does not allow him the mastery of his person and autonomy of his action that is given to Aeneas. Their separate identity from Dante deprives him of the special charisma and distinction a mortal can achieve through his privileged identification with an immortal, as in the case of Odysseus' identification with Athena. Hence Dante the traveler is destined to play the humble role of a powerless and helpless agent. But this is what constitutes the virtue of humility, the foundation of medieval Christian ethos.

Thematic Reference

If we cannot locate epic themes in Dante the traveler, where can we find them? What epic themes are really expressed by the *Commedia*? These questions concern the most difficult problem in textual interpretation: How is the thematic content of a text to be discovered and recognized? We may understand every line, every tercet, and every canto of Dante's epic, and yet fail to recognize its epic theme. What is overtly stated in a poem may not be its ultimate theme.

The thematic content of a poem or a story can be conveyed in two different modes: overt and covert, explicit and implicit, direct and indirect. When you read a simple detective story, you may assume that its thematic content is directly stated in the story, whether it be the theme of describing an exciting murder or detecting an elusive murderer. You may not look for any further thematic implication than what is overtly given in the story. By contrast, if you are reading Dostoyevsky's *Crime and Punishment*, you may not operate on such a simple assumption. Beyond what is explicitly stated, you may be tempted to discover a general theme implicitly exemplified in that particular story.

At this point, we should introduce the notion of thematic reference in analogy to the notion of semantic reference. A story can be said to refer to certain thematic ideas, whether those ideas are expressed directly or indirectly. When a story directly expresses its thematic ideas, its thematic reference can be said to be direct. When a story indirectly expresses its thematic ideas, its thematic reference can be said to be indirect. These two modes of thematic reference roughly correspond to two types of semantic reference. The semantic reference made by the use of a proper name is direct, while the reference by the use of a definite description is indirect. If I refer to Johannes Kepler as the scientist who discovered the elliptical orbit of Mars, I make an indirect reference. If I refer to him by using his name, I make a direct reference.

An indirect thematic reference involves at least two levels of thematic ideas, the immediate and the remote. For example, Aesop's fable of the hare and the tortoise refers immediately (or directly) to a race between the two animals and remotely (or indirectly) to the moral of the race.

The structure of this thematic reference can be described in another way: Aesop's story refers to a race between two animals, which in turn refers to a moral. The second thematic reference is made through the first one; the race described by the story functions as a mechanism of thematic reference just as the story does.

The difference between direct and indirect thematic references can be restated in terms of simple and complex systems of thematic reference. Thematic reference can be regarded as a simple system when it is made of only direct reference. It can be regarded as a complex system when it is made of direct and indirect references. Some travelogues can function as satires through their complex systems of thematic reference. For example, *Gulliver's Travels* refers explicitly to such exotic peoples as the Lilliputians, the Laputans, and the Houyhnhnms, and implicitly to Swift's own countrymen. Without this complex system of thematic reference, Swift's work would be as simple in its thematic implications as *The Book of Marco Polo*.

Like satires and fables, parables operate through a complex system of thematic reference. The parable of the sower refers not only to the sower and his activity in the ordinary sense, but also to a special kind of sower and his sowing of divine words. The former is its explicit thematic reference, and the latter is its implicit one. Some proverbs operate like parables. The proverb "A rolling stone gathers no moss" thematically refers not only to some stones and their rolling, but also to some human beings and their roving. Some maxims also operate in a system of complex thematic reference. "A bird in the hand is worth two in the bush" refers to a few other things worth having and chasing beside birds.

In an allegory, the literal sense establishes its direct thematic reference, and the allegorical sense its indirect thematic reference. Its complex system of thematic reference can be further complicated by having more than one level of indirect reference. As a fourfold allegory, the *Commedia* is said to have four senses: literal, allegorical, moral, and anagogical. Dante explains these four senses by giving four different readings of the following biblical passage: "When Israel went out of Egypt, the house of Jacob from a people of strange language; Juda was his sanctuary, and Israel his dominion."[4] According to him, the literal meaning of this passage is the escape of Israelites from Egypt in the time of Moses. Its allegorical meaning is our redemption from the kingdom of sin through Christ. Its moral meaning is the conversion of the soul from the misery of sin to the state of grace. Its anagogical meaning is the transport of the soul from the world of corruption to the liberty of everlasting glory. The literal meaning establishes the direct thematic reference, which in turn establishes the three levels of indirect thematic reference: allegorical, moral, and anagogical.

On the level of literal meaning, semantic and thematic references coincide; semantic meaning is identical with thematic meaning. This is not the case with the other three levels of meaning. From this we may conclude that direct thematic reference is established by the identity of the semantic and the thematic meanings, and that indirect thematic reference is dictated by the distance between those two levels of meaning.

Thematic reference is a pragmatic function, while semantic reference is a semantic function. This functional difference can be further elucidated by relating it to the functions of some rhetorical figures. Let us first see whether a metaphor serves a semantic or a pragmatic function. The sentence "The lion is the king of beasts" says something about lions and nothing about kings; its reference is not affected by its metaphor. The metaphor performs not the referential but the predicational function. Since the predicational function is semantic, a metaphor serves a semantic rather than a pragmatic function. Likewise, a metonym usually serves the semantic function of predication, for example, "He threw away the bottle" for "He gave up drinking." Analogy is also a semantic device—for example, the analogy of God to the sun. For these reasons, these rhetorical figures are systematically different in their functions from fables, parables, and allegories.

The identity of semantic and thematic meanings that produces a simple system of thematic reference is the normal operation of natural languages. Fables, parables, and allegories are definitely unusual ways of talking and writing. But this unusual mode of communication has long become the central principle for literary compositions. Although most literary works are composed of particular statements that refer to particular persons and events, they are generally taken to express general thematic ideas. A story need not be a parable, fable, or allegory to be taken to convey a general idea. In this case, the distance between semantic and thematic meanings is generated by the incommensurateness of its semantic form with its thematic content. This incommensurateness also appears in some nonliterary discourses such as proverbs, adages, and maxims, in which a particular statement is used to express a general idea.

A particular statement can never fully express a general idea. At best, the former can exemplify or intimate the latter. Hence it takes special talent to employ language as a literary medium, and this special talent can give literary utterances far greater significance than the significance of particular statments. For a particular statement that can convey a general idea has the power of generality as well as its particular applications. In this does Aristotle locate the seriousness of poetry, "Hence poetry is something more philosophic and of graver import than history, since its statements are of the nature rather of universals, whereas those of history are singulars" (*Poetics* 1451b5–7). By "its statements" he means its thematic implications. On the semantic level, the statements you can find in Greek tragedies are not any more general than those to be found in the historical works of Herodotus and Thucydides.

The determination of thematic reference is an essential feature of thematic interpretation, as essential as the determination of semantic reference is to semantic interpretation. In the case of direct thematic reference, thematic determination is also semantic determination. The thematic interpretation of a simple murder story is no more than its semantic interpretation; the thematic content of the story can be fully known by knowing the semantic functions of its words, phrases, and sentences. The same thing can be said about the interpretation of such legal documents as contracts and testaments. Since the expressions "thematic content" and "thematic interpretation" may not be appropriate to these documents, let us use the more general expressions "pragmatic content" and "pragmatic interpretation." The pragmatic interpretation of a contract or a testament is no more than its semantic interpretation, because a contract or a testament has only direct pragmatic reference.

The determination of direct thematic reference may not seem to involve any pragmatic operation, because it is equivalent to the determination of semantic reference. Semantic operation appears to be sufficient for the interpretation of directly expressed thematic ideas. But the semantic operation in question can be properly conducted within the framework of a pragmatic genre. Prior to giving the semantic interpretation of any text, one must decide to what genre it belongs. A legal text cannot be interpreted in the same manner as a fiction, nor can a scientific treatise be interpreted in the same way as a poem.

Every pragmatic genre has its own universe of discourse. "A universe of discourse" means a domain of objects that are talked about in any given discourse. For example, the universe of discourse for an astronomical treatise contains astronomical objects such as stars, planets, comets, meteors, quasars, black holes, space and time, etc. The universe of discourse for Greek myths may include mortals and immortals, centaurs and unicorns, nymphs and satyrs, etc. Some universes of discourse may consist of actual entities, while others may include only fictive objects. The same word can have different meanings in different universes of discourse. For example, the meaning the word "star" has in the astronomers' universe of discourse is different from the one it has in the astrologers' universe of discourse. To locate a text in a pragmatic genre is to situate it in its own universe of discourse.

Every universe of discourse has its own requirement for precision and its own degree of tolerance for vagueness. The expression "my cousin" may be precise enough to introduce someone in a social gathering, but may be too vague to be useful in contesting the legality of a testament. Every universe of discourse also has its own rules for pragmatic presuppositions and implicatures in addition to the common rules it shares with other universes of discourse.[5] For example, the legal expression "an act of God" does not presuppose the existence of God, whereas any theological talks about God's acts do presuppose it. When Daniel Defoe's *The Shortest Way with the Dissenters* was reclassified as a satire, it was given a set of implicatures quite different from the initially presumed ones. This change of implicatures was due to the change in the universe of discourse. But what is overtly stated in *The Shortest Way* remains the same in different universes of discourse.

Because of these serious semantic variations in the nature of the universes of discourse from one pragmatic context to another, one might be tempted to say that every pragmatic genre has its own semantic system. As a general practice in linguistics, however, only one semantic system is admitted for each natural language at any historical period, and that one system is defined in complete abstraction from all pragmatic genres and their universes of discourse. The different dialects of one natural language can be said to have different semantic subsystems, but those subsystems are again defined in abstraction from all pragmatic considerations.

The genre selection is an indispensable step in textual interpretation because it determines the universe of discourse. To that extent, Hirsch has done right to stress the importance of genre, although he has not clearly spelled out precisely what is accomplished by the genre selection. Since the genre selection is a pragmatic operation, no thematic interpretation can ever be fully carried out by semantic interpretation alone, even when it is concerned only with the problem of determining direct thematic references.

The determination of indirect thematic references is a much more complex pragmatic operation; it has to reach out for the thematic reference that lies well beyond the semantic level. How is this to be accomplished? An answer to this question can be formulated by using Heidegger's notion of projection, which has been adopted as a central element in Gadamer's theory of hermeneutic understanding. Gadamer says, "A person who is trying to understand a text is always performing an act of projection."[6] This notion of projection is especially true of thematic understanding, because the thematic reference of a text must be projected when it is not directly given.

This method of projection is by no means a unique invention of Heidegger and Gadamer. It has been known as the method of hypothetical construction. It is the same method as what Dilthey called "Kepler's inductive method." It is also the same as Piaget's corrigible schemata, whose constructive–corrective process has been recommended by Hirsch as the only viable method of textual interpretation. As Hirsch correctly says, this constructive–corrective method is a universal scientific method, whether the domain of scientific inquiry be the world of natural phenomena or of human activities.[7]

The process of thematic projection and construction is not much different from the process of projecting and constructing a scientific theory on the basis of observational data. What corresponds to scientific data is the text and its semantic meaning. Just as it is possible to propose competing theories for the account of one set of scientific data, so it is possible to project competing thematic interpretations on the basis of one semantic reading of a text. No doubt, each different semantic reading of a text can provide a different textual basis for thematic interpretations. For any given set of data in science, there is no a priori limit to the number of theories that can be proposed on the basis of those data. By the same token, there can be no a priori limit to the number of thematic interpretations that can be projected on the basis of any given text. Hence thematic projection always presupposes interpretive freedom.

During the past few decades, there has been much talk about interpretive freedom. But that talk has been quite confusing because the domain of this freedom has not been clearly circumscribed. Some have talked as though our interpretive freedom lies in the domain of semantic interpretation. For example, Stanley Fish asserts that even the formal units of a text are "always a function of the interpretive model one brings to bear; they are not in the text."[8] By "formal units" he seems to mean the semantic units such as words, phrases, or sentences. He seems to claim that one has complete freedom in carving up a text into these semantic units and in assigning semantic meanings to those units. This is a total freedom in semantic interpretation. Because of this freedom, he concludes, it is possible to produce the same reading from *Lycidas* and from *The Waste Land*. Normal Holland may be claiming the same semantic freedom by saying that a literary text is no more than "a certain configuration of specks of carbon black on dried wood pulp" devoid of all meanings.[9]

This semantic freedom inevitably turns every text into a document of private language. Two persons may never give the same semantic interpretation of the same text, except by coincidence. Fish tries to vindicate the viability of his solipsistic program of reading by appealing to the medieval allegorical practice: "Whatever one may think of this interpretive program, its success and ease of execution are attested to by centuries of Christian exegesis."[10] But the medieval tradition of allegorical exegesis never questioned the necessity of accepting the semantic basis of any text under interpretation. The objective of allegorical exegesis was to determine the indirect thematic reference and never the direct thematic references of any texts.

Our total freedom in semantic interpretation is bound to make each of our languages totally private to each of our solipsistic selves. Hence the vaunted semantic freedom shall bury us all in semantic solipsism.[11] Such freedom, though possible, is not worth the trouble of having and claiming it. The only freedom that can be meaningfully exercised is the pragmatic freedom of thematic interpretation, but this freedom presupposes the necessity of semantic unfreedom, that is, our bondage to the objectivity of any given semantic context. We have to share this semantic bondage with the author of every text we interpret. If we are to interpret Wordsworth's poems, we must read them in his English rather than in Cleanth Brooks's. This semantic objectivity alone can provide the textual foundation for our pragmatic freedom in thematic interpretation.

This semantic objectivity may very well be what Hirsch is seeking in his definition of verbal meaning as the principle of permanence in textual interpretation. In order to stress its semantic basis, he may have tried to characterize the nature of its permanence by equating his distinction of verbal meaning and significance with Frege's semantic distinction between sense and reference. If his doctrine of verbal meaning is accepted in this semantic sense, then the thematic interpretations of a text belong to the province of significance. The thematic meanings of a text can be said to change perpetually, because it is possible to propose new thematic meanings for any given text. For that reason, all thematic interpretations can be consigned to the province of significance, the source of all changes in Hirsch's theory of interpretation.

With this rendition of Hirsch's distinction between meaning and significance, we may have finally produced the best of all possible interpretations for his theory of interpretation. But this interpretation has one troublesome consequence. In Hirsch's theory, the distinction between meaning and significance is related to authorial intention. Authorial intention is claimed to control only the verbal meaning of a text, and its significance is acknowledged to fall always outside its control. Since the thematic meanings of a text are now assigned to the province of significance, they can never be said to be the objects of its author's intention. That is, no author is ever conscious of the thematic meanings of his works. This implication appears to be quite radical, perhaps too radical to be compatible with our normal understanding of authorial intention.

Hirsch himself provides enough textual evidence to show that his notion of authorial meanings is broad enough to include thematic meanings. He says that the verbal meaning of a text includes not only what is said overtly but also what is implied or connoted by it.[12] What is implied or connoted by a text is none other than its implicit thematic reference, which we have shown to be the central topic in any thematic interpretations of a literary work. If implicit thematic references are included in Hirsch's notion of verbal meaning, then all thematic meanings should be regarded as the objects of authorial intention. Hence our semantic interpretation of Hirsch's notion of verbal meaning is clearly incompatible with his own notion of authorial intention.

Perhaps some of the complexities in these tangled issues may be eliminated by refining the concept of authorial intention. All the distinctions we have introduced into our notion of thematic reference can be applied to our notion of authorial intention. In pragmatics, the notion of reference is inseparable from the notion of intention, since pragmatic references are established by the speaker's or author's intentions together with requisite pragmatic conventions. Corresponding to the distinction between the simple and the complex systems of pragmatic reference, there can be the distinction between the simple and the complex systems of pragmatic intentionality. The simple system of intentionality consists of explicit intentions; the complex system of intentionality consists of explicit and implicit intentions. Explicit pragmatic references are objects of explicit intentionality; implicit pragmatic references are objects of implicit intentionality.

The relation between intention and expression also has to be restated in accordance with these pragmatic distinctions. In normal speech acts, we have seen, their relation is that of identity. Now we can see that this identity can be either implicit or explicit. The explicit identity of intention and expression obtains in the domain of explicit reference, and their implicit identity in the domain of implicit reference. Their explicit identity cannot allow any room for the indeterminacy of meaning, but their implicit identity can. It is this room of indeterminacy that provides the pragmatic leverage for proposing many different interpretations of any given text on the level of its implicit thematic reference.

This distinction between the two modes of intentionality can clear up some confusions about the intentional fallacy. Against this fallacy, William Wimsatt and Monroe Beardsley have declared, "We argued that the design or the intention of the author is neither available nor desirable as a standard for judging the success of a work of literary art."[13] The validity and even the plausibility of this assertion depend on how the expression "the design or the intention of an author" is understood. The explicit intention of an author is what is explicitly stated in his text; it is clearly available. His implicit intention is not so readily available, because it is given implicitly in his text. It has to be projected and constructed on the basis of its explicit reference. Nonetheless it is implicitly available. Although available, these two types of authorial intention cannot serve as a standard of judgment. To use them as a standard of judgment amounts to judging a text by itself, because they are essential constituents in our interpretations of that text.

Wimsatt and Beardsley's objection to authorial intention as a standard of judgment applies neither to the explicit nor to the implicit authorial intention. The intention they have in mind appears to be some extraneous intention. After giving a piano recital, let us imagine, the pianist says to his audience, "Although my recital has turned out to be very poor, my intention has all along been to give you a very fine performance." That intention was extraneous to the performance; the former was not present in the latter, implicitly or explicitly. Hence this type of intention should be distinguished from the type that is implicitly or explicitly present in the performance. The latter can be called the intrinsic intention, if the former is called the extraneous intention.

In textual interpretation, intrinsic intentions are intrinsic to the text; they constitute its implicit and explicit thematic references. Insofar as these references can be said to be in the text, these intentions can also be said to be in it. But extraneous intentions are not in it; they are not to be found in the text. In some cases, extraneous intentions can be given outside the text. Even when the extraneous intention of an author becomes available extratextually, it cannot be used as a standard for judging his work. A literary text has to be judged on its own merit in the same way that the value of a musical performance is assessed on its own rather than in reference to the performer's extraneous intention. Hence the extraneous authorial intention is doubly extraneous; it is extraneous for textual judgment as well as for textual interpretation.

A textually extraneous intention need not be extraneous to the production of a text. Although an authorial intention fails to be translated into the implicit or explicit thematic reference of a text, it may initiate the production of that text. As far as the production of a text is concerned, an extraneous intention can be its ultimate cause. The pianist's extraneous intention was the ultimate cause for the production of his performance. When this productive causal relation holds between a text and an extraneous intention, this intention should be called the "productive intention." Since a work of literature is a manifestation of this productive intention, one may feel that the ultimate objective in literary interpretation is to discover the author's original thematic motive that led to the production of his work. Then one is bound to feel like Harold Bloom in his agnostic mood: "There is a dumbfoundering abyss between ourselves and the object, or between ourselves and other selves."

No literary text can ever indicate anything about the nature of its author's productive intention, unless it is translated into its implicit or explicit thematic reference. Hence it is impossible to determine, on the basis of textual evidence, which one of the thematic interpretations permitted by any given text coincides with the productive intention of its author. The countless number of possible thematic interpretations that can be projected onto any given text can generate the dreadful aura of a dumbfoundering abyss, because not one of those interpretations can be said to be any nearer or further from the productive intention of its author than any other. If any thematic interpretations of a text are taken to be expressions of its author's productive intention, they seem to float in the boundless abyss of thematic possibilities.

But there is no reason to be lost in this interpretive abyss and despair over the unreachable productive intention. When natural scientists construct scientific theories to interpret natural phenomena, they do not despair over the unreachability of the Creator's productive intention. Even God's productive intention may be extraneous to the nature of this universe; his creation may have turned out to be quite different from the way it was originally intended. At any rate, the productive intention of nature is extraneous to the scientists' interpretation of natural phenomena. By the same token, the author's productive intention is extraneous and irrelevant to the interpretation of his text.

The irrelevance of the productive intention for textual interpretation can be made manifest by the following hypothetical considerations. Suppose now that the productive authorial intention, which has failed to be expressed in a work of literature, is made extratextually available to the reader. Suppose further that the thematic idea contained in that authorial intention turns out to be better as an idea than any ideas the reader can propose in his interpretations of that work. Even then this idea cannot be accepted as a better interpretation of the work than any of the reader's. Whereas his interpretations have some thematic coherence with the text, the author's own idea does not (it has failed to be expressed in the work).

To say that one thematic idea is better as an idea than another thematic idea is by no means univocal. A thematic idea can be said to be good or bad for many different reasons, for example, its existential profundity or superficiality, or social relevance or irrelevance, or its historical significance or insignificance. Whatever criterion may be used for judging the merit of a thematic idea as an idea, the same criterion cannot be used for determining its value as an interpretation of a text. The value of a projected interpretation can be decided only on the basis of how well it coheres with a given text, just as the value of a proposed scientific theory can be decided on the sole criterion of how well it fits its data.

It is also possible to imagine a case in which the thematic idea contained in a productive authorial intention turns out to be much inferior, as an idea, to some of the ideas the reader can project in his interpretations. Even in this case, there is no reason to reject his own interpretations and accept the author's original thematic idea in their place. All thematic interpretations must be tested by the common measure of textual coherence, whether they are proposed by the author or by his interpreters.

The source of those interpretations is totally irrelevant to the test of their textual coherence. Some of our interpretations may even agree with the author's productive intention, but this coincidence is equally irrelevant for determining the merit of those interpretations.

Finally it is possible to imagine a case in which the reader can project the implicit thematic reference of a text and find out that this implicit reference has never been intended by its author. The author's productive intention was simple rather than complex; his thematic reference was meant to be explicit and never implicit. This discrepancy between the reader's interpretive intentionality and the authorial productive intentionality may very well be taking place in the readings of ancient texts such as Homeric epics. Although to impute some general thematic ideas to works of literature has long been a pragmatic convention, it is quite likely that this convention was totally alien to ancient bards. Even then it is still justifiable to project interpretations of those ancient texts beyond their explicit references, as long as the interpretations can be supported by those texts.

Given any text that describes a particular event or a series of particular events, it is always possible to reach out for its implicit reference to general thematic ideas, not because of any authorial intention, but because of the ontological nexus between a particular and a universal. A particular can always reflect the nature of a universal, because the nature of a particular is constituted by the manifestation of a universal. Even historical events are no exceptions to this ontological principle. Although every historical event is a particular occurrence, it can function as a vehicle for some universal signification. It is this ontological nexus between universals and particulars that enables authorial intention as well as parables and proverbs to operate in a complex system of pragmatic references.

To recognize a universal meaning in a particular entity is an act of recognition. But this act cannot be an act of intuition in textual interpretations any more than it can be in scientific investigations. The textual and the scientific data are usually so complex that the recognition of the universals reflected in those data requires an elaborate operation of theoretical projection and construction. When a text involves such a complex system of thematic references as Dante's *Commedia*, as shall soon be seen, its thematic projection and construction may require some ingenuity and subtlety. For this thematic operation, however, the extraneous authorial intention is simply extraneous and gratuitous.

CHAPTER NINE
Thematic Coherence

THE value of thematic coherence as the central principle of textual interpretation can perhaps best be illustrated by applying it to the thematic interpretation of Dante's *Commedia*. For this principle has probably been flouted more flagrantly in the traditional reading of that epic than anywhere else. We have already seen why Dante the traveler cannot stand up as an epic hero. The unheroic character of Dante the traveler belongs to the more or less explicit dimension of the *Commedia's* thematic content. Its recognition does not require very much of a projective construction.

We should now consider some thematic ideas that have been used in the traditional reading of the *Commedia* and that can be assumed to belong to its implicit thematic dimension. One of those ideas is the presumed theological framework of the *Commedia*. Unlike the behavior of Dante the traveler, its theological framework is never explicitly given. Hence its recognition requires an elaborate network of projection and construction. Perhaps in this network of projected thematic references, we may be able to find the epic theme of the *Commedia*, which cannot be located in its explicitly given thematic references.

Dante's Epic Theme

Since the *Commedia* is a theological poem, most Dante scholars have taken it for granted that it should have a theological theme and that it must have been derived from medieval Christian theology. Although this is a reasonable assumption, it does not settle the question of Dante's theological themes. In fact, it is no more than a preliminary for posing the question. For the tradition of medieval theology had had many strands and strains, whose varieties and differences became especially pro-

nounced during the twelfth and thirteenth centuries. Since most Dante
scholars have not been aware of this complexity, they have accepted
what has appeared to be an obvious solution: that Dante adopted the
theology of St. Thomas Aquinas. This solution has appeared to be obvious for two reasons. First, it appears to be a beautiful match between
the two great Gothic monuments in letters. Second, since the Thomistic
theology is usually characterized as the summa of all medieval theology,
it can be regarded as the ultimate source and authority for any post-
Thomistic poetic derivation of medieval theological ideas. On these
grounds, many Dante scholars have explicated the theological themes
of the *Commedia* in the context of Thomistic theology.

However, the textual contours of the *Commedia* cannot easily be
mapped into the framework of Thomistic theology. Like the metaphysical system of his master, Aristotle. Aquinas' system is emphatically
dualistic; it consists of a series of dyads such a natural vs. supernatural,
rational vs. irrational, sacred vs. secular, etc. In contrast, Dante's epic
is governed by the principle of triadic construction: it consists of three
canticles describing his journey with the aid of three successive guides
through a three-storied universe, beginning with his encounter with the
three beasts of the Delectable Mountain and ending with his beatific
vision of the Three Persons of the Holy Trinity. Even the smallest poetic
unit of the *Commedia* is a trinitarian composition, the *terza rima* or three-
line stanza, which is used without a single deviation from the first to the
last canto. The trinitarianism of Dante's epic and the dualism of Aquinas'
theology produce an obvious mismatch between the text and its presumed thematic content.

Nevertheless, most Dante scholars have long maintained the tradition
of imposing Thomistic dualism on Dante's trinitarian epic, and have
produced a series of unsightly textual exegeses. A conspicuous example
is the allegorical account of Dante's three guides. Dante the traveler is
guided first by Vergil through *Inferno* and *Purgatorio* right up to the
entrance of the Terrestrial Paradise, and then by Beatrice from the top
of *Purgatorio* through the ten heavens of *Paradiso* to the Mystical Rose
of the Empyrean, where he is handed over to his final guide, St. Bernard
of Clairvaux, with whose aid and prayer he concludes his long journey
with the beatific vision. Since the trinitarian relation of Dante's guides
cannot be accommodated within the dualistic system of Thomistic theology, most Dante scholars have concentrated their exegeses on the first
two guides and simply left the third guide out of their accounts.

According to traditional exegetes, Vergil is an allegorical representation of natural reason, while Beatrice represents revealed or supernatural theology. This is in perfect accord with the Thomistic distinction between the natural and the supernatural orders. However, this perfect accord between Dante and Aquinas produces some anomalous readings of the *Commedia*. For example, if Vergil stands for natural reason, how can he guide Dante's soul through *Purgatorio*, the realm of grace? The realm of grace is a supernatural domain, which stands well above the reach of natural reason. Even the task of guiding Dante through *Inferno* is well beyond the capacity of natural reason. Dante makes it clear that no mortal creature can ever, on his own, traverse the different regions of Hell. Most Dante scholars would have defended their position by claiming that Vergil the guide performs these supernatural feats with the aid of grace bestowed on him on Dante's behalf.

However, this defense rests on a self-contradictory theological notion. Natural reason ceases to be natural as soon as it is aided by the supernatural power of grace. To inject grace into the working of natural reason is the essence of the theological doctrine called the infusion of grace, which transforms man's natural powers into supernatural ones. Hence Vergil the guide cannot stand for natural reason if he is aided by the power of grace. As an allegorical representation of natural reason, Vergil is theologically too anomalous to be accommodated within the teachings of medieval Christianity. He concludes this anomalous role by crowning and mitering Dante the pilgrim on the top of Purgatory (*Purgatorio* 27.142). That is, he confers the awesome power of temporal and spiritual autonomy on the sanctified Christian soul, which is an incredible role for natural reason.

The role of Vergil in the *Commedia* is too fantastic to fit the Christian conception of natural reason, and yet very few Dante scholars have sensed the awkwardness of his allegorical function, because they have all read the *Commedia* within the secure theological framework of St. Thomas. Only rarely has a perceptive soul, like Charles Singleton, had the boldness to question the traditionally imputed allegorical role of Vergil.

Is it not clear that Virgil can not and does not always speak and act as Reason, with a capital initial, and that to try to make him do this is to try to rewrite the poem according to a conception of allegory which the poem does not bear within itself?[1]

The interpretation of Beatrice as the symbol of revealed theology does not fare much better than that of Vergil as the symbol of natural reason. To be sure, the elaborate arrangement of Beatrice's Pageant on the Terrestrial Paradise appears to be the initial confirmation of this interpretation: the four beasts surrounding the Chariot apparently stand for the four Gospels; the twenty-four elders preceding the Chariot, for the twenty-four books of the Old Testament; the seven persons following the Chariot, for the seven books of the Acts, the Epistles, and the Apocalypse. The Pageant appears to represent the unfolding of revealed theology through the Old and the New Testments. In that event, the Chariot would be no more than a vehicle of transportation for Beatrice as revealed theology.

At the end of the Procession, however, the Chariot is subject to a series of assaults by an eagle, a fox, and a dragon, which are supposed to represent the tribulations of the Christian church (*Purgatorio* 32.109–35). In that event, the Chariot should stand for the Church, a far more awesome function than merely the transportation for revealed theology. Beatrice's Pageant itself should be regarded as the procession of the Church, a much graver event than the unfolding of revealed theology. The latter is only one feature of the former. Furthermore, Beatrice's position as the sole occupant of the Chariot betokens a much weightier allegorical role for her than that of representing revealed theology. She represents the leadership of the whole Church, too complex and too concrete a role to be discharged by such an abstract entity as revealed theology. For these reasons, some Dante scholars have been tempted to view her allegorical role as something more substantial than that of representing revealed theology. For example, Pierre Mandonnet has felt the need to elevate her allegorical role to that of the supernatural order (*ordre surnaturel*) itself.

The problem of interpreting the allegorical role of Dante's third and final guide, St. Bernard, has been an embarrassment to most Dante scholars. Since they have exhausted the dyadic schema of Thomistic theology in their allegorical account of Vergil and Beatrice, they have nothing left to say about the allegorical role of St. Bernard. They do not even have a place left for the poor saint to stand on. Thus Dante's third and final guide has been left allegorically naked and cold, while Vergil and Beatrice have been smothered under ill-fitting and ever-mounting allegorical adornments.

Beatrice replaces Vergil as Dante's guide to continue his work; St. Bernard replaces Beatrice to conclude her work (*Paradiso* 31.65). However great the missions of Vergil and Beatrice may have been, theirs are meant to be only a preparation for what St. Bernard is destined to accomplish for Dante. Hence we can never expect to understand the allegorical roles of Dante's first two guides without understanding that of his final guide. As long as St. Bernard is to remain allegorically naked and vacuous, the voluminous exegeses on Vergil and Beatrice will add up to nothing.

This strange story of Dante's three guides is only one example of the countless textual distortions that have been forced on Dante's trinitarian epic by dogmatically squeezing it into the dualistic Thomistic framework. Many years ago, I came to be distressed by these distortions and took upon myself the task of freeing Dante's masterpiece from the Thomistic shackles. I had to replace the dualistic Thomism with a trinitarian thematic framework for the *Commedia*. I found it in the theology of the Holy Trinity and in the Platonic doctrine of the tripartite human soul. These two doctrines had been intimately associated in medieval Christian teachings. Since the time of the early Church Fathers, the three parts of the soul (intellect, feelings, and appetites) had been assumed to be the best allegorical image of the Holy Trinity on earth. By placing the *Commedia* in this triadic framework of the Trinity and the tripartite soul, I presented a systematic trinitarian reading of Dante's epic in my *Fragile Leaves of the Sibyl*.[2]

This triadic framework perfectly matches the trinitarian texture of the *Commedia*. For example, the threefold relation of Dante's three guides appears to be almost dictated by this triadic framework. I have shown that they allegorically represent the workings of the Holy Trinity in the salvation of a human soul. Vergil stands for the Son; Beatrice for the Holy Spirit; and Bernard of Clairvaux for the Father. Vergil's mission for Dante represents the visible mission of the Second Person for every human soul; that is, to teach it how to die in the world of sin (*Inferno* and how to be born again in the world of grace (*Purgatorio*). Beatrice's mission represents the invisible mission of the Third Person; that is, to sanctify the reborn soul and to guide its journey to the heavenly mansion of the Father.

These two missions are the missions of salvation. In order to highlight the allegorical significance of Vergil's and Beatrice's missions, Dante uses two words, *mia salute* (my salvation), in his final descriptions of these two guides: "Virgilio a cui per mia salute die'mi" (Vergil, to whom I gave myself up for my salvation), and "O donna . . . /che soffristi per la mia salute/in inferno lasciar le tue vestige" (O lady . . . /who for the sake of my salvation/didst endure to leave thy footprints in Hell) (*Purgatorio* 30.51; *Paradiso* 31.79–81).

The magic word *salute* is one of those special words rarely used in the *Commedia*. To be exact, it is used only fourteen times in the composition of its one hundred cantos. The use of the two words *mia salute* together is even rarer; they are used together only in these two instances. By this unmistakably stringent poetic device, Dante is trying to tell us that Vergil and Beatrice allegorically stand for the Son and the Spirit, the only two agents of salvation known in Christianity. To hand over the mission of salvation to either natural reason or revealed theology would be an act of heresy or lunacy in any part of Christendom.

It is the Father who sends out his Son on his visible mission and his Spirit on his invisible mission. He does not himself go out on any mission of salvation, but remains in his heavenly mansions. His function is not to redeem fallen souls from the sinful world, but to receive, with the beatific vision, the souls redeemed by the Son's visible mission and the Spirit's invisible mission. Like this heavenly Father, Bernard of Clairvaux waits for Dante in the Empyrean and concludes the work of Vergil and Beatrice by elevating his soul to the ecstatic vision of the Holy Trinity. This ultimate character of the Father's function in the Christian scheme of salvation is highlighted in Bernard's two descriptions of his own role. When the saint replaces Beatrice as Dante's guide, he tells Dante that he has taken over her position in order to bring Dante's longing to its final goal (*Paradiso* 31.64–66). Just before presenting his eloquent prayer to the Queen of Heaven for her intercession on Dante's behalf, the saint tells Dante that his prayer is to bring Dante's long journey to its conclusion (*Paradiso* 31.94–96.). In the meantime, the saint is described as a tender father and is addressed as the holy father (*Par.* 31.63; 32.100).

This is only a brief summary of my trinitarian interpretation of Dante's three guides. The most important point, however, is that the framework of trinitarian theology is not limited to any one feature of the *Commedia*, but pervades the entire epic. I have tried to demonstrate this point by giving a topological account of Hell, Purgatory, and Paradise in the *Commedia*. The topology of these three realms has been the most baffling problem in Dante scholarship ever since the composition of this great epic. Despite the structural grandeur of these three realms, which has often been compared to the grandeur of Gothic cathedrals, there seems to be no relation at all between the topological structures of the three worlds.

There are nine Circles in Hell, seven Terraces on Purgatory, and ten Heavens in Paradise. The nine-tiered structure of Hell must somehow be related to the seven-tiered structure of Purgatory, because one is for the condemnation of sinners while the other is for their purgation. But it seems to be impossible to detect any topological relation between them. The nine Circles of Hell represent nine sins, and the seven Terraces of Purgatory represent seven sins. Since Dante nowhere indicates any relation between these two systems of sins, his Hell and his Purgatory stand structurally aloof from each other. The topological relation of Paradise to Hell and Purgatory is even more opaque than that of Hell to Purgatory. Whereas Dante closely associates the subdivisions of Hell and Purgatory with virtues or sins, he does not do this for the ten Heavens of Paradise. Furthermore, the number of Heavens coincides neither with the number of Circles in Hell, nor with that of Terraces in Purgatory. Thus Dante's three worlds seem to fall away from each other structurally.

In my *Fragile Leaves of the Sibyl*, I have shown how this topological problem of the *Commedia* can be solved by disclosing the real structure of Dante's three worlds, which are hidden under their surface structures. I have demonstrated how the real structures of those three worlds are organized in accordance with the triadic principle that governs the triadic structure of the human soul.[3] This common structural principle enables Dante's three worlds to function as the unified medium for systematically exhibiting various types of behavior emanating from the three parts of the human soul.

This makes the *Commedia* a summa (systematic summation) of all human characters and conducts, passions and dispositions, attractions and aversions. This grand panorama of the human soul is not presented for its own sake, but as the allegorical medium for representing the workings of the Trinity. This is in perfect accord with the medieval belief that the three parts of the human soul constitute the most eminent image of the Three Persons of the Holy Trinity on earth. Thus I have shown that the Holy Trinity is the ultimate theme for Dante's trinitarian epic, and that its three Persons are his epic heroes.

The trinitarian theological framework that constitutes the implicit thematic reference of the *Commedia* is by no means Dante's invention. Ever since St. Augustine's systematic treatise on the Trinity, the trinitarian framework had functioned as the foundation for all medieval theological discourses. Even St. Thomas' summae are no exception to this tradition. What is not so obvious or prominent in Thomistic theology is the allegorical dimension of trinitarianism, that is, the theological notion that the nature and operation of the Holy Trinity are allegorically represented in the whole creation. The trinitarian allegorical sensibility thrived during the twelfth century and reached its fullest bloom in the theology of St. Bonaventure. The Seraphic Doctor sees and feels everything through the Platonic triadic schema, just as consistently as the Angelic Doctor perceives it through the Aristotelian dyadic schema. In Bonaventurian theology, the Three Persons of the Holy Trinity and their triune relation constitute the ultimate paradigm, which is supposed to be allegorically reflected in every grade of the whole creation. This is the allegorical essence of what has been known as Bonaventure's exemplarism.[4]

Bonaventure's trinitarianism constituted the mainstream of the Gothic ethos, and Thomistic theology went against this mainstream in two crucial regards. First it adopted the Aristotelian dyadic outlook against the traditional triadic one. Then it tried to replace the allegorical mode of theological discourse with the analogical mode. These two Thomistic innovations had far-reaching theological implications and consequences.

The dyadic schema of St. Thomas is used to demarcate clearly the natural from the supernatural order. By using this demarcation, the Angelic Doctor secures the domain of human autonomy in the natural order. Human beings have the power to fulfill their natural end, Thomas Aquinas holds, although they do not have the power to fulfill their supernatural end. This is a far clearer recognition of human power and dignity, albeit limited, than the traditional Christian teaching, which had systematically stressed human impotence without a clear discrimination of the natural from the supernatural order.

The radical character of recognizing human autonomy, albeit partial, can best be shown by comparing the Thomistic conception of man with Dante's conception. The Delectable Mountain Dante the traveler tries to scale at the outset of his epic journey represents the kingdom of natural end and bliss, and a Thomistic man would have the power to climb it on his own. But the Dantesque man does not have the power to accomplish even this modest task; his attempt to climb the Delectable Mountain only turns him into a helpless victim of three beasts. Hence the *Commedia* embodies the medieval notion of human impotence and dependence far more emphatically than the Thomistic conception of humanity. With its

recognition of partial human autonomy, the Thomistic conception constituted the transition from the medieval notion of total human impotence
and dependence to the Renaissance notion of total human autonomy or
sovereignty.

As was shown in the last chapter, allegories operate with complex
systems of thematic reference, while analogies operate with simple systems. Hence the theology of analogy is a more direct way to talk about
God than the theology of allegory, although analogy is not as direct as
literalism. The semantic mechanism of indirect signification is not admitted in any parts of literal discourses. In analogy, indirect signification
is admitted only in its predicational function; in allegory, it is admitted
in its referential function as well. Hence literal theology is a more direct
way to talk about God than analogical theology, which is in turn a more
direct way than allegorical theology.

The difference between the direct and the indirect ways to talk about
God concerns the cognitive and existential posture of human beings
toward God. If we feel that God is radically different from human beings
and that he cannot be known in the same way as his creatures can, we
are likely to adopt the indirect modes of theological discourse. However,
if we feel that God is more or less like us and that he can be known more
or less the same way as his creatures, then we are likely to take up more
or less direct modes of theological inquiry. Since the indirect modes of
theological discourse more emphatically presuppose the difference between God and his creatures than the direct modes, the former are likely
to express a greater sense of human humility toward the Creator than
the latter. Even in the mode of discourse, Thomistic theology constituted
the historical transition from the medieval allegorical tradition to the
univocalism and literalism of the Renaissance.[5]

Since these two innovations by the Angelic Doctor went directly
against the mainstream of the Gothic ethos, they could not but offend
many of his contemporaries. Especially because these innovations were
presented as appropriations of the ideas newly imported from the Islamic
Aristotelian tradition, they provoked suspicion and distrust among cus-
todians of the medieval tradition, and called forth a series of extraordinary
surveillances culminating in the Condemnation of 1277. The acceptance
of Thomistic theology as an orthodox doctrine by the Catholic church
did not take place until the Council of Trent, well after the demise of
Gothic culture and the death of Dante. Although Dante wrote after
Aquinas, his *Commedia* is just too Gothic and too Bonaventurian to

accommodate any unique features of Thomistic theology. Dante's allegorical sensibility, his trinitarianism, and his conception of human power all go against the fundamental innovations introduced by the Angelic Doctor.

The *Commedia* and the Modern Ethos

My trinitarian interpretation clearly makes the *Commedia* an epic of God. In that interpretation, whatever is overtly stated in the *Commedia* is shown to function only as an allegorical medium for the manifestation of the Trinity engaged in the momentous task of creation and redemption. This God-centered reading of the *Commedia* goes against the traditional man-centered reading of it. The assumption that Dante the traveler is the epic hero of the *Commedia* and that its main theme is his epic journey for the salvation of his soul is the heart of this man-centered reading. According to this reading, Dante's three worlds mainly present a grand panorama of human conduct and passion, in which God seldom makes his presence felt. As far as its thematic substance is concerned, the *Divina Commedia* has been read as a *Commedia umana*. In this epic of humanity, God functions only as a remote source of necessary and occasional aid. He never occupies the center of the epic action.

In support of this man-centered reading of the *Commedia* and in objection to my God-centered interpretation, John A. Scott invokes Dante's own authority: "si vero accipiatur opus allegorice, subiectum est homo prout merendo et demerendo per arbitrii libertatem iustitiae praemiandi et puniendi obnoxius est" (However, if the work [the *Commedia*] is taken allegorically, the subject is man, as by his merits or demerits in the exercise of his free will he becomes answerable to the rewarding or punishing justice).[6] This passage is from paragraph eight of Dante's dedicatory epistle to Can Grande. Although the authenticity of this epistle has been disputed, we shall disregard that dispute for the moment. Instead we shall try to resolve one question only: If the quoted passage is indeed Dante's own pronouncement, does it dictate the man-centered reading of the *Commedia*?

Dante seems to declare categorically that the subject of his epic is man, specifically man as the agent of his own free will. In the exercise of this free will, Dante seems to assume, man is given mastery over his actions and his destiny. Even God must stay outside the domain of human free will and can come into Dante's man-centered epic only as the agency of justice for rewarding or punishing man in accordance with his merit or demerit. This interpretation of the quoted passage is to impute the Pelagian heresy to Dante, perhaps the most serious heresy in Christianity after the denial of the existence of God and his omnipotence.

In fact, many Dante scholars have given the Pelagian reading to Dante's pronouncements on human will in the *Purgatorio*. In response to Dante's question on the cause of evil in the world, Marco Lombardo tells him that the cause lies not in the power descending from the heavens but in the human free will (*Purgatorio* 16.58–84). In explaining the nature of love to Dante, Vergil says that man deserves neither praise nor blame for his primary desires (*prima voglia*) because they arise in him instinctually. But these instinctual desires are placed under the control of man's innate freedom, which can distinguish good from evil and which can counsel on matters of choice. This principle of counsel and choice is the ground for man's merit and demerit (*Purgatorio* 18.55–72). These remarks indeed appear to confirm Scott's reading of Dante's dedicatory epistle to Can Grande.

Nevertheless, the Pelagian heresy was such a serious issue for medieval Christendom that we should take extreme caution in attributing it to Dante or any other medieval Christians. The seriousness of this heresy lies in the claim that man has the complete freedom to do good and evil and that the merit and demerit in the exercise of this free will determine his reward and punishment after death. This doctrine is incompatible with the orthodox Christian teaching that the grace of God is indispensable for the salvation of man—that is, man can never achieve eternal bliss through his merit alone.

The seriousness of the Pelagian heresy comes from the fact that it infringes on the sovereignty of God's will. If God must reward or punish man in accordance with the merit or the demerit that he has earned in the exercise of his own free will, the exercise of divine will is being dictated by that of human will. In that event, human will is the agent of action, while divine will is only the agent of response. The question of who shall be rewarded and who shall be punished will ultimately be determined by human rather than divine will. Because of this serious implication, the Pelagian heresy was consistently and emphatically condemned, from Augustine through Aquinas to Martin Luther.

Especially in medieval Christendom, most theologians made careful attempts to formulate the doctrine of human free will without infringing on the unlimited sovereignty of God's will and the absolute indispensability of his grace for human salvation. For example, St. Thomas affirms the necessity of grace for salvation: man can neither avoid nor arise from sin without grace (*Summa theologiae*, part 1-2, question 109, answers 7 and 8). But human merit can never be the cause of grace; grace is never given to anyone because he merits or deserves it (pt. 1-2, q. 112, a.1). God alone is the cause of grace; his sovereign will alone determines who will and who will not get it.

St. Thomas recognizes the need to prepare the human soul for grace, but he says that even this preparation is made by God's grace, which moves the human free will (pt. 1-2, q. 112, a.2). He admits that the justification and salvation of the ungodly require the movement of free will. Even God cannot justify the ungodly unless their conversion comes from their free will. But the Angelic Doctor points out that this movement of their free will is only a manifestation of the justifying grace (pt. 1-2, q.112, a.3). In response to the question whether or not a man can deserve eternal life through his own works, the Doctor replies that he can if his meritorious works have proceeded from the grace of the Holy Spirit; he cannot if they have proceeded from his free will alone (*ibid.*).

To be sure, few medieval theologians had ever flatly denied the existence and operation of free will. Hence the intractable theological question was not whether or not man was endowed with free will, but whether his free will was to be conceived as a totally autonomous agency or as only a partially autonomous one subservient to the operation of divine will. The former conception was the essence of Pelagius' claim; the latter was the foundation of the orthodox Christian dogma as advocated by St. Augustine against Pelagius. All of Dante's pronouncements on human will are consonant with the orthodox teachings of the medieval Church. In his dedicatory epistle to Can Grande, Dante himself affirms the universal supremacy of God's existence and essence: God alone is the cause of his own existence and essence (or powers), while every other entity in the universe derives its existence and essence (or powers) from God immediately or mediately (paragraphs 20 and 21). Of course, since human free will is one of the powers that constitute human essence, it must come from God.

Even Dante's pronouncements on free will in the *Purgatorio* are carefully qualified so as to forestall their Pelagian misreadings. After explaining the doctrine of free will, Marco Lombardo tells Dante that the human soul can fulfill its free destiny only under the spiritual leadership of the Church and the temporal leadership of the Empire, the two divinely instituted organs for the administration of grace to this world. These two institutions have fallen into confusion since the usurpation of the emperor's secular authority by the pope, and the lack of leadership has been the ultimate cause of sin and evil in this world (*Purgatorio* 16.94–114). The indispensability of the divinely instituted leaderships for the proper exercise of free will simply means the dependence of human will on grace.

As Dante's guide and teacher, Vergil performs for Dante the traveler what the Empire and the Church are supposed to perform for mankind. Vergil concludes his mission by telling Dante:

> Non aspettar mio dir più, nè mio cenno.
> libero, dritto e sano è tuo arbitrio,
> e fallo fora non fare a suo senno:
> per ch'io te sopra te corono e mitrio.

> No longer expect word or sign from me.
> Free, upright, and whole is thy will,
> and it would be a mistake not to act on its wisdom:
> Therefore over thyself I crown and miter thee.

> (*Purgatorio* 27.139–142)

The crown and the miter are the symbols of the emperor's temporal authority and the pope's spiritual authority. Vergil exercises these two authorities in his education of Dante in such a manner that Dante fully appropriates them into his own being by the time they reach the top of Purgatory. Consequently, to crown and miter Dante the pilgrim comes to be the final act of Vergil as his mentor.

Under the tutelage of Vergil, Dante learns that the human soul has lost its freedom through sin and can regain it only through grace. In every Circle of Hell, Dante is shown that the human soul can never be freed from the bondage of sin and evil without grace. On every Terrace of Purgatory, he learns that the end of purgation is to regain the freedom of the soul, and that no act of purgation can be performed without the power of grace. As a testimony to the indispensability of grace, the entire mountain of purgation quakes and shouts praises to the Lord (*Gloria in excelsis deo*) rather than to the penitent souls for their merits and struggles, every time one of them regains its freedom by completing its penance (*Purgatorio* 20:133–38; 21.58–72).

The dependence of human will on divine will is perhaps most emphatically manifested through Dante's own experience in his epic journey. Prior to the arrival of Vergil, Dante tries to scale on his own the Delectable Mountain, only to be thwarted by three beasts; that is, only to realize how helpless and powerless his good intention is in coping with his sinful dispositions. At this critical juncture, Vergil comes to his aid in response to Beatrice's entreaty. The central function of Vergil and Beatrice as Dante's guides and teachers is to administer grace to his helpless and powerless will and to restore its health and freedom. Vergil concludes his mission by pronouncing the perfection of Dante's free will. At the conclusion of Beatrice's mission, Dante addresses her as the one who has drawn him from servitude to liberty (*Paradiso* 31.85). Every step of Dante's pilgrimage is sustained by the power of grace.

Even Vergil's lecture on free will is presented only as a partial view of the profound mystery available to human reason (*Purgatorio* 18.46). He tells Dante to seek a fuller account of this mystery of faith from Beatrice (*Purgatorio* 18.48, 73–75). Beatrice opens her discourse on free will in the First Heaven, where Dante meets the inconstant who failed to keep their vow because of others' violence (*Paradiso* 4.64–114). First of all, she tells him what a rare thing it is to have a firm will (*Paradiso* 4.87). She reveals the complexity of the mystery of free will by using the distinction between the absolute will (*voglia abssoluta intende*) and the other (*altra*) or conditioned will (*Paradiso* 4.113–14). That is, although the conditioned will can be subject to external force and violence, the absolute will is absolutely inviolable.

Beatrice explains to Dante that the great value of a religious vow lies in the sacrifice of free will, because it is the sacrifice of the greatest gift from God (*Paradiso* 5.19–27). To be accurate, this sacrifice of free will is not limited to those who take religious vows; it is the fundamental act of conversion for any Christian. This is what is meant by the Christian teaching that humility is the foundation of all Christian virtues. The act of humility is to sacrifice one's will and subordinate it to the will of God. This supreme act of sacrifice constitutes the most fundamental phase of Christian penance in Purgatory. The penitents of the First Terrace are engaged in this act by reciting the Lord's Prayer ("Thy will be done on earth as it is in heaven") (*Purgatorio* 11.1–24).

After her discourse on free will in the First Heaven, Beatrice surprisingly makes no further attempt to explicate the nature of this mystery to Dante. Instead, in almost every region of Paradise, she shows him how the power of grace ordained and sustained the earthly mission of every blessed soul Dante meets in Paradise. In the Heaven of the Sun, for example, he is told how St. Francis and St. Dominic were ordained as the two princes of the Church to be entrusted with the great mission of rejuvenating the decadent Church by "the providence, which governs the world" (*Paradiso* 11.28–36). In the Heaven of Jupiter, Dante learns that the mystery of grace can save even those born before Christ (Ripheus) and those who have never heard of him during their first lives on earth (Trajan) (*Paradiso* 20.100–126).

The human soul must aspire to salvation before it can be saved, but it can aspire to salvation only when its will is moved by grace (*Paradiso* 20.111). Even the efficacy of human prayer does not come from its power to alter the eternal will of God, but lies in its affirmation and manifestation of divine will (*Paradiso* 20.52–54). The success of human intercession is not a victory over divine will, but a victory of and for divine will: it is conquered because it wills to be conquered, and to be conquered in this manner is to conquer through its benevolence (*Paradiso* 20.97–99). This is the doctrine of predestination (*Paradiso* 20.130).

As a result, Dante comes to realize the impossibility of understanding the doctrine of free will apart from the doctrines of grace and predestination. Moreover, this inseparability is shown to Dante in the Heaven of Jupiter, which allegorically portrays the nature and grandeur of divine justice. If divine justice is understood in this context of the inseparable divine and human will, it cannot be limited to the modest function of meting out reward and punishment in accordance with the merit and demerit that the human beings have earned through the independent exercise of their free will.

If the exercise of human free will is absolutely dependent on grace, there is no way to do justice to man as the subject of Dante's epic without accounting for the operation of divine will. As soon as the operation of divine will is accepted as the foundation of all human merits and demerits, the world of Dante's epic will be seen as a God-centered one, in which the exercise of human will is ultimately dependent on divine will. To say that man in the exercise of his free will is the subject of the *Commedia* does not automatically make humanity the center of that epic. The world of Dante's epic can be seen as man-centered only if human free will is admitted as the autonomous force in that epic, which cannot allow the intrusion of divine will into the domain of human actions. Everything depends on how the relation between human and divine will is understood, that is, whether it should be understood in the Augustinian or the Pelagian manner.

The sovereignty of human will became an overriding concern during the Renaissance, although no one dared to revive formally Pelagius' doctrine of the autonomy of human will. The Renaissance philosophers and humanists alike took it for granted that man has the power to do good or evil with his autonomous will alone. This was one tacit agreement among the various schools of Renaissance thought such as Platonists (e.g., Ficino and Pico), Aristotelians (e.g., Pomponazzi), and humanists (e.g., Erasmus). In order to attack this new anthropocentric ethos of the Renaissance and to reaffirm the old theocentric Christian ethos, Martin Luther composed his *De servo arbitrio* (The Enslaved Will). In this regard, he was a true champion of medieval Christianity and an implacable critic of the Renaissance ethos.

The man-centered reading of the *Commedia* projects the man-centered Renaissance ethos as the ultimate theme of that epic. In justification of this reading, many have hailed Dante as the supreme poet of his vernacular tongue in celebration of the Renaissance secular ethos, and his *Commedia* as an immortal monument to the vitality of that ethos. For the same reason, Erich Auerbach has labeled him a poet of the secular world.[7] As a great poet of the secular and the profane, he is often teamed up with Petrarch and Boccaccio to make the celebrated trio of Italian Renaissance literature. Thus the Renaissance secular ethos as well as Thomistic theology is found in the traditional reading of the *Commedia*. But these two themes are incompatible with each other, because Thomistic theology is still God-centered. Hence the traditional reading of the *Commedia* is doubly incoherent. It is not only incoherent in relation to the text, but also contains mutually incoherent themes.

In order to save Dante's immortal epic from these thematic and textual incoherences, I have proposed my trinitarian reading. I know of no other reading that can demonstrate the coherence of Dante's text. I have learned the principle of interpretive coherence from the New Critics. As a matter of fact, I gratefully admit, my *Fragile Leaves of the Sibyl* was a systematic attempt to apply my New Haven lessons in the New Criticism to the thematic explication of the *Commedia*. I do not know of any other systematic attempt to extend the spirit of the New Criticism to the interpretation of this epic.

The principle of textual and thematic coherence may very well turn out to be the most enduring legacy left by the New Critics. Its importance has often been overlooked because it has tended to be overshadowed by their excessive concern with such provincial matters as poetic paradox and irony. Due to this provincial concern, they have usually mistaken the detection of these poetic traits for the ultimate goal of their practical criticism. Consequently, some of them have assumed that to apply their method to the reading of the *Commedia* is to demonstrate the existence of paradox and irony in that epic. But they have never questioned how essential is the existence of paradox and irony to its textual and thematic unity.[8]

When I. A. Richards, at the inception of the New Criticism, conducted the historical experiment of having his students analyze poems without revealing their authorship, he was trying to have them respond to the texts of those poems without any extratextual considerations and be faithful to what is truly in those texts.[9] This spirit of textual fidelity was all along meant to be a faithful servant to the principle of interpretive coherence. Richards' historical experiment was conducted to determine his students'. competence to grasp the entire range of their thematic references, implicit as well as explicit. This entire range of thematic references cannot be fully articulated without appealing to the principle of textual and thematic coherence. For this reason, this principle has always served as the foundation of practical criticism for all those who have espoused the spirit of I. A. Richards' historical experiment. My trinitarian explication of the *Commedia* is one of the endless fallouts from that experiment.

CHAPTER TEN
Thematic Tradition

THE impositions of Thomistic theology and the Renaissance ethos on the *Commedia* are examples of our natural temptation to read unfamiliar texts in the context of familiar thematic ideas. The Renaissance ethos has long been familiar to us because it is the fountainhead of our modern ethos. Even Thomistic theology can be classified as part of our familiar intellectual legacy, because of its adoption as the official teaching of modern Catholic church. At any rate, it is much more familiar to most of us than Bonaventurian theology. For these reasons of familiarity, Dante scholars have felt relatively at home in adopting these ideas as thematic frameworks for reading Dante's epic, and seldom noticed their incoherence with his text.

To impose one's familiar ideas on unfamiliar texts amounts to transposing those texts from their original cultural contexts to one's own context. To read the *Commedia* in the thematic framework of the modern ethos is to transpose it from the context of the medieval ethos to that of the modern ethos. The thematic interpretation of a text always involves the contextual operation of placing the text in a cultural context. Hence cultural context is inseparable from the pragmatic context for textual interpretation.

Hermeneutic Circle

The role of cultural context in thematic interpretation can be articulated by using Dilthey's notion of the hermeneutic circle: the whole can be understood only through the understanding of its parts, but the parts can be understood only through the understanding of their whole. The thematic projection and construction of a text can be made by treating it as a part of the culture that has produced it, but the nature of that culture can be understood through interpretation of those texts that have been produced in it. The thematic interpretation of a text is not simply a textual operation; it is a contextual operation as well. This contextual side of thematic interpretation has been overlooked by the New Critics, because they have taken it for granted that the thematic interpretation of a text involves nothing but the text. Cleanth Brooks never suspected that his textual interpretation of a Lucy poem would ever require the contextual operation of placing it in any historical context.

The contextual misplacement of a text usually produces a systematic distortion of its thematic content, because the thematic ideas operative in one cultural context can be systematically different from those operative in another cultural context. This thematic distortion by contextual misplacement can also be produced in mathematics and science, for example, by reading a non–Euclidean geometrical treatise in the Euclidean context, or a Ptolemaic treatise in the Newtonian context. Although this type of contextual misplacement is unlikely to take place in mathematics and science, it is one of the most frequent occurrences in readings of literary texts. Whether one is reading Dante or Homer, Shakespeare or Wordsworth, one is most likely to read them in the thematic context of one's own age rather than theirs.

To avoid the contextual misplacement and distortion of a text by reading it in its original context has been the central objective of the German hermeneutic tradition. This objective was formally stated in Schleiermacher's *Erster Kanon*: The explanation of any given text and the determination of its meaning should be made in its original linguistic context.[1] This hermeneutic objective was reaffirmed by Dilthey's characterization of interpretive understanding (*Verstehen*) as the threefold process of transposition (*Hineinversetzen*), reconstruction (*Nachbilden*), and reexperience (*Nacherleben*); that is, to interpret a text is to reconstruct its original context and reexperience its original meaning by transposing oneself from one's own cultural context to the reconstructed cultural context of the text.[2]

Schleiermacher's and Dilthey's hermeneutic objective presupposes a high level of contextual mobility; that is, that the reader can readily move around from one historical context to another. In fact, this presupposition has long been the fundamental premise of the entire German hermeneutic tradition. But this premise has received a serious critique from Heidegger and his student Gadamer. Heidegger initiated this critique by transposing the notion of hermeneutic circle from the domain of cognitive objects to that of cognitive subjects.[3] According to him, we are all caught in our own historically given context or horizon. Just as the conditions of our existence are historically given, so are the conditions of our understanding and interpretation. These historically given conditions determine the finitude of our understanding, and there is no way to transcend this circle of finitude. This circle of historically circumscribed understanding is the Heideggerian hermeneutic circle. If we can understand or interpret anything, Heidgger holds, we can do so only within this circle, which is constituted by the historical horizon of our own existence.

If Heidegger is right, we cannot transpose ourselves from our own historical context to that of Dante and reexperience his *Commedia* as it was experienced by him and by his audience. If we are to understand and experience his epic, we can do so only in our own historical context, which determines the way we see and feel things. Someone living in twentieth-century America or Europe cannot see and feel things the way medieval Christians or Renaissance Italians did. Our understanding and experience are inexorably context-determined, context-dependent, and context-bound.

By using the notion of Heideggerian hermeneutic circle, Gadamer has tried to revamp the entire discipline of hermeneutics.[4] In this attempt, he places his main emphasis on the context-boundness and context-dependence of a human subject and his understanding. No one, he maintains, can transcend his own context, in which he has been placed by his tradition and history. He advocates this notion of a context-bound subject in opposition to the notion of a context-free subject, which had been operative in the old German hermeneutic tradition: namely, a subject allegedly capable of transporting himself to any historical contexts without any constraints from his own context. He calls the latter notion "the naive assumption of historicism, namely, that we must set ourselves within the spirit of the age, and think with its ideas and its thoughts, not with our own, and thus advance towards historical objectivity."[5] He attributes this naive assumption to "the questionableness of Romantic hermeneutics."

Romantic hermeneutics, Gadamer says, had inherited this assumption of objective reason from the Enlightenment. The Enlightenment had operated with the conviction that human reason can divest itself of all prejudices and biases, and render itself into an absolutely objective medium for understanding. If human reason can do this, it is none other than what has been known as the "absolute reason." The Romantics had embraced this notion of reason in spite of their criticism of the Enlightenment. But an absolute reason is impossible, according to Gadamer: "Reason exists for us only in concrete, historical terms, that is, it is not its own master, but remains constantly dependent on the given circumstances in which it operates."[6]

The questionable element in the notion of absolute reason is its underlying assumption that we are absolutely free in shedding our own beliefs and values and in taking up the beliefs and values of others. We can easily see the dubiousness of this assumption if we try to drop our own beliefs and values and replace them with Dante's beliefs and values. It is just impossible to force ourselves into believing many of the things Dante had taken for granted, such as the geocentric universe, the quintessence of heavenly bodies, or the administering angels. It is equally impossible to stop believing or valuing what we believe or value. If we do not have this freedom of beliefs and values, we cannot freely transpose ourselves from one historical context to another. In that case, we are bound to understand everything only from, in, and through our own historical context. This contextual immobility, if true, entails contextual relativism—that is, the view that our historical understanding and textual interpretation are always relative to our historical context.

Gadamer's hermeneutic program has been taken to advocate and defend contextual relativism by many of his followers and critics alike. But he says many things that are clearly incompatible with any simple version of relativism. Although I have myself given a relativistic account of his position and its critique, I propose to reexamine his text and figure out where he really stands.[7] Perhaps the best place to open this textual reexamination is his remarks on the operation of prejudgments in our understanding, which have been taken by many as the fundamental premise for his contextual relativism.

Gadamer has adopted the notion of prejudgments from Heidegger's theory of understanding. Heidegger's theory was addressed to one of the most sensitive issues in Husserl's phenomenology, namely, the question of the point of beginning for phenomenological investigations. Husserl had located the main source of our errors in the preconceptions and presuppositions we unconsciously and uncritically take into our cognitive acts. Those preconceptions and presuppositions generally distort our understanding by not allowing the objects of our cognition to reveal their nature. In order to neutralize their effects, he had proposed the program of phenomenological investigations. This program is to approach the objects without presuppositions and preconceptions, and let the objects reveal themselves freely to us. This phenomenological enterprise seemed to dictate that its beginning could be made by divesting our consciousness of all its presuppositions and preconceptions. Hence Husserl called phenomenology a science without presuppositions.

Heidegger came to see that his teacher Husserl's view of phenomenological approach as presuppositionless was erroneous for two reasons. First, it is impossible for human beings to divest themselves of all presuppositions and preconceptions before confronting the objects of their cognition. Second, even if it were possible to do so, it would be undesirable. If we are to confront the objects of our cognition without any preconceptions and presuppositions, we shall be completely vacuous subjects to which no objects can reveal anything. Therefore Heidegger has concluded that preconceptions and presuppositions are the indispensable preconditions for any acts of understanding.[8] The real question for true phenomenological understanding is not whether we should operate with or without preconceptions and presuppositions, but how we can secure the right ones.

Although Heidegger recognizes various elements in our preconditions for understanding, Gadamer brings them all under one label of "prejudgments" (*preajudicium* or *Vorurteil*). He holds that the nature of our prejudgments is dependent on our historical context because our prejudgments are given and determined by our historical context. That is, the context-boundness of our understanding is due to the context-boundness of our prejudgments. The assertion that our understanding is always dependent on our prejudgments is meant to be not a methodological recommendation but an ontological description.[9] Gadamer's statements about the operation of prejudgments are only meant to describe what always and inevitably takes place in our understanding.

Although we have to approach all our texts with the prejudgments provided by our own historical context, Gadamer holds, we can still have the right kind of prejudgments for the interpretation of those texts. According to him, right prejudgments are provided by the continuity of tradition. For example, we have the right prejudgments·for reading Dante's *Commedia* because those prejudgments have been handed down to us from the time of Dante through the continuity of Western European tradition. If we had been reared in some non-European tradition untouched by Western European culture, we would never have the right kind of prejudgments for reading and understanding Dante. Our capacity to understand even his Italian, let alone his complex theology, is clearly a cultural legacy that has come down to us through the continuity of our tradition.

In the domain of beliefs and values that can operate as prejudgments, tradition is a principle not only of continuity but also of discontinuity and diversity. The tradition of Western Europe has produced, since Dante's time, many sets of beliefs and values quite different from his. Hence most of those beliefs and values may not be right prejudgments for understanding his *Commedia*. As has been shown, Thomistic theology and the Renaissance ethos have turned out to be wrong prejudgments for the thematic interpretation of Dante's epic, although both of them are products of the same tradition that produced the *Commedia*. Consequently tradition cannot always guarantee the rightness of our prejudgments.

Gadamer admits that there is no such thing as "the unbroken stream of tradition," and that there is always a tension between the familiarity of a tradition and its strangeness. Hence tradition can provide wrong as well as right prejudgments. What then is the criterion for discriminating the right from the wrong ones? To this question, Gadamer offers a phenomenological solution: the rightness and the wrongness of prejudgments can be shown by "the things themselves." Wrong prejudgments are wrong because they do not reveal the nature of things as they truly are. When our prejudgments turn out to be wrong, they have to be revised again and again until they become right. Hence the reading of a text is a continuous series of revisions to a project of interpretation until it can deliver "the unity of meaning."

> This constant process of new projection is the movement of understanding and interpretation. A person who is trying to understand is exposed to distraction from fore-meanings that are not borne out by the things themselves. The working-out of appropriate projects, anticipatory in nature, to be confirmed "by the things" themselves, is the constant task of understanding. The only "objectivity" here is the confirmation of a fore-meaning in its being worked out. The only thing that characterizes the arbitrariness of inappropriate fore-meanings is that they come to nothing in the working-out. But understanding achieves its full potentiality only when the fore-meanings that it uses are not arbitrary.[10]

Gadamer's criterion for determining whether a fore-meaning can or cannot be worked out appears to be the principle of textual coherence.

The fore-meanings that turn out to be incoherent with their texts are inappropriate and arbitrary; they have to be rejected or revised. Even the notion of the unity of meaning (*die Einheit des Sinnes*) that is employed by Gadamer in determining the appropriateness of fore-meanings belongs to the principle of coherence. An interpretation of a text can be said to establish the unity of its meaning if the interpretation provides a consistent and coherent reading of the text. Gadamer's project of understanding and interpretation is to be guided by the things themselves (*die Sache selbst*) and by the texts themselves. Whenever there is any conflict between our prejudgments (or fore-meanings) and the things (or texts) themselves, it is not the things but our prejudgments that have to be revised and rejected. At every phase of our inquiry, the integrity of objects must be respected and our preconceptions must never be allowed to distort the nature of those objects.

Gadamer's project of understanding and interpretation turns out to be thoroughly phenomenological. For this reason he stresses the openness of his project; that is, the need to stay open to new possibilities and interpretations.[11] When this phenomenological ideal of openness is realized in the openness of our dialogue, he maintains, it elevates its proceedings well beyond the level of subjective opinions.[12] This phenomenological stance is further reinforced by his firm stand against "the tyranny of hidden prejudices" and "the spell of our own fore-meanings." These subjective obstacles can and must be eliminated for the sake of understanding the things (*Sache*) or texts in terms of themselves.[13]

All of these statements can be taken as faithful expressions of phenomenological spirit. There is no shred of relativism in any of them. On the contrary, the emphasis is always given to the objects of cognition (the things or texts themselves) and the concern for understanding them in their own terms. The fact that our prejudgments are given by our own historical context cannot by itself make our understanding and interpretation context-bound. Our understanding and interpretation can be said to be bound by them only if they are immune to our criticism and revision. As long as we have the power to test the adequacy of our prejudgments in reference to the objects of our cognition, and as long as we have the freedom to revise or reject them for the sake of understanding those objects on their own terms, we have all we need to secure the objectivity of our understanding and interpretation.

Gadamer's contextual relativism determines only the initial conditions for our understanding and interpretation, that is, only the point of their departure. The context-boundness of those initial conditions is indisputable; every project of inquiry and understanding, hermeneutic or scientific, can begin only where the agents of inquiry and understanding are situated. This indisputable fact is perfectly compatible with any version of objectivism. The real issue between objectivism and relativism concerns not the point of departure, but of arrival; that is, the question of how far we can go in comprehending the nature of our objects. Although Gadamer seldom addresses himself to this question, he shows no inclination to set any limit on our capacity of comprehension.

According to Gadamer's account, even the nature of our historical horizon is very flexible. Our horizon is not anything like a tight cognitive prison that can make all of us prisoners to our own beliefs and values. Gadamer rejects outright the notion of "a truly closed horizon." The openness of our horizon is of course essential to the openness of Gadamer's phenomenological attitude. Our project of understanding and interpretation can be revised because the boundaries of our horizon can be enlarged. By the time we have devised a suitable project of reading the *Commedia*, we shall have extended our horizon to include Dante's beliefs and values. Although Gadamer never uses the expression "the openness of the horizon," he says as much in his stress on the perpetual mobility of our horizon: "The horizon is, rather, something into which we move and that moves with us. . . . Thus the horizon . . . is always in motion."[14]

This mobility of our horizon prevents us from being imprisoned in our initial perspectives or in the tradition that provides those perspectives, as Gadamer says.

> It is not only that historical tradition and the natural order of life constitute the unity of the world in which we live as men; the way that we experience one another, the way that we experience historical traditions, the way that we experience the natural givenness of our existence and of our world, constitutes a truly hermeneutic universe, in which we are not imprisoned, as if behind insurmountable barriers, but to which we are open.[15]

Our horizon is not a cognitive prison, but a hermeneutic vantage point whose limits can be removed and whose defects can be repaired.

It is clearly unjustifiable to level the charges of contextualism and relativism against Gadamer. The charge of objectivism is the only one that can justly be made against a man out to understand the objects on their own terms. In what sense, then, can we still say that Gadamer's hermeneutics is committed to contextual relativism? This is the most compelling question we have to face in understanding the complexity of Gadamer's hermeneutics.

Interpretation and Application

The principle of contextual relativity appears to enter his program through the unique role he assigns to the art of application. Traditionally, the art of interpretation has been regarded as independent of the art of application. This independence presupposes a clear demarcation between the two domains of hermeneutics: the domain of understanding and interpreting the meaning of a text and that of applying the result of our understanding and interpretation.[16] The unique feature of Gadamer's hermeneutic program is the rejection of this traditional demarcation. Gadamer insists on the inseparability of interpretation from application, and the centrality of application in every phase of a hermeneutic enterprise.[17]

Gadamer's unique stance on the hermeneutic role of application appears to go bluntly against our common-sense knowledge. We can surely interpret a text without taking on the task of its application. The separation of interpretation from application appears to be not only possible but also natural and obvious. Their natural separation seems to have allowed and fostered what has been known as antiquarianism in the humanities. If Gadamer is right, hermeneutics can provide no breathing room for antiquarians. For these reasons, E. D. Hirsch reaffirms the traditional demarcation between interpretation and application, by relegating the art of application to the domain of significance and by retaining only the art of understanding and interpretation in the domain of verbal meaning.[18]

Whatever may be said against Hirsch, he must always be given credit for respecting sound common sense. To respect sound common sense could not have been anything great or laudable in any normal age. But it is becoming an extraordinary deed in our abnormally fashion-conscious age, in which every trendy fashion seems to gain its ephemeral existence through its arrogant pretense not only of outmoding every other fashion but also of superseding even sound common sense. Now it takes extraordinary courage and wisdom to hold on to common sense, the courage to go against the reigning fashions and the wisdom to see through their high-flown pretenses.

Gadamer tries to prove his unusual position by appealing to the inseparability of interpretation and application in legal hermeneutics.[19] When a judge interprets a law, he does so by applying the law to a new case. This may appear to be an unfair example, because the function of interpretation in the courts of law may be an exception to the general hermeneutic practice. This inseparability of interpretation and application may not apply even to the hermeneutic practice of legal historians, since their function is not the application of law to any particular cases in the present, but the determination of the meaning of law in the past. Gadamer is undaunted by this probable objection. To determine the meaning of a law even for a legal historian, he holds, is to determine the range of its application. To find out the ancient meaning of a Roman law is to find out what range of actual and possible applications the law had in the ancient context. There is no way to find out the meaning of law without appealing to the notion of legal application.

Gadamer then shows that the same hermeneutic principle of inseparability also operates in theological hermeneutics. He concedes that the role of application in theological hermeneutics is not exactly the same as in legal hermeneutics. The proclamation of the word of God, which is the central function in theological hermeneutics, does not operate like a legal verdict. But he accepts Bultmann's view that "scriptural hermeneutics presupposes a relationship to the content of the Bible." A Jewish theologican cannot share the same relationship to the Old and the New Testaments with a Christian. Whereas the former regards the Old Testament as complete in itself, the latter takes the New Testament as the fulfillment of the Old Testament. Gadamer calls these two relationships to the Bible presuppositions for interpreting the Bible. These presuppositions of a Jew and a Christian are again different from the one a Marxist makes in looking on the Bible as a reflection of class interests.[20]

Gadamer's category of presuppositions is now becoming somewhat overextended. We can perhaps avoid some serious confusion by introducing a distinction within that category. Some presuppositions are needed for explicating the meaning of a text; they can be called textual presuppositions. Then there are presuppositions concerning the truth of the interpreted meaning; they can be called extratextual presuppositions. For example, the trinitarian theology is a textual presupposition for projecting the thematic meaning of the *Commedia*. But the question whether that theology is true or false is extratextual. Hence the presupposition of its truth value is extratextual.

The meaning of a text can never settle the question of its truth value. One can determine the meaning of a text without determining its truth value. Two persons can agree on the meaning of a text without agreeing on its truth value. The determination of textual meaning concerns only the text, but the determination of its truth value has to go beyond and outside the text. The principle of interpretive coherence applies to the determination of textual meaning, but not to its truth value. A text can be coherent in its meaning without being true.

Not all extratextual presuppositions concern the truth value of a text. Take Charles Morris' example of a short story written for the sake of making money. The author's ulterior motive for writing the story is extratextual. To attribute such an ulterior motive to its author in reading the story is to make an extratextual presupposition. But the presupposition in question is unlikely to affect our understanding of its meaning. This does not mean that the author's ulterior motives always remain extratextual. Suppose that an author writes a short story with the ulterior motive of flattering a special group of people. The presupposition of this motive can render intelligible some special references and exaggerations which may remain senseless without its presupposition. Hence the distinction between textual and extratextual presuppositions is strictly functional.

When a Jew and a Christian read the Old Testament, they can share exactly the same textual presuppositions, and yet cannot agree on their extratextual presuppositions. Even a Marxist can share the same textual presuppositions for reading the Old Testament with a Jew and a Christian, and yet maintain the claim that the text extratextually represents an old class struggle. It is also possible that a Marxist may, through his ideological bias, distort the textual meaning of the Old Testament, and may not share the same textual presuppositions for reading it with a Christian or a Jew. In that event, he is neither phenomenological nor respectful of the principle of textual coherence. Gadamer labels such an anti-phenomenological posture of interpretation as "dogmatism." There is no reason to assume that every Marxist is dogmatic. With sufficient ingenuity, an undogmatic Marxist can still maintain a Marxist extratextual presupposition for the Old Testament without resorting to the shady tactic of distorting its textual meaning.

By "application" Gadamer means the use of extratextual presuppositions. His claim on the inseparability of interpretation and application means that the interpretation of a text can never be conducted without presupposing a set of extratextual presuppositions. When we read a Sherlock Holmes story, for example, we cannot read it without presupposing that it is either a true story or a fiction. Likewise, we can never read a science fiction without presupposing its truth value. The suspension of our beliefs is often said to be required for reading fictions, but the act of suspension is dictated by extratextual presuppositions. That is, we do suspend our beliefs for reading a text because we recognize the incompatibility of our beliefs with the presumed truth of the text.

Whenever we approach a text, we cannot avoid making presuppositions about its truth value. In certain cases, we may be doubtful about the truth value of a text and be forced to suspend our judgment about it. Even then we are taking a definite stance toward its truth value, namely, that it is undecidable. The notion of truth value is inseparable from our notion of meaningful statements and discourses. Even in a casual conversation, we cannot dissociate the notion of truth value from whatever is said and heard. As was shown in chapter 6, this notion of truth value is interchangeable with the notion of reference. We can never properly respond to a statement without presupposing its system of reference, that is, without presupposing whether it refers to an actual, imaginary, or fictive entity. Hence some extratextual presuppositions are essential constituents of pragmatic contexts.

Gadamer's notion of hermeneutic application is quite unusual; it gravely deviates from the traditional notion. In fact, what has appeared to be his unusual stance on the inseparability of interpretation and application only reflects his unusual notion of application. If hermeneutic application is defined as the use of extratextual presuppositions and if some of these presuppositions are accepted as essential conditions of pragmatic context, then it follows logically that interpretation is inseparable from application.

Although his notion of application is unusual, Gadamer is consistent in its usage. Let us reconsider the relation of legal interpretation and application. The application of a law to a particular case is extratextual, although it is not extralegal. The application establishes a relation between a legal text and what lies outside the text, namely, particular cases. This extratextual relationship makes the interpretation of a law its application. Hence Gadamer's notion of application can be defined as any operation that involves some extratextual relation. By this definition, the interpretation of the word of God is always its application; it is the proclamation of the word to the people standing outside the text of the word.

Gadamer appears to be aware of the discrepancy between his and the standard notions of application, and makes some effort to clarify it. He compares his notion of application to Aristotle's notions of *techne* and *praxis*.[21] According to Aristotle, our life consists of three levels of knowledge: theoretical, practical, and productive. Whereas the first of these is concerned with pure theories and no applications, the other two involve applications of knowledge. The production of things involves the application of technical knowledge (*techne*); the practical life involves the application of practical knowledge (*praxis*), that is, ethical and political precepts.

Although both praxis and techne are matters of application, Aristotle points out, there is one fundamental difference between these two domains of application. Whereas we can learn or forget a *techne*, we can neither learn nor forget practical knowledge. Our practical knowledge is inseparable from our very existence, and this inseparability is the inseparability of practical knowledge from its application. By contrast, technical knowledge can easily be separated from its application. The traditional notion of application is much more like the notion of technical application than that of practical application. But Gadamer stresses that his notion of application is categorically different from the notion of technical application and that it is very much like Aristotle's notion of practical application.

Hermeneutic Experience

Gadamer's notion of application is central to his redefinition of the nature of hermeneutic experience.[22] In the German hermeneutic tradition, hermeneutic experience has been taken for granted as the ultimate objective of interpretation. In Dilthey's threefold notion of hermeneutic understanding, for example, to reexperience the original meaning of a text is the ultimate aim for reconstructing its original context and transposing oneself to it. Now the problem of reconstruction is quite different from the problem of transposition. It is possible to reconstruct the original meaning of a text and the beliefs and values of its original context without accepting them as one's own. But it is impossible to transpose oneself to the original context of a text without accepting its beliefs and values. If to transpose oneself to another historical context means nothing more than to imagine oneself to be in it without sharing its beliefs and values, then hermeneutic transposition cannot be distinguished from hermeneutic reconstruction.

If the operation of transposition is to be distinguished from that of reconstruction, transposition should be defined in terms of extratextual presuppositions about the truth values of thematic ideas. If we can accept the truth of thematic ideas contained in the *Commedia*, we can be said to transpose ourselves to Dante's historical context. However, if we cannot accept their truth, we cannot be said to transpose ourselves to his context, even though we can reconstruct the original meaning of his *Commedia* and its original context. If we can transpose ourselves to his context, we can experience his *Commedia* as it was experienced by him and by his audience. By the same token, if we cannot transpose ourselves to his context, we cannot reexperience the original meaning of the *Commedia*. For this reason, Gadamer holds that the nature of hermeneutic experience is governed by the principle of application, that is, the extratextual presuppositions and commitments we inevitably make in projecting and constructing the meaning of a text and its historical context.

As far as the truth of beliefs and values was concerned, Dilthey's *Weltanschauung* philosophy was committed to contextual relativism. Every historical context has its own beliefs and values which constitute its *Weltanschauung*, and there is no objective criterion for comparing and evaluating different *Weltanschauungen*. Beliefs and values can be said to be true (valid) or false (invalid) only in their own historical context and its *Weltanschauung*. Hence Dilthey's hermeneutic program maintained neutrality toward the question of truth and limited itself to the task of understanding the meaning of a text as an expression of a historical past. Gadamer rejects this neutral attitude toward truth: "a text is not understood as a mere expression of life, but taken seriously in its claim to truth."[23]

To take a neutral position on the question of truth is possible intellectually but not existentially. It is an intellectual stance to recognize the acceptability of Dante's geocentric view in the medieval context, but an existential one to accept its truth in one's own context. The former is existentially neutral, and the latter is not. This is the fundamental difference between our existential and intellectual stances. In this regard, our existential response is very much like our praxis (ethical practice) as conceived by Aristotle; neither of them can be separated from the domain of our own existence.

The claim that our existential stance is always determined by our present context does not imply that our own beliefs and values can never be changed as a consequence of reading some ancient texts or understanding their historical contexts. But this sort of change is radically different from the one that can be intentionally performed for the sake of reading ancient texts and understanding their historical contexts. Whereas the latter is meant to be an act of immediate intention, the former is understood to be an effect of our experience. Insofar as the change takes place as an effect of our experience, it still belongs to our own context because our experience is always an occurrence in our context. Whatever emerges in the causal chain of our experience belongs to the existential dynamics of our own historical context. Hence our existential attitude toward the questions of beliefs and values, whether changing or unchanging, is context-bound.

This claim on the context-boundness of our existence need not commit what Hirsch calls the fallacy of homogeneous past, another dubious affront to sound common sense.[24] There is indeed no better reason to assume that all Christians living in the medieval Christendom had homogeneous beliefs and values than to assume that all those living in the present context share the same set of beliefs and values. Even after making all allowances for individual differences and subcontextual variations, however, it appears to be a reasonable supposition to assume that our beliefs and values are given by our context, because nobody seems to be born fully equipped with a set of innate beliefs and values. We may shape and reshape our beliefs and values, and even go against the prevailing ethos of our context. Even then we can perform these existential acts only on the basis of our initial beliefs and values given by our historical context and in response to the events taking place in that context. This is what is meant by Heidegger's notion of being existentially situated in a historical context.

Accepting this Heideggerian view of human existence, Gadamer stresses the fundamental difference between our intellectual attitude toward the meaning of a text and our existential response to its truth. We can take a neutral stance on the question of textual meaning and reconstruct it in its own historical context. But we cannot take such a neutral stance on the question of textual truth because we can respond to it only with our own beliefs and values. These beliefs and values are extratextual and extracontextual in the reconstruction of textual meaning and its original context. They lie outside the text and its context; they belong to our own context. Hence they function as extratextual and extracontextual presuppositions for textual interpretation and contextual reconstruction.

The difference between our intellectual attitude toward the meaning of a text and our existential response to its truth value can be restated by amending Dilthey's notion of transposition. The transposition of oneself to another historical context is possible on the intellectual plane, but impossible on the existential plane. The intellectual transposition is inseparable from the intellectual operation of reconstructing textual meaning and its original context. The existential transposition is indispensable for the existential event of experiencing the reconstructed meaning and its truth. Since the existential transposition is impossible, the only way to experience a text and its meaning is to transpose them to our own context. That is, our hermeneutic experience is existentially bound by our own context.

This is Gadamer's existential reformulation of Dilthey's hermeneutics, which provides, for the first time, the existential foundation of hermeneutics. But this existential dimension of Gadamer's hermeneutics cannot be separated from its phenomenological dimension. The phenomenological dimension is concerned with the projection and construction of textual meaning; the existential dimension is concerned with the hermeneutic experience of that meaning. The former is the domain of understanding and interpretation; the latter is the domain of application. The former governs the operation of textual and contextual presuppositions; the latter, the operation of extratextual and extracontextual presuppositions. But these latter presuppositions are not extracontextual to our own context, but only to the text and its context. Gadamer's hermeneutics has these two features, existential and phenomenological, because it is derived from Heidegger's existential phenomenology.

The difference between the two dimensions of Gadamer's hermeneutics can be restated by using the traditional notion of hermeneutic appropriation. This traditional notion has been chiefly concerned with an intellectual operation. When we confront an ancient text out of its own historical context, we may find it unintelligible and strange. By reading it in its original context and understanding it as an expression of ancient life, we may make it intelligible and meaningful. This intellectual operation has been known as appropriation in the traditional hermeneutics.

Hence the traditional notion of appropriation belongs to the operation of reconstruction. To make a text intelligible in terms of its own historical context does not affect the existential question of its truth for us. That question can still remain alien to us—that is, unappropriated, as Gadamer points out.

> The text that is understood historically is forced to abandon its claim that it is uttering something true. We think we understand when we see the past from a historical standpoint, that is, place ourselves in the historical situation and seek to reconstruct the historical horizon. In fact, however, we have given up the claim to find, in the past, any truth valid and intelligible for ourselves.[25]

In Gadamer's hermeneutics, appropriation cannot be limited to the intellectual and phenomenological plane. It must also take place on the existential plane of hermeneutic experience. The unique feature of his hermeneutics is not only his claim that existential appropriation can take place only in our own context, but also his thesis that the central element in existential appropriation is the truth value of textual meaning. Two persons who agree on the textual meaning of the *Commedia* can still have different reading experiences of that epic, if they assign different truth values to its textual meaning. By the same token, we can have different hermeneutic experiences in reading the book of Genesis, depending on whether we take it as a revelation of divine truth or a legacy of a mythical past. In Gadamer's view, our presupposition for the truth value of textual meaning is the fundamental condition for determining the nature of our hermeneutic experience, and this presupposition is context-bound because it is our existential response.

In accordance with this spirit of existential appropriation, Gadamer tries to reshape the very concept of understanding (*Verstehen*) by labeling hermeneutic understanding as "the experience of truth" (*die Erfahrung von Wahrheit*).[26] In the traditional hermeneutics, understanding had been assumed to be the experience of meaning (*Bedeutung*), that is, the meaning of a text rather than its truth. On the intellectual and phenomenological plane, truth can be claimed or asserted, but cannot be experienced. The experience of truth can take place only on the existential plane. This experience of textual truth is the heart of Gadamer's hermeneutic experience.

While existential appropriation is mainly concerned with the question of textual truth, phenomenological appropriation is concerned with the question of reconstructive method. All methodological discussions in traditional hermeneutics have been addressed to the problem of phenomenological appropriation, that is, the method of reconstructing the original meaning of a text in its original context. There can be no methodological discussion, Gadamer seems to assume, about the problem of existential appropriation—that is, the method of accepting or rejecting textual truth—because its acceptance or rejection, being an existential response and decision, requires no method.

Of these two dimensions of his hermeneutics, Gadamer insists, the existential appropriation is the ultimate end, and the phenomenological appropriation is its means. He maintains that this relation of hermeneutic means and end has long been confused in the traditional hermeneutics, where the reconstruction of the past has been mistaken as the ultimate hermeneutic goal.[27] To rectify this confusion of means and end in hermeneutics is Gadamer's main concern, which is indicated in the title of his book, *Truth and Method*. By placing truth ahead of method, he wants to reinstate the primacy of the truth of textual meaning over the method for its reconstruction.[28] He explicitly states his concern in the introduction.

> The hermeneutic phenomenon is basically not a problem of method at all. It is not concerned with a method of understanding, by means of which texts are subjected to scientific investigation like all other objects of experience. It is not concerned primarily with the amassing of ratified knowledge which satisfies the methodological ideal of science—yet it is concerned, here too, with knowledge and with truth. In understanding tradition not only are texts understood, but insights are gained and truths acknowledged.[29]

The question of primacy should not be mistaken for the question of separability. The two operations of appropriation, existential and phenomenological, are inseparable. In fact, they must be conducted simultaneously. The simultaneous performance of these two operations produces what Gadamer calls the horizon-fusion (*Horizontverschmelzung*).

> Every encounter with tradition that takes place within historical consciousness involves the experience of the tension between the text and the present. The hermeneutic task consists in not covering up this tension by attempting a naive assimilation but consciously bringing it out. This is why it is part of the hermeneutic approach to project an historical horizon that is different from its own. On the other hand, it is itself, as we are trying to show, only something laid over a continuing tradition, and hence it immediately re-

combines what it has distinguished in order, in the unity of the historical
horizon that it thus acquires, to become again one with itself.

The projecting of the historical horizon, then, is only a phase in the
process of understanding, and does not become solidified into the self-
alienation of a past consciousness, but is overtaken by our present horizon
of understanding. In the process of understanding there takes place a real
fusing of horizons, which means that as the historical horizon is projected,
it is simultaneously removed.[30]

The projection of a past historical horizon is to spell out fully the
tension between the text and the present, without which the text can be
naively misappropriated by being unconsciously read in the present rather
than in its own historical horizon. But to leave the tension as articulated
in the projection of a past horizon cannot be the end of our hermeneutic
experience. Taken as an end in itself, the projection of a past horizon can
result only in its alienation from our own existence. But the tension
between the projected horizon and ours, Gadamer says, is overcome by
the fusion of the former into the latter.

Thus Gadamer's hermeneutic program requires the operation of two
historical contexts: the context of the interpreted object and the context
of the interpreting subject. The former is the context of reconstruction
and the latter is the context of reexperience. Since Gadamer's hermeneutics requires the operation of these two contexts, it should be called
a double-context program in distinction from the single-context program
of the traditional hermeneutics. The German hermeneutics from Schleiermacher to Dilthey has been assumed to require the use of only one
context, the context of the interpreted object; the context of the interpreting subject is supposedly left behind by the subject's transposition
of himself from his own context to the context of his text.

Gadamer's double-context program generates a most sensitive problem in hermeneutics: How do the two contexts interact with each other?
He tries to cope with this problem with the metaphor of fusion: the two
contexts are said to fuse into one. Unfortunately this metaphor can give
misleading impressions. First, it can imply either that the context of the
object is fused into the context of the subject, or that the context of the
subject is fused into the context of the object. The second mode of
context-fusion may produce something like the experience of Don Quixote; the man of la Mancha may be said to have fused the context of his
own world into the context of medieval knight-errantry. But this quix-
otic mode is incompatible with Gadamer's existential hermeneutics. In

his program, the context of the subject always functions as the primary context, into which the context of the object must be fused.

Another misleading impression that is liable to be given by Gadamer's metaphor of fusion concerns the speed and degree of horizon-fusion. His metaphor seems to imply that the fusion of two horizons is immediate and complete, consequently the overcoming of the hermeneutic tension between the present and the past is also immediate and complete. These implications are clearly incompatible with our hermeneutic experiences. The fusion of a projected horizon into ours can be immediate and complete only if we can immediately and completely accept all the beliefs and values of that horizon. But this is not usually the case. In our reading of ancient texts, we are most likely to find both elements: those that can be accepted into our present context and those that cannot be so accepted. Hence Gadamer's notion of horizon-fusion can be better articulated by admitting the distinction between positive and negative fusions.

Positive fusion is existential acceptance into our present context; negative fusion is existential rejection of and exclusion from it. These two modes of fusion can also be called positive and negative appropriations. These two modes are operative in Bultmann's program of demythologizing the *New Testament*: Jesus Christ's message on repentance and responsibility can be accepted into our present context, but its mythological wrappings cannot be so accepted.[31] Furthermore, the discrimination of the acceptable from the unacceptable elements is by no means always obvious, because their acceptability and unacceptability can, in some cases, be determined not directly but through the test of their coherence and incoherence with our present context.

The fusion of a past horizon into the present can be assumed to be totally positive if only the continuity of tradition is recognized, as seems sometimes to be the case with Gadamer's conception of tradition. But the recognition of its discontinuity dictates the recognition of negative fusion and appropriation. Without negative fusion and appropriation, the hermeneutic tension between the old and the new historical contexts can only be apparent and can never be real. Existentially, there can be no real difference and conflict between any two historical contexts, and tradition can only be continuous and homogeneous. The total homogeneity of tradition will eliminate the need for projecting a historical horizon beyond the present one and the need to fuse the former into the latter. Consequently Gadamer's double-context program will operationally dwindle to a single-context program.

By recognizing the discontinuity of tradition, however, we can restore the vitality and profundity of Gadamer's double-context program. If every historical context is at once continuous and discontinuous with our present context, the fusion of the former into the latter is always positive and negative at the same time. By recognizing these two features of horizon-fusion, we are only reliving the two inseparable processes in the development of our cultural tradition.

The elements of every cultural tradition are perpetually subject to the process of rejection and retention, combination and separation. This perpetual process of self-renewal brings about the continuity and discontinuity of tradition, and the hermeneutic tension between the past and the present. To relive this tension in the reading of our texts is the essence of hermeneutic experience, the experience of their meanings and their truths as they are accepted and rejected, remembered and forgotten, owned and disowned in the continuous development of our tradition.

CHAPTER ELEVEN
Thematic Dialectic

THE thematic ideas of a literary work are derived from its cultural context, which constitutes the existential context of its author. For example, as we have seen, the thematic ideas of the *Commedia* are derived from Dante's existential context. The contextual nexus of thematic ideas does not apply only to such monumental works as Dante's epic. In my *Cultural Thematics*, I have shown that the thematic ideas of such relatively casual works as Boccaccio's stories are also emphatically rooted in their author's cultural context, just as emphatically as the thematic ideas of such serious works as Dante's and Petrarch's epics.[1]

Just as an interpreter of a literary text cannot situate his act of interpretation in any other context than his own, so an author of a text cannot derive his thematic ideas from any other context than his own. An author may propose certain thematic ideas in a deliberate opposition to the dominant ideas of his own historical context. Even in that case, the emergence of his thematic ideas belongs to the existential dynamics of his existential context. Hence the thematic ideas of a literary text are doubly existential; they are linked to the existential context of the author as well as of the interpreter.

The operation of thematic ideas in the existential contexts of authors and interpreters constitutes the thematic tradition. Every act of textual composition and interpretation is a constitutive act in the formation and development of thematic tradition, because it is an act of thematic committment—that is, the act of selecting and rejecting, elevating and downgrading, combining and separating a set of thematic ideas that constitute the thematic content of a cultural tradition. Hence every act of composition and interpretation is a participation in the thematic development of a cultural tradition, and its ultimate understanding requires the understanding of the dynamics of this development.

Cultural Themes

Every culture embodies a cluster of ideals. Contemporary American culture, for example, embodies such diverse ideals as the total freedom of individuals, their equality, the removal of all repressions and restraints, the instant gratification of needs and wants, and the glorification of youth and power. These culture-bound ideals may be called cultural themes in analogy to musical or literary themes. This analogy is justifiable, because the thematic problems in a dramatic production or a musical composition are ultimately derived from the thematic problems in the context of real life. The derivation in question may be literal and direct, as in dramatic production, or it may be only symbolic and imitative, as in musical compositions.

The thematic dimension of art and literature chiefly reflects the thematic character of human existence. This may be one of the points Aristotle had in mind in labeling art as mimesis. A work of art turns out to be an attempt to work out its thematic problems because it reflects our way of being human, which consists in a series of existential projects for resolving the perpetual conflict of cultural themes. Thematic understanding of art and life has its roots in the matrix of cultural themes.

Every society has its own cultural themes. For example, an agrarian society is governed by a set of cultural themes different from the cultural themes of an industrial society. The difference between two different agrarian or industrial societies can also be described in terms of the difference between their respective cultural themes. Furthermore, the cultural themes in any given society are organized in a recognizable pattern. This thematic pattern of a culture has usually been the object of investigation in cultural morphology; it has been referred to as the cultural form or pattern.[2]

The notion of cultural form or pattern has a close affinity with Dilthey's notion of objective mind. The former may have been derived from the latter. The most serious misunderstanding of Dilthey's notion has been the assumption that the objective mind of a community or a historical era has a monolithic unity. This fallacy of monolithic unity or homogeneity has frequently been committed not only by the advocates but also by the critics of the notion of cultural forms or patterns. But Dilthey's notion of objective mind is meant to be taken on many different levels of generality and particularity. The notion of cultural forms or patterns must be used in the same flexible manner.

The nature of each culture's thematic pattern can be described by enumerating all its thematic components and their structural relations. But this is an extremely cumbersome and perhaps unmanageable enterprise, because every culture embodies an enormous number of themes and subthemes. Cultural morphologists have generally tried to capture the unique character of each cultural form by highlighting its salient or dominant themes. This selective procedure resembles our cognitive process of distinguishing different persons and recognizing their individualities. Every person has a potentially infinite number of personal traits, and it is impossible to enumerate and recognize them all. Instead of getting lost in this plethora of personality traits, we rely on the salient or dominant traits in our recognition and description of different persons.

A good example of this selective procedure can be found in Ruth Benedict's *Patterns of Culture*. She describes the cultural pattern of the Pueblos of New Mexico by highlighting their spirit of moderation. By using Nietzsche's distinction between the Apollonian and the Dionysian ethos, she labels their spirit of moderation "Apollonian": "The Southwest Pueblos are Apollonian . . . Apollonian institutions have been carried much further in the Pueblos than in Greece."[3] The Pueblos do not seek any extraordinary or excessive experiences even in their use of drugs and alcohol; they do not tolerate the operation of any shamans because the shamans are the agents of the Dionysian excess and exuberance. Instead, they rely on the institution of priests, whose behaviors are governed by the well-established rules and rituals of the community.[4] In this description of the Pueblan cultural pattern, Benedict is simply delineating their dominant cultural theme and its operation in their culture.

Ruth Benedict employs the same method to characterize the cultural patterns of Dobu Island and the Kwakiutl of Vancouver Island. The dominant theme of the latter's culture is the Dionysian ethos, the dialectical opposite of the cultural theme of the Pueblos. The life of the Kwakiutl is governed by the ideal of exuberance and abandon; the experience of ecstasy and frenzy is the central aim of its rituals and dances.[5] The dominant cultural theme of the Dobuans is the domination and exploitation of each other by treachery; they cannot allow the notion of fidelity to enter even into the relation between husband and wife.[6] Everybody is out to take everybody else by every conceivable means of trickery and treachery. Because of this governing ideal, all Dobuans are perpetual victims of suspicion and paranoia.[7]

If the patterns of a culture can be described by delineating its dominant theme, cultural morphology may appear to be a much more feasible program of research than has been generally conceded. It has been said by many that cultural morphology as a research program cannot be applied to the advanced cultures of civilized societies, because these cultures do not have the same kind of simple patterns that the primitive cultures have. At best, it can be used to delineate the simple patterns of primitive cultures. In this criticism, the word "pattern" is taken in its normal sense, namely the overall structure through which the various components of a culture are organized. In that case, the pattern of an advanced culture would, by definition, be a complex overall structure, perhaps too complex to be adequately described with the normal anthropological resources. However, if the pattern of a culture is determined by its dominant theme or themes, there should not be any insurmountable obstacles to applying cultural morphology to the complex cultures of advanced societies. For the operation of dominant cultural themes cannot be limited to the simple cultures of primitive societies.

Perhaps we can use the notion of cultural themes for a thematic explication of European culture.[8] For many centuries, the dominant theme of medieval Christian culture was the notion of the *contemptus mundi*. The most enduring architect of this idea was St. Augustine. He formalized the emphatic demarcation between the carnal and the spiritual world, the visible and the invisible, the corruptible and the incorruptible. He taught his fellow Christians that the domain of nature and matter had been corrupted and defiled through the fall of Adam, and that to despise and renounce this defiled domain of nature was the necessary condition for securing and retaining the integrity and sanctity of one's spiritual being.

In the twelfth century, this Augustinian ideal was challenged by its opposite; many Christians began to regard nature as the domain of order and beauty rather than as that of disorder and defilement. In *De planctu naturae*, for example, Alan of Lille exalts the position of Dame Nature as "Child of God and Mother of Things." This exaltation was in tune with the worship of ladies and the tradition of courtly love on the one hand, and the adoration of the Blessed Virgin on the other. In contrast to this elevation of the feminine principle, the Augustinian tradition had denigrated it by identifying it with the flesh, the corporeal, and the corruptible.

The rising interest in the temporal world eventually transformed the monastic tradition. When St. Benedict founded this monastery at Monte

Cassino, the cloistered life was meant to be a life of renunciation, the spiritual life sheltered from the defilement of the mundane world. During the twelfth century, many monastic orders began to take an active interest in mundane affairs; for example, the Cistercians sponsored and carried through numerous projects of reclamation. By the thirteenth century, the monastic world was coming under the domination of the new breed of this-worldly monks, the Franciscans and the Dominicans. This new breed boldly rejected the old Benedictine ideal of building walls against the mundane world, and started to tear them down in order to find their religious vocations in the secular world.

This secular cultural theme was the mainspring of the twelfth-century renaissance, one of the central ingredients in the constitution of the Gothic culture, and the fountainhead for the Renaissance and the modern ethos. This does not mean that the Augustinian theme of the *contemptus mundi* was completely overpowered by this new cultural theme. On the contrary, it remained one of the dominant themes of Christian culture. As we shall see later, the interplay of these old and new cultural themes was the main source of vitality for the Christian culture during these turbulent centuries.

While this set of cultural themes was concerned with man's attitude toward the natural order, there was another set, that was concerned with the nature of man and his relationship with his fellow human beings. In the Augustinian tradition, man was conceived as a totally helpless creature who could not do anything good or decent without God's grace. Because of this impotence inherent in his sinful nature, as we have seen, humility (the sense of his utter powerlessness) was extolled as his highest virtue, while pride was condemned as his gravest sin.

As an isolated individual, the medieval Christian regarded himself as so powerless and so worthless that he felt he could not properly participate in any form of life, whether it be secular or religious. Hence the medieval Christian culture placed great emphasis on communal bonds. Feudalism was developed as a nexus of fidelity and loyalty between lords and their vassals, and between knights and their peers. The Church was represented as the Mystical Body of Christ; medieval Christians were assumed to participate in the life of grace only as members of this Mystical Body. They believed in the communion of saints.

The cultural theme of a powerful individual began to assert itself in the twelfth century in the emergence of such strong personalities as Bernard of Clairvaux and Peter Abelard. This strong individualism eventually produced the celebrated Renaissance man, confident of controlling all his affairs, accountable to no other authority than his own, and dependent on no power other than his own. This was the emergence of the sovereign individual. Whereas the Augustinian individual was keenly conscious of his powerlessness and helplessness, this new sovereign individual was proudly conscious of his own powers. The old theme of the humility of man was replaced by the new theme of the dignity of being human, as in Giovanni Pico della Mirandola's *De hominis dignitate*.

Since this new sovereign individual was determined to control his environment and shape his own destiny, he conceived of himself as a master artisan or artist. This is one of the reasons why the role of the artist was dramatically exalted during the Renaissance. The Renaissance man developed a fanatic obsession with *fortuna*, because her power could not be kept under the control of this master artisan. She could always infringe on his sovereignty at her pleasure. The flow of fortune is the routine of life for anyone who lives with a keen awareness of his own impotence. However, to someone proudly conscious of his own power and control, nothing can be more distressing and degrading than the fortuitous blow of fortune. Hence the Renaissance man lived with constant dread of fortune, and was willing to sacrifice anything to preserve his sovereignty against the rage of fortune.

The notion of man as the master artisan was implemented in the various spheres of the Renaissance culture. Most notably, it was manifested in Renaissance politics; for example, in the emergence of artful politicians, the Borgias and the Medici, who tried to control political affairs with the new instruments of force and fraud, the qualities of the lion and the fox. This new political art of the sovereign individual was formalized in Machiavelli's *The Prince*. The economic counterpart of the Renaissance prince was the Renaissance entrepreneur, the new artful individual willing to take the risk of initiating a new enterprise and establishing his own private kingdom in the chancy world of emergent capitalism.

The notion of artful control was also the main impetus for the development of Renaissance magic and science. The common motive behind their development was the ambition to tap and control all the powers available both in heaven and on earth. The mastery of all natural and supernatural forces was one of the inevitable goals lying before the sovereign individual. This goal of mastery and control is embodied in Francis

Bacon's immortal maxim, "Knowledge is power." The evident implication of this maxim is that knowledge is not an end in itself but only
a means for power. This instrumental view of knowledge, which has
become familiar and obvious with us, was a radical break with the classical view of knowledge.

The ancient Greeks and Romans had distinguished between theoretical
and practical knowledge. The former was to be sought for its own sake,
and the latter for its use. But they had always regarded the pursuit of
knowledge for its own sake as a nobler end than its pursuit for its use.
In their conception of practical knowledge, it would have been improper
to exalt power and control as its ultimate end. In their view, the true
object of knowledge was the unalterable nature of reality, such as the
nature of man or the universe. There was no reason to assume that
knowledge of this unalterable nature could give men any power and
control over it. Hence the Stoic maxim, "Follow nature (reality)," ap-
propriately summed up their conception of the ethical function of human
knowledge. The ultimate benefit to be derived from the knowledge of
reality was to prepare and enable a human being to accept the nature of
reality in stoic fortitude. Of course, this Stoic maxim preached a message
diametrically opposed to the one to be enunciated in Bacon's maxim.

The notion of the sovereign individual was also the cultural theme that
governed the development of the Reformation. The sovereign individual
was compelled to seek the mastery and control not only of his external
world, but also of the world of his interiority. The sovereignty of his
interiority was embodied in Luther's doctrine of inviolable religious
conscience, that is, Christian freedom: "Neither pope, nor bishop, nor
anyone else, has the right to impose so much as a single syllable of
obligation upon a Christian man . . . for we are free from all things."
Since no true Christian could recognize another Christian as his religious
authority, every Christian had to exercise his own authority and minister
to his own religious needs. This new idea of religious freedom and
equality was formalized in the protestant conception of universal
ministership.

The relation of the sovereign individual to his community was exactly
the reversal of the relation of the Augustinian man to his community.
Whereas the latter had felt totally powerless and helpless apart from his
communal nexus, the former could not maintain the inviolable sovereignty of his own self without denying his dependence on his community.
The ancients had conceived man as essentially communal; his nature was

inconceivable apart from his communal existence. This communal view of human nature is expressed in Aristotle's maxim, "Man is by nature a political animal." Since human existence was assumed to be essentially communal, Aristotle regarded his *Politics* as the necessary extension of his *Ethics*.

During the Renaissance, this communal view of human nature began to be replaced by the atomistic view: the original nature of human existence has no connection at all with any communal nexus and all communities have been introduced as artificial inventions of convenience and necessity. This view of human nature and political order was eventually formalized in Hobbes's *Leviathan*.

Hegel's Thematic Triad

Now I would like to present another feature of cultural themes, namely, their interplay. Since cultural themes are expressions of cultural ideals or values, they are seldom indifferent to one another. The affirmation of one may dictate the repudiation of another; the realization of the latter may demand the acceptance of a third. Different cultural themes may complement each other; they may conflict with each other. In many different forms, cultural themes can play themselves against one another.

It is this notion of thematic interplay that has been lacking in cultural morphology. Without this notion, the morphological approach could not cope with the dynamic dimension of cultural systems. At best it could produce static taxonomies. This has been the most grievous deficiency in cultural morphology, far more grievous than all the technical difficulties of implementing morphological programs. Now that the notion of cultural forms has been restated in terms of cultural themes, it is feasible to articulate the dynamics of those cultural forms as the interplay of cultural themes.

By adapting Hegel's notion of historical dialectic, we may call the interplay of cultural themes "thematic dialectic." We may even use Hegel's triadic schema of thesis—antithesis—synthesis in explicating the dynamics of thematic dialectic. However, many have argued that Hegel's triadic schema harbors an irreparable logical flaw. If thesis and antithesis are contradictory of each other, many critics have pointed out, their synthesis or reconciliation must be impossible because the reconciliation of contradictories is logically impossible.

Of course, if the contradiction of thesis and antithesis is only apparent, then their reconciliation may indeed be possible. But Hegel has emphatically and repeatedly said that their contradiction is not apparent but real. If their contradiction is real, his critics have objected, Hegel's dialectical logic is a self-nullifying system, as J. N. Findlay says.

> And it can be readily shown that a language-system which admits even *one* contradiction among its sentences, is also a system in which *anything whatever* can be proved, so that the *whole* of such a system becomes self-nullifying, and infected with contradiction.[9]

If the triadic schema is self-nullifying, it is bound to destroy the logical consistency of Hegel's dialectical system. Then how does Hegel manage to use the triadic schema as the dialectical framework for his system? This has been the most scandalous question in Hegel scholarship, and has called forth many serious and perilous answers.

The most radical of all these answers has been to hold that Hegel never uses the triadic schema, that he even scorns Kant's use of it, and that he resolves each dialectical conflict on its own merit and without appealing to any single formula. A recent proponent of this view, Gustav Mueller, says that "the Hegel legend of thesis–antithesis–synthesis" has been one of Marx's ruthless fabrications.[10] If true, this radical account can indeed spare the presumed logical embarrassment from Hegel's system, and restore credibility and respectability to his dialectical moves. This respectable solution, however, involves some serious consequences.

The claim that Hegel makes no use of the triadic schema blatantly goes against textual evidence. It is just impossible to wade through any of Hegel's writings or any part of them without running into such triads as that of Logic–Nature–Spirit, Being–Nonbeing–Becoming, Universal–Particular–Individual, Physics–Chemistry–Biology, Family–Civil Society–State, Archaic Art–Classical Art–Romantic Art, Religion of Nature–Religion of Freedom–Absolute Religion, Art–Religion–Philosophy, or Subjective Spirit–Objective Spirit–Absolute Spirit. To say that these triads do not involve the use of the triadic schema of thesis–antithesis–synthesis is simply incredible, although it may be respectfully motivated.

This incredible claim, if true, eliminates the logical matrix for Hegel's dialectical fireworks. As we have seen in chapter 7, Hegel's system is meant to be, before anything else, a systematic account of conflict. It is meant to demonstrate the dialectical formula for all conflicts; that is, every conflict is the opposition of a thesis and its antithesis and their opposition is resolved in their reconciliation through a synthesis. To deny Hegel's use of this triadic schema is to deny that his system has any universal principle of conflicts and resolutions. In that case, his system can accept conflicts and resolutions only as a series of fortuitous, unaccountable events, and cannot be, in this regard, different from any pedestrian view. Thus we settle for the obvious safety of a pedestrian outlook in place of the grave risk inherent in Hegel's Olympian flight and vision. This is perhaps the most perilous consequence in all Hegelian scholarship.

For these considered reasons, sensible Hegel scholars do not even think of denying Hegel's use of the triadic schema. All of them proceed on the premise that the use of this schema is inseparable, one way or another, from his writings. Their disputes center around the problem of determining what real value should be given to the use of this dialectical schema. W. T. Stace recognizes its value only as an ideal that is too high even for Hegel to live up to.

> It must not be supposed that Hegel has actually succeeded in rigorously applying these principles throughout his system. The description of the dialectical method given above is an *ideal* description, a description of what the method aims at being or ought to be. In practice it is sometimes difficult to see how this description applies to some of Hegel's actual triads.[11]

This is a pious response to the scandalous problem. It rests on the pious assumption that Hegel's triadic schema is logically possible. For what is logically impossible cannot be exalted as an ideal. One can stand on this assumption only by closing one's eyes to the logical scandal in Hegel's triad.

The presumed failure on Hegel's part to live up to his own ideal has been claimed by some Hegel admirers to be his virtue of dialectical resilience and resourcefulness. Although Hegel has only one dialectical schema on the theoretical level, he is said to use it, on the practical level, in endlessly different ways, resourcefully modulating and modifying the same formula to meet the special problems and conditions in each case. Richard Kroner expresses this view: "The theme of thesis, antithesis, and synthesis, like the motif of a musical composition, has many modulations and modifications."[12] This view is even more pious than Stace's.

Whereas Stace takes a reverent attitude only toward Hegel's lofty ideal and laments over his failure to live up to it, Kroner exalts Hegel's ideal and practice in a seamless unity. In spite of this difference, both of them stand on the same pious assumption that Hegel's triad is logically sound. This is a serious logical oversight.

The unique merit of Findlay's response lies in his forthrightness. He neither refuses to recognize the logical scandal in Hegel's triad, nor resorts to the dubious tactic of denying Hegel's use of the triad, nor tries to hide Hegel's problem behind the facade of his presumably unfathomable resilience and resourcefulness. He has pronounced his verdict on Hegel's dialectical method as follows.

> If the painful analysis of this book has established anything, it is that there is no definite method called the dialectical. . . . In a rough manner the triplicity or triadicity stressed by Hegel . . . is merely an expository integument, and one that often positively masks, rather than reveals, the actual course of his thinking.[13]

This verdict on Hegel's dialectic has been resoundingly vindicated by the very fact that the recent resurgence of Hegel scholarship has not been able to produce even one convincing work to resurrect his dialectical logic.

What then is the nature of the dialectical method Hegel really uses in his own practice? Findlay finds it impossible to give a uniform characterization of it, because Hegel's uniform label of triadicity covers so many different types of dialectical moves. As it were, Hegel the practitioner of dialectic was the first revisionist of his own dialectical theory. No wonder, then, that every revival of dialectical method in post-Hegelian development has been a revision of his triadic schema, whether the revision be intentional or unintentional.

Some notable examples of Hegelian revisionisms are Karl Marx's dialectical materialism, Kierkegaard's existential dialectic, and Max Weber's cultural dialectic.[14] We can discriminate two aspects of Hegel's doctrine from each other, which these revisionists have tried to modify: the substantive and the procedural. Within Hegel's doctrine, the substantive aspect (or subject matter) of historical dialectic is claimed to be the ideas that constitute the controlling forces of historical movements (for example, the formative ideas of the Enlightenment or the French Revolution), while its procedural aspect is claimed to be the triadic schema of dialectical opposition and reconciliation.

Karl Marx rejects ideas as the substantive force of historical dialectic, and installs the social classes in their place. In his revised formula, historical dialectic is not the conflict of ideas, but the battle between the exploiting and the exploited classes. This dialectic of class struggle cannot be resolved in the reconciliation of the contending classes, for one of them must be vanquished and eliminated by the other. In Marx's hand, Hegel's schema of reconciliation is replaced by the schema of elimination.

Kierkegaard recognizes the domain of ethical choice as the only substantive ground for dialectical interplay. He repudiates Hegel's dialectical schema of synthesis and reconciliation because it is inappropriate and inapplicable to the domain of ethical choice. He maintains that the problems of ethical choice and decision can be handled only through the logic of *either/or*. Thus he formulates the stringent dialectic of existential choice, in which the act of accepting something always involves the painful decision to reject something else. Kierkegaard's dialectical schema is a schema of rejection and elimination as much as Marx's.

Max Weber reappropriates ideas as the motive forces of history, for example, in his notion of worldly asceticism as the controlling force of capitalism in its incipient stage.[15] Besides the idea of worldly asceticism, Weber admits many other cultural ideals such as the ideals of rationality, charisma, and authority, into the domain of his socio-cultural dialectic. But he is skeptical of Hegel's logic of dialectic, its triadic schema, and its optimistic doctrine of reconciliation. In that regard, Weber's schema of cultural dialectic is meant to be as realistic as Marx's and Kierkegaard's, whereas Hegel's expresses the Romantic ethos of universal reconciliation. While the latter stands on the hopeful assumption that every conflict can be resolved in a harmonious reconciliation, the former manifest the brutal recognition that the resolution of every conflict involves the painful procedure of elimination and exclusion.

Thematic Resolution

My purpose is not to discuss the merits and demerits of these revisions vis-à-vis those of their original, but to show that my notion of thematic dialectic is another revision of Hegel's inexhaustible idea. Every cultural theme has its dialectical opposite. For example, the cultural theme of regarding nature as an object of contempt and defilement is dialectically opposed to that of adoring it as an object of beauty and sanctity. These two cultural themes are incompatible with each other, because they are contraries. That is, if one of them is to be realized, the other must be rejected. The opposition of these two cultural themes may be called thematic exclusion or contrariety. Theirs is the dialectic of incompatible or incommensurate themes.

This type of thematic opposition should be distinguished from another type, which may be called "thematic tension" (or "competition"). For example, the cultural theme of being concerned with the other world is not necessarily incompatible with the cultural theme of being concerned with this world, because one does not logically exclude the other. That is, it is possible for someone to be concerned with both worlds. But these two cultural themes can be in competition with each other, and their competition can create tension. Nevertheless, theirs is the dialectic of compatible or commensurate themes.

When two cultural themes are in competition with each other, their conflict can be resolved in many different ways: they can be kept in equilibrium, or one can be renounced or suppressed for the sake of the other, or one can be subordinated to the other. The first of these three modes may be called resolution by equilibrium; the second mode, resolution by suppression; and the third mode, resolution by subordination.

Resolution by equilibrium treats the two competing cultural themes as equals and maintains their balance. For example, the conflict between the private interests of individuals and the public interests of their community can be resolved in this manner. Both interests can be regarded as equally important, and their conflict can be resolved by maintaining a proper balance between them. Lévi-Strauss regards binary opposition as the standard method for achieving and maintaining social equilibrium in primitive societies.[16] The competition of two cultural themes takes the form of binary opposition, and their balance or equilibrium also takes the same form. Hence the binary opposition that governs the operation of primitive thought and societies can be regarded as one version of resolution by equilibrium. Aristotle's notion of the golden mean belongs to the same type of resolution.

Resolutions by suppression and subordination can be illustrated by the medieval ideal of the *contemptus mundi*: concern for this world was to be totally suppressed for the sake of concern for the other world. By the twelfth century, this resolution was being replaced by another: secular concern was not to be totally suppressed but only to be subordinated to religious concern. This is resolution by subordination. Resolution by suppression was acceptable and reasonable, as long as the medieval Christians took no strong interest in the natural order. Once they started taking a positive attitude toward nature, this resolution became difficult to accept and maintain, and had to be replaced by resolution by subordination. Since resolution by subordination emerged to cope with much stronger secular interests than did resolution by suppression, the former produced much greater tension in the medieval Christian sensibility than the latter. This greater tension began to give new vitality to the Christian West in the twelfth century, and produced such intense personalities as Bernard of Clairvaux and Peter Abelard.

The allegorical sensibility that bloomed in the twelfth and the thirteenth centuries was one way to resolve the thematic tension between the secular and the religious concerns. If the beauty of nature was to be appreciated for its own sake, this secular attitude was bound to create a tension with the religious concern. However, this tension could be avoided by taking the beauty of nature as the allegorical medium for reflecting the beauty of the supernatural order. The subordination of secular interest to religious concern through allegory reached its fullest bloom in St. Bonaventure's theology of allegory, and Dante's figural allegory in the *Commedia*. Bonaventure's theology was to see the allegorical reflection of the Holy Trinity in every natural object and historical event; Dante's figural allegory was to portray the workings of the Trinity through the allegorical medium of the entire universe and its history. Gothic cathedrals are visual monuments to the same allegorical ethos; they were the attempts to capture the sense of the supernatural order in the natural medium.

St. Thomas' doctrine of the natural and the supernatural orders was also a way to resolve the conflict between secular and sacred concerns by subordinating the former to the latter. But there is a delicate point of difference between his way and Bonaventure's. Although both recognized positive values for the natural order, these positive values were quite different. Bonaventure saw the positive value of nature mainly in her function as allegorical medium. It was essentially an instrumental value. However, Aquinas took the bold step of recognizing the intrinsic value of nature in addition to her instrumental value. This was the main reason why he was considered a radical theologian by his contemporaries. Although Aquinas insisted on the subordination of the intrinsic value of the natural order to that of the supernatural order, the very recognition of the former was a scandal and blasphemy to the conservative Christians who could recognize no intrinsic values outside the supernatural order.

In addition to these three ways to resolve thematic conflicts, there are three other ways: the two competing themes can be unified or fused into one, one of them can be eliminated, or one can be absorbed into the other. These three ways may be called resolution by fusion, resolution by elimination, and resolution by absorption. These additional three ways are quite different from the original three. Whereas the original three recognize the existence of two competing cultural themes and try to deal with the demands of both, these additional three accept the legitimacy of only one theme and its demand in their resolutions. The former produce dualistic resolutions; the latter result in monistic resolutions. These monistic resolutions became influential during the Renaissance.

The resolution by fusion was especially popular among the Renaissance Platonists such as Nicholas of Cusa and Ficino. Those who adopted this mode of resolution discarded the medieval demarcation between the natural and the supernatural orders, and began to conceive those traditionally divided realms as one unified order or universe. This unified view of reality had been prepared by Duns Scotus's doctrine of univocity, which was the most radical transformation of medieval theology. Medieval theologians had in general recognized an emphatic distinction between two types of discourse: the discourse of finite beings and that of the infinite being. They also maintained that our natural language was designed for the discourse of finite beings, and that it was unsuited to the discourse of the infinite being. However, since natural language was the only language we have, they believed that special ways of using natural language had to be devised for talking about the infinite God. Bonaventure's doctrine of allegory and Aquinas' doctrine of analogy were attempts to formalize these special ways to use natural language for the discourse of the infinite being. Repudiating this venerable tradition of two pragmatics, Duns Scotus advocated his doctrine of univocity, namely, the startling claim that both the finite and the infinite could be handled in one universe of discourse.[17]

Resolution by elimination was popular among the Renaissance naturalists and Aristotelians. Boccaccio was one of the outstanding naturalists; Pomponazzi was one of the eminent Aristotelians. The Renaissance naturalists and Aristotelians denied the existence of the other world, and thereby abolished the ontological ground for concern with the supernatural order. They resolved the medieval thematic conflict by eliminating one of the competing cultural themes, that is, by denying its existence. This mode of resolution should not be confused with resolution by suppression. In the suppression of secular interests for the sake of religious concern, the existence and operation of the former are as firmly recognized as those of the latter.

Whereas resolution by elimination produces a monistic framework, resolution by suppression retains its dualistic framework. The former dictates the adoption of one semantic order in place of two; the latter necessitates the continued use of two semantic orders. Boccaccio and Pomponazzi could dispense with allegory and analogy even more resolutely than could Nicholas of Cusa and Ficino, but Augustine and Fulgentius were in need of two semantic orders as much as were Bonaventure and Dante. Of course, this question of semantics is relevant only to the thematic dialectic of the natural and the supernatural concerns.

To illustrate resolution by absorption, let us consider the conflict between the cultural theme of individual interests and that of communal interests. We have already noted the possibility of resolving this thematic dialectic by maintaining their equilibrium. But this resolution became inapplicable and inoperable with the emergence of the sovereign individual, because the sovereign will of the individual could not be retained and preserved in such an equilibrium. It dictated the subordination of communal interests to the individual will, but even this resolution was not quite perfect from the standpoint of individual sovereignty, because it could not fully eliminate the thematic tension between the individual and the communal interests.

A perfect resolution of this thematic conflict was for the sovereign individual to absorb the communal interests and make them his own. This mode of resolution underlies Hobbes's thesis that people can form a commonwealth only by subjecting their wills to the will of one person: "therein to submit their wills, everyone to his will, and their judgments, to his judgments. This is more than consent, or concord; it is a real unity of them all, in one and the same person" (*Leviathan* pt. 2, ch. 17). The same spirit of absorption is enunciated in Louis XIV's political credo, "L'État, c'est moi." The unity of the king and his state is established by the absorption of the state into the king. If successful, this resolution cannot allow any room for futher tension between the individual and the communal interests.

In resolution by absorption, the relation of the individual and the community can be reversed; the individual interests can be absorbed into the communal interests. This is the mode of resolution that operates in today's totalitarian states, in which the interests of individuals are claimed to be indistinguishable from the interests of the state. In the case of Nazism, the two modes of resolution by absorption were jointly used: the individual interests of all citizens were absorbed into the interests of the state or the race, which in turn were absorbed into the interests of the *Führer*.

Resolution by absorption should not be confused with resolution by fusion. Although both modes produce monistic results, they differ in one important respect. In resolution by fusion, the two competing cultural themes operate as equals; both lose their original identities in the process of fusion and gain a new joint identity. In resolution by absorption, the two competing themes operate as unequals; only one can retain its original identity and integrity, while the other must lose them.

Each of these three modes of monistic resolution can find a counterpart in one of the three modes of dualistic resolution. Resolution by fusion corresponds to resolution by equilibrium; in both, the competing cultural themes are treated as equals. Resolution by elimination resembles resolution by suppression; ultimately, no intrinsic values are recognized for either the eliminated theme or the suppressed one. Resolution by absorption corresponds to resolution by subordination; in both resolutions, one of the competing themes is given dominance over the other, although positive values are recognized for both.

These various forms of resolution are for dealing with the conflict of two cultural themes, the dyadic conflict. There may be more complex forms of thematic conflict than the dyadic one: for example, triadic conflict, tetradic conflict, etc. These complex thematic conflicts may, however, still operate in the dyadic form; for example, in a thematic conflict involving three cultural themes, two themes may be jointly opposed to the third. That is, the deep structure for this apparently triadic conflict may really be dyadic, and its resolution can employ any one of the various modes for resolving the dyadic conflict. Even if its deep structure is as complex as its apparent structure, the various modes for resolving the dyadic conflict can be still adapted to its resolution. To be sure, their adaptation will make them much more complex.

So far we have investigated the thematic dialectic of the compatible and the commensurate. The thematic dialectic of the incompatible and the incommensurate presents an altogether different problem of resolution. As we have seen, this is the conflict of contrary or contradictory themes. Since it is logically impossible to accommodate both in the resolution, one or both of the themes must be eliminated. That is, there are only two modes of resolution for this type of thematic dialectic: the elimination of one of the themes, and the elimination of both. These two modes are Kierkegaard's *either/or* and Zen Buddhists' *neither/nor*. All the other modes of resolution we have examined are inapplicable to the thematic dialectic of the incompatible or incommensurate.

Thematic Consequence

In addition to these two types of conflicts and their resolutions, there is a third problem in thematic dialectic, which may be called the problem of consequence. The resolution of a thematic conflict establishes the dominance of some cultural theme or themes, which can produce certain thematic consequences. These consequences can also take various forms: thematic continuance, thematic expansion, thematic reaction, thematic reversal, thematic repression, and thematic deterioration.

Thematic continuance means continuing the thematic dominance established by any given resolution. Thematic expansion means expanding it from one sphere of culture to another. Let us take the example of medieval monastic discipline: its dominant cultural theme was to conquer and control the desires and passions of the interior world. During the eleventh and twelfth centuries, this cultural theme of control and conquest began to be expanded from the interior to the exterior world. For example, the Cistercians implemented their massive reclamation projects by transferring the spirit of control and conquest from their interiority to the exterior world of agriculture. The Crusades were also manifestations of this expansion; they were meant to transfer the spirit of control and conquest to the Holy Land. Gregory VII's momentous reorganization of the Church was the transference of the same cultural theme to the province of ecclesiastical institutions.

The emergence of nation-states continued this transference to the province of secular political institutions; its extension to economic institutions produced entrepreneurs and their capitalism. Even the spirit of control and conquest over nature, which has governed the development of modern science and technology, may have come about as the expansion of the spirit of control and conquest from the interior world to the exterior one. As we have seen, this spirit of control and conquest over the external world was an essential feature of the cultural theme of being a sovereign individual. Now we can see that the monastic theme of self-conquest and self-control had been the fountainhead of this cultural theme.

Thematic reaction is reaction against the dominance of the reigning cultural themes. For example, the strong interests in nature that emerged in the twelfth century may have been a reaction against the dominance of the *contemptus mundi*. Many forms of antiscientism in our world today are reactions against the dominance of science and scientism in our culture. This notion of reaction is quite similar to Hegel's notion that every thesis generates its antithesis, or that every synthesis becomes a thesis by positing its own antithesis. The generation of antithesis looks like the emergence of thematic reaction, but there is an important point of difference between the two. Whereas the generation of antithesis is dictated by logical necessity, the emergence of thematic reaction is a matter of historical contingency. The former occurs necessarily and instantaneously with the emergence of a thesis or a synthesis; the latter may occur at any time or never.

Thematic reversal is a somewhat more complicated process than thematic reaction. The former is one of Hegel's favorite ideas; his well-known example is the reversal that takes place in the dialectical relation between master and slave. The master becomes so dependent on the slave that the former loses his mastery over the latter and becomes enslaved to his service, while the slave gains mastery over the master through the latter's enslavement.[18] Max Weber was especially fascinated with this mode. He believed that a cultural ideal usually contains, in its success, the germ of its own reversal or destruction.[19] That is, the realization of a cultural ideal tends to generate its opposite ideal and cultural force that will eventually destroy its original ethos and force. For example, the ethos of asceticism was the instrumental force for accumulating wealth and converting it into capital during the initial period of European capitalism, but the accumulated wealth and the resulting luxury eventually turned against the ethos of asceticism and destroyed it.[20]

A thematic reversal is taking place in our technological mastery over nature. Through modern science and technology, modern European culture has established its mastery over nature. But in the meantime this culture has become completely dependent on science and technology.

The sovereign individual of the modern West started out as the master of science and technology, but is ending up as its slave. Even the emergence of the sovereign individual may have come about as the dialectical reversal of the medieval theme of Christian humility. The medieval Christian may have come to recognize his hidden powers by living through long centuries of a powerless existence.

Thematic repression is the repression of some cultural themes by the domination of the reigning cultural themes. Let us take one example from the sovereign individual. Since he is bent on planning, regulating, and controlling every phase of his life, he inevitably represses his sense of naturalness and spontaneity. This phenomenon of repression should not be confused with that of subordination or suppression, which we saw in the resolutions of thematic conflicts. Whereas both subordination and suppression are intended, repression is unintended. The sovereign individual has no intention of repressing his sense of naturalness and spontaneity. In fact, he may even be distressed over its repression.

A sovereign individual cannot allow the existence and operation of another sovereign individual within the sphere of his power and control. For he can maintain his sovereignty only by controlling and manipulating all other persons with whom he comes into contact. Consequently, the only personal relationship he can tolerate is one of total control over other persons and their total subjection to his command. He cannot establish friendship with another person in its traditional sense, that is, a relationship of trust and respect between two open and caring individuals. The natural relation of sovereign individuals is the Hobbesian state of nature, *bellum omnium in omnes*, "where every man is enemy to every man" (*Leviathan* part 1, ch. 13). Even when they bind themselves into a political community, they do so solely for the sake of promoting their own security and convenience.

Classical and medieval literature abound in memorable stories of great friendships, such as Achilles and Patroclus, Damon and Pythias, Roland and Oliver, etc. This tradition became extinct with the emergence of sovereign individuals. None of the one hundred stories in Boccaccio's *Decameron* has friendship for its central theme; few of Shakespeare's numerous heroes are capable of deep friendship. In this regard, Coriolanus occupies a special place among Shakespearean heroes. He is so immersed in his own egocentric being that he can never establish a loving and caring relationship with another human being. With a few exceptions, all Shakespearean heroes embody Coriolanus's egocentric personality in different ways. Their irredeemable egocentricity is not an incidental but the central feature of their tragic character.

Thematic deterioration is the deterioration of the dominant cultural themes. During the past few decades, for example, many of the dominant modern cultural themes have declined and deteriorated, e.g., the work ethic, self-reliance, self-discipline, etc. This is why many have said that we are entering the post-modern age, or even a post-Christian culture. The end of the Middle Ages saw a similar deterioration of old cultural themes.

The deterioration of old cultural themes is sometimes accompanied or even dictated by the emergence of new ones. New themes can emerge as a creation of a new age or as a transformation of old ones to meet new needs. New cultural themes can also be introduced from other cultures. At any rate, new cultural themes present new thematic conflicts and problems, which demand new thematic development and resolutions, which in turn produce new thematic consequences and configurations.

Thematic Reflection

This is an outline of my own thoughts on thematic dialectic. I have already said that my notion of thematic dialectic is an adaptation of Hegel's notion of historical dialectic. Let us now compare my revision with its original. Hegel holds that every dialectical conflict is reconciled through the synthesis of thesis and antithesis. Reconciliation through synthesis is equivalent to resolution by fusion. Whereas the latter is one of many possible ways of resolving dialectical conflicts in my theory, the former is the only way of doing it in Hegel's system.

Since Hegel recognizes only one way to resolve every dialectical conflict, he is compelled to hold that every historical development is determined by logical necessity. Hegel has often been accused of historical determinism, but logical necessitarianism is a far stronger claim than historical determinism. My view that there is more than one way to resolve any thematic conflict is not necessarily incompatible with historical determinism, although the latter is not logically entailed by the former. Although there are six or seven modes of resolution available for any given thematic conflict, the selection of one for its resolution may be determined by historical causes and conditions operating on that thematic conflict.

In Hegel's system, however, there is only one way to resolve all dialectical conflicts. The outcome of every dialectical struggle is necessarily predetermined by this one logical formula of dialectical synthesis. This is what I mean by "logical necessitarianism." Logical necessitarianism entails historical monotony, because every resolution or every historical development endlessly repeats one mechanical formula. However, if thematic conflicts can be resolved in many different ways, historical processes can present a greater range of diversity and variety.

Hegel's logical necessitarianism is not limited to his doctrine of dialectical reconciliation, but is already contained in his conception of dialectical conflict itself. We have recognized two types of dialectical conflict: the dialectic of the incompatible and incommensurate, and that of the compatible and commensurate. Hegel presents every pair of theses and antitheses as contraries or contradictories, that is, as the conflict of the incompatible and the incommensurate. If dialectical conflict is conceived in this manner, there can be only one format for every conflict.

Take the example of the dialectical conflict between art and religion. Hegel claims that their conflict is necessary, and that it is reconciled in philosophy.[21] The conflict between art and religion can be claimed as a necessary one only if art and religion are conceived as contraries, which is indeed a dubious view. The conflict between art and religion is possible but not necessary. In chapter 7 we saw that with the supremacy of aesthetic values, art really began to take over the function of religion during the Romantic era. That is, there was serious conflict and competition between art and religion in Hegel's own day. But that conflict was dictated by the unique aesthetic ethos of Romantic Europe. Until the Romantic exaltation of art in place of religion, Western Europe had seldom seen any serious conflict between the two.

Since Hegel conceives the conflict between art and religion as a conflict of contrariety, he cannot allow the possibility of conflict between art and other things besides religion or between religion and other things besides art. For example, he can neither account for the conflict between art and ethics or politics, nor for the conflict between religion and philosophy. In Hegel's system, philosophy can never be in conflict with art or religion, because the former can only be the synthesis of the latter. Art can never be in conflict with ethics or politics because it is the contrary of neither ethics nor politics. This rigidity of dialectical conflict is dictated by Hegel's conception of it as the logically necessary conflict of contrary or contradictory ideas. My thematic conception of dialectic interplay eliminates this Hegelian rigidity by reconceiving its conflict as the existentially contingent one between competing cultural themes. For example, the claims and demands of art can come into conflict with those not only of religion, but also of ethics, economics, politics, science, philosophy, or any other thematic claims and demands of culture.

Hegel's logical conception of dialectical conflict presents an immediate problem for its resolution. As we have already seen, such a conflict is the conflict of the incompatible and the incommensurate (contradictories and contraries). The *reconciliation* of contraries or contradictories is logically impossible. We have also seen that the only way to resolve such a conflict is to eliminate one (*either/or*) or both (*neither/nor*) of the conflicting themes. This is the line of thought that underlies Kierkegaard's logic of *either/or*. He took seriously Hegel's claim that every dialectical conflict is the conflict of contraries or contradictories. The logic of elimination also underlies Marx's doctrine of resolution: the class conflict or struggle can be resolved only by eliminating the exploiting class. Marx came to this conclusion perhaps because he also took seriously Hegel's characterization of dialectical conflict as the conflict of the logically incompatible.

However, Hegel cannot be content with resolution by elimination, because he is eager to preserve both thesis and antithesis. This appears to be a logically impossible project, but his logic of *both/and* and his doctrine of synthesis are meant to accomplish this project. That is, *both* thesis *and* antithesis are claimed to be preserved in their synthesis. In this synthesis, however, the original conflict of the incompatible and the incommensurate (contraries and contradictories) is transformed into the conflict of the compatible and the commensurate. This is exactly what happens in Hegel's dialectic of master and slave; their incompatibility is resolved by their being transformed as essential constituents of a higher consciousness and being.

In every dialectical maneuver, Hegel starts out with the conflict of the incompatible or incommensurate and then shows it to be that of the compatible or commensurate in its reconciliation. He appears to have formulated this schema of dialectical maneuver, because he took his model from Kant's cosmological antinomies in the *Critique of Pure Reason* and Plato's ontological antinomies in his dialogue *Parmenides*. Each of Kant's cosmological antinomies consists of two contrary propositions, for example, "The world is finite," and "The world is infinite." Kant points out that both assertions have the support of equally valid arguments. Plato's ontological antinomies take the same format as Kant's cosmological antinomies, e.g., "Being (reality) is one," and "Being is many." Evidently, Hegel takes at face value Kant's claim that both thesis and antithesis are equally valid. In that event, the only way to resolve their conflict is to find their synthesis, in which both claims will be accepted as partial truths.

However, there is no necessity to accept Kant's claim that both thesis and antithesis are equally valid. Once freed from the constraints of this claim, Plato's ontological antinomies and Kant's cosmological antinomies can be resolved in either of two ways. It is plausible to hold that Being is one in reality and many only in appearance, or that the world is finite in reality and infinite in appearance. This is the resolution by subordination; one thesis is subordinated to the other. It is also plausible to hold that Being is one and not many, or that the world is finite and not infinite. This is resolution by elimination; one thesis is eliminated or rejected in favor of the other. Of course, it is logically possible to reverse the relation of subordination or that of elimination.

These various ways of resolving theoretical conflicts are in fact used in natural science. Let us consider the conflict between the two views of the photon and other small particles. In one view, they are regarded as waves; in the other, they are regarded as particles. The notion of microscopic objects that obey the laws of quantum mechanics can be regarded as the synthesis of these two conflicting views; the wave-like and the particle-like properties can be explained as two different manifestations of the ultimate nature of those microscopic objects. Although this Hegelian reconciliation is widely accepted among physicists, it is by no means the only acceptable resolution. Louis de Broglie has claimed that the particle-like properties constitute the primary characteristics of photons, while the wave-like properties constitute its secondary characteristics. Then, there are some physicists who have reversed de Broglie's position. These two theories are attempts to resolve the conflict in question by subordinating one view to the other.

Resolution by reconciliation or subordination is useful only if both competing theories are assumed to be equally or partially valid. In some cases, however, one or both of the competing theories can be totally false. In those cases, resolution by elimination can be the only sensible one. Which of the various forms of thematic resolution can be used for any given dialectical conflict can be determined only by our understanding of the complex relations of its thematic components with each other and to their historical context. Hence it is impossible to prescribe a universal formula for the resolution of all thematic conflicts such as Hegel's triadic schema. The universality in his schema inevitably produces dialectical rigidity in our thematic understanding. In order to avoid this rigidity, I have stressed thematic flexibility and diversity in my revision of Hegel's dialectical schema, by replacing his logical necessity with existential contingency as the center of all thematic conflicts.

We should also avoid another of Hegel's serious errors, his belief in the ontological sovereignty of the dialectical process. He maintains that the dialectical process of conflicting ideas is not only autonomous (never influenced by anything outside the realm of those ideas), but also determines everything else in human history. Of course, this is a causal claim, which can be validated only by empirical investigations. In my view, cultural themes may be determined by the economic, political, or natural environment; conversely, the former may determine the latter. There may be causal connections between cultural themes and human genetic constitutions. These questions of causal interactions are open questions, which can be settled only by empirical investigations.

Whatever causal nexus cultural themes may have, they still constitute the content of existential context because cultural themes are existential concerns. Hence to understand the thematic dialectic of a culture is to understand the existential dynamics of its thematic context and content. Every thematic conflict is an existential conflict; the possibilities of its resolution are existential possibilities. The selection of these possibilities is an existential choice and decision, which determines the shape of human existence in that culture. Whatever consequences may follow from them, they are bound to have existential repercussions. In short, thematic context is existential context; thematic dialectic is existential dialectic.

To stress the existential dimension of thematic dialectic is by no means to advocate existential individualism, that is, the view that the existing individuals do experience and resolve their thematic conflicts in their existential solitude. Although Heidegger has exalted existential solitude as the privileged essence of authentic existence, no individual can ever act without involving himself in the context of his community as long as he understands himself and his problem through the language of his community. By our linguistic bond, as Gadamer says, all of us are thematically situated in the context of our community and its tradition. We can work out our thematic problems only in this context.

By restating the dynamics of thematic dialectic in existential terms, we can finally avoid Hegel's mystical assumption of Absolute Spirit as the primary agent of historical dialectic. Existential decisions and responses belong to the existing individuals, whether they are made individually or collectively, authentically or inauthentically. Hence there can be no monolithic homogeneity in the thematic development of any historical period. On the contrary, every thematic conflict is likely to produce conflicting alliances and allegiances among the members of a community. Some of them may advocate one mode of resolution, while others support another mode. Only the aggregate outcome of their thematic decisions and agonies can be mistaken as the operational result of a supra-individual subject.

The postulation of a supra-individual subject is not only theoretically unjustifiable, but also methodologically gratuitous and pernicious. It gives the misleading impression of thematic homogeneity among the various sectors and members of a community by concealing their intricate thematic divisions and alliances behind a mystical facade. Moreover it removes the sense of existential anxiety and personal involvement from the thematic stance every human subject has to take in the confrontation of his or her own existential problems. Any thematic analysis that fails to capture this sense of anxiety and involvement is functionally incomplete. For no thematic account of any text or its context can ever fulfill its ultimate pragmatic function until it is linked to the historical matrix of existential subjects. It is this existential link that gives the ultimate significance to all our hermeneutic exercises and experiences.

Notes

1. TEXT AND CONTEXT

1. Norman N. Holland, *5 Readers Reading* (New Haven: Yale University Press, 1975), p. 12.

2. *Ibid.*, pp. 113–28.

3. Norman N. Holland, "Stanley Fish, Stanley Fish," *Genre* (1977), 10:434.

4. Stanley E. Fish, "Interpreting the *Variorum*," *Critical Inquiry* (1976), 2:477–78. All expressions in which Stanley Fish appears to attribute any acts to the text, e.g., "the text encourages," or "the text disallows," are intended to refer to the text not as an independent entity, but only as an object constituted by the reader's interpretive strategies.

5. Norman N. Holland, *Poems in Persons* (New York: Norton, 1973). Stanley E. Fish, "Literature in the Reader: Affective Stylistics," *New Literary History* (1970), 2:123–62.

6. Geoffrey H. Hartman, *The Fate of Reading and Other Essays* (Chicago: University of Chicago Press, 1975), p. 5.

7. *Ibid.*

8. Gerald Graff, "Fear and Trembling at Yale," *The American Scholar* (1977), 46:472.

9. I. A. Richards, *Practical Criticism, a Study of Literary Judgment* (London: Paul, Trench, Trubner, 1929).

10. W. V. Quine, *Ontological Relativity and Other Essays* (New York: Columbia University Press, 1969), pp. 26–68.

11. For Edmund Husserl's theory of phenomenological constitution, see his *Cartesian Meditations: An Introduction to Phenomenology*, Dorion Cairns, trans. (The Hague: Nijhoff, 1960), pp. 56–88, and Robert Sokolowski, *The Formation of Husserl's Concept of Constitution* (The Hague: Nijhoff, 1964).

12. Holland, *5 Readers Reading*, p. 40.

13. Cleanth Brooks, *The Well Wrought Urn: Studies in the Structure of Poetry* (New York: Harcourt, Brace, 1947).

14. The title essay in Geoffrey H. Hartman, *Beyond Formalism: Literary Essays, 1958–1970* (New Haven: Yale University Press, 1970), pp. 42–57.

15. E. D. Hirsch, *Validity in Interpretation* (New Haven: Yale University Press, 1967).

16. Friedrich E. D. Schleiermacher, *Hermeneutik*, Heinz Kimmerle, ed. (Heidelberg: Carl Winter, 1959), p. 90.

17. Hans-Georg Gadamer, *Truth and Method*, Garrett Barden and John Cumming, eds. and trans. (New York: Seabury, 1975), trans. based on the second German edition.

2. INTENTION AND EXPRESSION

1. E. D. Hirsch, *Validity in Interpretation* (New Haven: Yale University Press, 1967), pp. 46–47.

2. Edmund Husserl, *Logical Investigations*, J. N. Findlay, trans., 2 vols. (London: Routledge, 1970), trans. based on the second German edition.

3. *Ibid.*, Investigation 1, ch. 2.

4. Lewis Carroll, *Through the Looking Glass*, ch. 6.

5. Hirsch, *Validity in Interpretation*, p. 13.

6. Husserl, *Logical Investigations*, Investigation 1, sec. 1.

7. *Ibid.*, secs. 2–4.

8. *Ibid.*, secs. 11–12.

9. *Ibid.*, sec. 13.

10. *Ibid.*, sec. 11.

11. Edmund Husserl, *Ideas: General Introduction to Pure Phenomenology*, W. R. Boyce Gibson, tr. (London: Allen and Unwin, 1931), sec. 94.

12. Husserl, *Logical Investigations*, Investigation 1, secs. 18–20.

13. *Ibid.*, sec. 7.

14. This is one of the forceful points Jacques Derrida makes in his critique of Husserl's theory of signs. See his *Speech and Phenomena and Other Essays on Husserl's Theory of Signs*, David B. Allison, tr. (Evanston: Northwestern University Press, 1973).

15. Friedrich E. D. Schleiermacher, *Hermeneutik*, Heinz Kimmerle, ed. (Heidelberg: Carl Winter, 1959).

16. *Ibid.*, p. 80.

17. *Ibid.*, p. 81.

18. *Ibid.*, p. 87.

19. *Ibid.*, pp. 74, 87, 109, 136.

20. *Ibid.*, p. 87.

21. *Ibid.*, p. 109.

22. *Ibid.*, p. 81.

23. *Ibid.*, p. 82.

24. In this skeletal account of Martin Luther's biblical hermeneutics, I am relying on James Samuel Preus, *From Shadow to Promise: Old Testament Interpretation from Augustine to the Young Luther* (Cambridge: Harvard University Press, 1969), pp. 242–45.

25. Schleiermacher, *Hermeneutik*, p. 80.

26. *Ibid.*, p. 108.

27. David C. Hoy, *The Critical Circle: Literature, History, and Philosophical Hermeneutics* (Berkeley: University of California Press, 1978), p. 33.
28. E. D. Hirsch, *The Aims of Interpretation* (Chicago: University of Chicago Press, 1976), pp. 20–25.
29. *Ibid.*, p. 26.
30. H. P. Grice, "Meaning," *The Philosophical Review* (1957), 66:387.
31. Hirsch, *The Aims of Interpretation*, p. 34.
32. Harold Bloom, *The Anxiety of Influence: A Theory of Poetry* (New York: Oxford University Press, 1973).

3. CONTEXT AND MEANING

1. E. D. Hirsch, *Validity in Interpretation* (New Haven: Yale University Press, 1967), pp. 227–28.
2. *Ibid.*, p. 228.
3. Cleanth Brooks, *The Well Wrought Urn: Studies in the Structure of Poetry* (New York: Harcourt, Brace, 1947), p. 236.
4. David C. Hoy, *The Critical Circle: Literature, History, and Philosophical Hermeneutics* (Berkeley: University of California Press, 1978), p. 21.
5. E. D. Hirsch, *The Aims of Interpretation* (Chicago: University of Chicago Press, 1976), p. 24.
6. Isabel Hungerland, "Contextual Implication," *Inquiry* (1960), 3:223. Charles L. Stevenson discusses the same point in his essay "On the Reasons That Can Be Given for the Interpretation of a Poem," in Joseph Z. Margolis, ed., *Philosophy Looks at the Arts* (New York: Scribner's, 1962), pp. 121–39. In the legal world, the presumption of normality is embodied in the objective bystander's test. For example, if two parties to a contract disagree in construing some of their contractual terms, the courts generally resolve this sort of legal dispute by appealing to the criterion: how would those disputed terms be construed by an objective bystander?
7. *G.S.* 7:164–88. *G.S.* is an abbreviation of Wilhelm Dilthey's *Gesammelte Schriften*, 12 vols. (Leipzig: Teubner, 1921–1965). For a good summary of his hermeneutic theory, see Richard E. Palmer, *Hermeneutics: Interpretation Theory in Schleiermacher, Dilthey, Heidegger, and Gadamer* (Evanston: Northwestern University Press, 1969), pp. 98–123. For his theory of the human studies, see Rudolf A. Makkreel, *Dilthey, Philosopher of the Human Studies* (Princeton: Princeton University Press, 1975); Michael Ermarth, *Wilhelm Dilthey: The Critique of Historical Reason* (Chicago: University of Chicago Press, 1978); and H. P. Rickman, *Wilhelm Dilthey, Pioneer of the Human Studies* (Berkeley: University of California Press, 1979).
8. *G.S.* 7:150.
9. Hirsch, *Validity in Interpretation*, p. 4.
10. Hirsch, "The Norms of Interpretation—A Brief Response," *Genre* (1969), 2:58.
11. *G.S.* 7:251.

12. *G.S.* 7:151. Here is another description of objective mind: "Its domain ranges from the style of life and the forms of social intercourse to the complex goals molded by society, to customs, the law, the state, religion, art, science and philosophy" (*Ibid.* 7:208). Dilthey's idea of objective mind has been appropriated by George Herbert Mead in his theory of "the generalized other." For details, see *Works of George Herbert Mead* (Chicago: University of Chicago Press, 1972), 1:154–64.

13. *G.S.* 7:208.

14. *G.S.* 5:242–58.

15. *G.S.* 5:144.

16. *G.S.* 7:86, 320.

17. *G.S.* 7:205–06.

18. *G.S.* 7:84.

19. *G.S.* 7:84–85.

20. This monistic conception of expression and its content may also be called the monistic view of intentionality. This monistic view has been espoused by many contemporary philosophers in their revolt against the Cartesian dualism of mind and body. For example, Ludwig Wittgenstein says, "An intention is embedded in its situation, in human customs and institutions." In Dilthey's language, an intention is embedded in the objective mind. Besides the monistic conception of intentionality, Wittgenstein's many other basic ideas, such as the ideas of the form of life (*Lebensform*), conventions, and language are fundamentally the same as Dilthey's, because Wittgenstein has drawn them from the German tradition of *Geisteswissenschaften*. For Wittgenstein's ideas, see his *Philosophical Investigations*, G. F. M. Anscombe, trans. (New York: Macmillan, 1953). For his relationship with the German tradition, see Allan Janik and Stephen Toulmin, *Wittgenstein's Vienna* (New York: Simon and Schuster, 1973). For the relevance of Wittgenstein's ideas to the social sciences, see Peter Winch, *The Idea of a Social Science and Its Relation to Philosophy* (London: Routledge, 1958), and Karl-Otto Apel, *The Analytic Philosophy of Language and the Geisteswissenschaften*, Harald Holstelilie, trans. (Dordrecht: Reidel, 1967).

Maurice Merleau-Ponty also advocates the monistic conception of intentionality in his doctrine of embodiment: "The consciousness of the body invades the body, the soul spreads over all its parts, and behavior overspills its central sector" (*Phenomenology of Perception*, Colin Smith, trans., London: Routledge, 1962, p. 75). He rejects the view that the bodily motion is a *representation* of the soul, because this view implicitly assumes the dualism of soul and body, intention and behavior. Instead he argues for the unity of the two. He also argues that the behavior of the body can be understood only in the contexts of the style of behavior and of its background, which play the role of the context of interaction and situation in his theory of behavior.

21. *G.S.* 7:208.

22. *Ibid.* 7:207.

23. *Ibid.* 7:211.

24. *Ibid.* 7:220. It is quite misleading to call Kepler's method "induction." In order to distinguish his method from the inductive method, Charles Peirce calls it the method of abduction or retroduction. For details, see *Collected Papers of*

Charles Sanders Peirce, Charles Hartshorne and Paul Weiss, eds. (Cambridge: Harvard University Press, 1960), 1.68–74.

25. *G.S.* 7:235.

26. P. F. Strawson, "Intention and Convention in Speech Acts," *The Philosophical Review* (1964) 73:452. This article was reprinted in his *Logico-Linguistic Papers* (London: Methuen, 1971), pp. 149–69.

4. SEMANTICS AND PRAGMATICS

1. Hans-Georg Gadamer, *Truth and Method*, Garrett Barden and John Cumming, eds. and trans. (New York: Seabury, 1975), pp. 345–66.

2. For details, see Pieter Seuren, ed., *Semantic Syntax* (Oxford: Oxford University Press, 1974), and W. J. Hutchins, *The Generation of Syntactic Structures from a Semantic Base* (Amsterdam: North-Holland, 1971).

3. Stanley Fish, "Literature in the Reader: Affective Stylistics," *New Literary History* (1970), 2:123–62.

4. Ludwig Wittgenstein, *Philosophical Investigations*, G. E. M. Anscombe, trans. (New York: Macmillan, 1953), pt. 1, sec. 19.

5. For the distinction between pure and descriptive semantics, see Rudolf Carnap, *Introduction to Semantics* (Cambridge: Harvard University Press, 1942), pp. 11–12.

6. J. L. Austin, *How to Do Things with Words* (Cambridge: Harvard University Press, 1962). John R. Searle, *Speech Acts: An Essay in the Philosophy of Language* (Cambridge: Cambridge University Press, 1969).

7. Bertrand Russell, *An Inquiry into Meaning and Truth* (London: Allen and Unwin, 1940), and *Logic and Knowledge* (London: Allen and Unwin, 1956); Alfred Tarski, *Logic, Semantics, Metamathematics*, J. H. Woodger, trans. (Oxford: Oxford University Press, 1956); Rudolf Carnap, *The Logical Syntax of Language*, Amethe Smeaton, trans. (London: Routledge, 1937); and *Meaning and Necessity: A Study in Semantics and Modal Logic* (Chicago: University of Chicago Press, 1947).

8. Ferdinand de Saussure, *Course in General Linguistics*, Wade Baskin, trans. (New York: Philosophical Library, 1959), pp. 7–20. For further elucidation of the distinction between *langue* and *parole*, see Jonathan D. Culler, *Ferdinand de Saussure* (Harmondsworth: Penguin Books, 1976), pp. 22–29.

9. Saussure, *Course in General Linguistics*, p. 19.

10. *Ibid.*, p. 9.

11. *Ibid.*, p. 19.

12. It is quite possible that Saussure was misled by his analogy of the *langue:parole* relation to the symphony: performance relation. From the fact that a symphony as a composition can exist apart from its performances, he probably assumed that *langue* could exist apart from *parole*. If *langue* can have independent existence, it can function as an independent object of scientific researches.

13. Saussure, *Course in General Linguistics*, p. 10.

14. *Ibid.*, p. 9.

15. N. S. Trubetzkoy, *Principles of Phonology*, Christiane Baltaxe, trans. (Berkeley: University of California Press, 1969); Roman Jakobson et al., *Preliminaries to Speech Analysis: The Distinctive Features and Their Correlates* (Cambridge: MIT Press, 1952, 1961); Roman Jakobson and Morris Halle, *Fundamentals of Language* (The Hague: Mouton, 1956).

16. A. J. Greimas, *Sémantique structurale* (Paris: Larousse, 1966).

17. Zellig Harris was Noam Chomsky's teacher, and the influence of structural linguistics came to Chomsky through Harris. For Harris' syntactic theory, see his *Structural Linguistics* (Chicago: University of Chicago Press, 1961). For Chomsky's theory, see his *Syntactic Structures* (The Hague: Mouton, 1957); *Aspects of the Theory of Syntax* (Cambridge: MIT Press, 1965); and *Topics in the Theory of Generative Grammar* (The Hague: Mouton, 1966).

18. Greimas, *Sémantique structurale*, pp. 176–80.

19. Robert Scholes makes a similar criticism. See his *Structuralism in Literature: An Introduction* (New Haven: Yale University Press, 1974), p. 106.

20. Julia Kristeva, *Le Texte du roman: Approche sémiologique d'une structure discursive transformationnelle* (The Hague: Mouton, 1970), p. 129.

21. *Ibid.*, p. 132.

22. Roman Jakobson, "Linguistics and Poetics," in Thomas A. Sebeok, ed., *Style in Language* (Cambridge: MIT Press, 1960), pp. 350–77.

23. *Ibid.*, p. 358.

24. Jakobson and Halle, *Fundamentals of Language*, p. 58.

25. There have been a few attempts to unravel the meaning of this assertion; for example, Jonathan D. Culler, *Structuralist Poetics: Structuralism, Linguistics, and the Study of Literature* (Ithaca: Cornell University Press, 1975), p. 56; and Terence Hawkes, *Structuralism and Semiotics* (Berkeley: University of California Press, 1977), p. 79. Unfortunately none of these attempts seems to be convincing or satisfactory.

26. Jakobson, "Linguistics and Poetics," p. 358.

27. *Ibid.*

28. *Ibid.*

29. *Ibid.*, p. 358.

30. *Ibid.*, pp. 358–59.

31. *Ibid.*, p. 359.

32. Roman Jakobson, "Qu'est-ce que la poésie?" *Poétique* (1971), 2:307, translated from the Czech by Marguerite Derrida. This English translation is quoted from Marjorie G. Grene, *Philosophy in and out of Europe* (Berkeley: University of California Press, 1976), p. 136.

33. Jackobson, "Linguistics and Poetics," p. 350.

34. Roland Barthes, "Science versus Literature," *The Times Literary Supplement* (September 28, 1967), reprinted in Michael Lane, eds., *Introduction to Structuralism* (New York: Basic Books, 1970), pp. 410–16.

5. PRAGMATIC ASCENT

1. *Collected Papers of Charles Sanders Peirce*, Charles Hartshorne and Paul Weiss, eds. (Cambridge: Harvard University Press, 1960), 2.228.

2. Charles Morris, *Foundations of the Theory of Signs* (Chicago: University of Chicago Press, 1938), p. 6.

3. Rudolf Carnap, *Introduction to Semantics* (Cambridge: MIT Press, 1942), p. 9.

4. The use of the word "syntax" as a linguistic term goes back to Chrysippus and his *peri tēs syntaxeōs tōn legoménōn* (concerning the syntax of language) in the third century B.C.

5. Morris, *Foundations of the Theory of Signs*, p. 33.

6. Carnap, *Introduction to Semantics*, p. 10.

7. Charles Morris, *Signs, Language and Behavior* (New York: Prentice-Hall, 1946), p. 219.

8. *Ibid.*

9. Morris, *Foundations of the Theory of Signs*, p. 33.

10. *Ibid.*, p. 52.

11. Carnap, *Introduction to Semantics*, p. 13.

12. Morris, *Foundations of the Theory of Signs*, pp. 7, 53.

13. *Ibid.*, p. 54.

14. Morris, *Signs, Language and Behavior*, p. 92.

15. Yehoshua Bar-Hillel, "Indexical Expressions," *Mind* (1954), 63:357–79. This article is included in his *Aspects of Language* (Jerusalem: Magnes, 1970), pp. 69–88. My references are to this volume.

16. Strawson, "On Referring," *Mind* (1950), 59:322–44. This article is included in his *Logico-Linguistic Papers* (London: Methuen, 1971), pp. 1–27. My references are to this volume.

17. Strawson, *Logico-Linguistic Papers*, p. 9.

18. Bar-Hillel, *Aspects of Language*, p. 84.

19. Richard Montague, "Pragmatics," in Raymond Klibansky, ed., *Contemporary Philosophy* (Florence: Nuova Italia, 1968), 1:102–22; "Pragmatics and Intensional Logic," in Donald Davidson and Gilbert Harman, ed., *Semantics of Natural Language* (Dordrecht: Reidel, 1972), pp. 142–68.

20. Strawson, *Logico-Linguistic Papers*, pp. 11–13.

21. Frege, "On Sense and Reference," in Peter T. Geach and Max Black, eds., *Translations from the Philosophical Writings of Gottlob Frege* (Oxford: Blackwell, 1960), pp. 56–78.

22. Edmund Husserl, *Logical Investigations*, J. N. Findlay, trans., 2 vols. (London: Routledge, 1970), Investigation 1, secs. 12–13.

23. Beside the works mentioned above, another laudable attempt at referential pragmatics is Richard Martin, *Toward a Systematic Pragmatics* (Amsterdam: North-Holland, 1959). There is one special system of signs, for which the notion of referential semantics appears to be suitable. That is cartomancy, which can have its own syntax, semantics, and pragmatics. Its semantics is the assignment of meaning to each card. Its syntax determines how different cards can be combined to generate a sentence, and this combination is generally determined by spreading out a stack of cards on a table. A sentence thus generated may read "A benevolent dark-haired man will do wonders for you." This reading still belongs to the semantic level. Who is referred to by the expression "a benevolent dark-haired man" has yet to be determined. Now suppose that its reference is fixed by identifying the man so described as the uncle of the person whose

fortune is being told. This is the interpretation of the cards, which belongs to the pragmatics of cartomancy. For details, see M. I. Lekomceva and B. A. Uspenskij, "Describing a Semiotic System with a Simple Syntax," in Daniel P. Lucid, ed. and trans., *Soviet Semiotics* (Baltimore: Johns Hopkins University Press, 1977), pp. 65–76.

The demarcation of semantics from pragmatics in cartomancy is made exactly the same way as what I have called the "Strawsonian demarcation." In the standard conception of semantics, however, the determination of reference is as much semantic as the determination of sense or meaning. Suppose that you know the meaning of the expression "the tallest buildings in New York City" without knowing which buildings are referred to by this expression. If you find out that it refers to the World Trade Center towers, you are still performing a semantic act. The interpretation of cards involves two levels of semantic operation: the assignment of standard meanings to each card and each permissible combination of cards; and the determination of reference for the standard meanings produced by the distribution and combination of cards.

The pragmatic act in cartomancy is the act of telling a fortune, which is usually done by fixing the reference of a general statement. The semantic determination of reference is used as a means for this pragmatic act. The semantic operation of fixing the reference for a statement can be performed without involving the notion of telling a fortune.

24. This criticism is made against Strawson's distinction between the meaning of a sign and its use by Herbert Hochberg in his "On Referring and Asserting," *Philosophical Studies* (1969), 20:81–88.

25. The German word *bedeuten* can be translated as "mean" or "refer." Husserl's *Bedeutung* is usually translated as "meaning," while Frege's *Bedeutung* (in his *Über Sinn und Bedeutung*) is translated as "reference."

26. Ludwig Wittgenstein, *Tractatus Logico-Philosophicus* (London: Routledge, 1922), 3.203.

27. *Ibid.*, 2.01, 2.11, 4.22.

28. Wittgenstein, *Philosophical Investigations*, G. E. M. Anscombe, trans. (New York: Macmillan, 1953), pt. 1, secs. 26–88.

29. *Ibid.*, secs. 7–88.

30. *Ibid.*, sec. 43.

31. J. L. Austin, *How to Do Things with Words* (Cambridge: Harvard University Press, 1962), pp. 4–5.

32. *Ibid.*, pp. 94–107.

33. John Searle, *Speech Acts: An Essay in the Philosophy of Language* (Cambridge: Cambridge University Press, 1969), pp. 57–61.

34. Charles Morris, *Signification and Significance: A Study of the Relations of Signs and Values* (Cambridge: MIT Press, 1964).

35. E. D. Hirsch, *The Aims of Interpretation* (Chicago: University of Chicago Press, 1976), p. 146.

36. E. D. Hirsch, *Validity in Interpretation* (New Haven: Yale University Press, 1967), p. 211.

37. *Ibid.*, pp. 78–89.

38. *Ibid.*, p. 49.

39. *Ibid.*, p. 81.
40. Alfred N. Whitehead and Bertrand Russell, *Principia Mathematica*, 2d ed., 3 vols. (Cambridge: Cambridge University Press, 1925–27), 1:340–46.

6. PRAGMATIC NORMS

1. J. L. Austin, *How to Do Things with Words* (Cambridge: Cambridge University Press, 1962), p. 104.
2. Richard Ohmann, "Speech Acts and the Definition of Literature," *Philosophy and Rhetoric* (1971), 4:14.
3. *Ibid.*, p. 17.
4. Mary L. Pratt, *Toward a Speech Act Theory of Literary Discourse* (Bloomington: Indiana University Press, 1977), pp. 89–99.
5. *Ibid.*, p. 91.
6. Pioneering works in this field are Saul Kripke, "Naming and Necessity," in Donald Davidson and Gilbert Harman, eds., *Semantics of Natural Language* (Dordrecht: Reidel, 1972), pp. 253–356; David K. Lewis, *Convention* (Cambridge: Harvard University Press, 1969), and *Counterfactuals* (Cambridge: Harvard University Press, 1973).
7. Teun van Dijk, "Pragmatics and Poetics," in Teun van Dijk, ed., *Pragmatics of Language and Literature* (Amsterdam: North-Holland, 1976), p. 31.
8. The relation of possible worlds to the actual world is well explained by Raymond Bradley and Norman Schwartz in their *Possible Worlds: An Introduction to Logic and Its Philosophy* (Indianapolis: Hackett, 1979), pp. 1–8.
9. Teun van Dijk, "Pragmatics and Poetics," p. 36.
10. Pratt, *Toward a Speech Act Theory*, pp. 3–37.
11. Samuel Levin, "Concerning What Kind of Speech Act a Poem Is," in Teun van Dijk, eds., *Pragmatics of Language and Literature*, pp. 141–60.
12. John Ross, "On Declarative Sentences," in Roderick Jacobs and Peter Rosenbaum, eds., *Readings in English Transformational Grammar* (Waltham, Mass.: Xerox College, 1970), pp. 222–72.
13. Levin, "Concerning What Kind of Speech Act," p. 150.
14. *Ibid.*, p. 151.
15. Since literary works are devoid of illocutionary forces and perlocutionary effects, Richard Ohmann has classified them as locutions in his "Speech, Literature and the Space Between," *New Literary History* (1974), 5:52. But this is a wrong classification. The notion of locution does not involve the notion of creation; it is the notion of merely uttering words without using them for any purpose. The act of literary creation definitely involves the use of words for literary functions.
16. Charles Morris, "Pragmatism and Logical Empiricism," in Paul Schlipp, ed., *The Philosophy of Rudolf Carnap* (La Salle: Open Court, 1963), p. 88.
17. In Paul Schlipp, ed., *The Philosophy of Rudolf Carnap*, p. 861.
18. Jürgen Habermas, *Communication and the Evolution of Society*, Thomas McCarthy, trans. (Boston: Beacon, 1979), p. 1. The essay, "What is Universal Pragmatics?" is included in this volume.

19. *Ibid.*, p. 2.

20. This point comes out more clearly in Habermas' critique of Chomsky in his "Towards a Theory of Communicative Competence," *Inquiry* (1970), 13:360–75. The charge of monologism against Chomsky is due to his misunderstanding of Chomsky's theory, which abstracts the study of syntax from the context of monologue as much as from the context of dialogue.

21. Habermas, *Communication*, p. 29.

22. *Ibid.*, p. 33.

23. For a representative work in sociolinguistics, see Dell Hymes, *Foundations in Sociolinguistics* (Philadelphia: University of Pennsylvania Press, 1974). The expression "communicative competence" was introduced by Hymes in *On Communicative Competence* (Philadelphia: University of Pennsylvania Press, 1971).

24. H. P. Grice, "Logic and Conversation," originally delivered as a part of the 1967 William James Lectures at Harvard University. It has been printed in two anthologies: Donald Davidson and Gilbert Harman, eds., *The Logic of Grammar* (Encino, Calif.: Dickenson, 1975), pp. 64–75; and Peter Cole and Jerry Morgan, eds., *Syntax and Semantics* (New York: Academic Press, 1975), 3:41–58.

Grice's difficulties in establishing conversational maxims are well discussed by Joseph Margolis in "Literature and Speech Acts," *Philosophy and Literature* (1979), 3:39–52.

25. Robin Lakoff, "The Language of Politeness," *Papers from the Ninth Regional Meeting of the Chicago Linguistics Society* (Chicago: University of Chicago Linguistics Department, 1973), pp. 292–305.

26. A. P. Martinich, "Conversational Maxims and Some Philosophical Problems," *Philosophical Quarterly* (1980), 30:215–28.

27. For the history of the idea of *prepon* and *decorum*, see Max Pohlenz, "*To Prepon*," *Nachrichten von der Gesellschaft der Wissenschaften zu Göttingen, Philologisch-Historische Klasse* (1933), 1:53–92.

28. Hymes, *Foundations in Sociolinguistics*, pp. 95–98.

7. PRAGMATIC FUNCTIONS

1. Cleanth Brooks, *The Well Wrought Urn: Studies in the Structure of Poetry* (New York: Harcourt, Brace, 1947).

2. T. K. Seung, *Cultural Thematics: The Formation of the Faustian Ethos* (New Haven: Yale University Press, 1976), pp. 134–36.

3. Rosalie Colie, *Paradoxia Epidemica: The Renaissance Tradition of Paradox* (Princeton: Princeton University Press, 1966).

4. This exalted and pervasive function of poetry was not a phenomenon unique to ancient Greece, but rather a common one in most oral traditions. In ancient China, for example, *The Book of Odes* was a highly revered sacred text.

5. The succession of seers, poets, and philosophers as spiritual leaders of ancient Greece is well chronicled in F. M. Cornford, *Principium Sapientiae: The Origins of Greek Philosophical Thought* (Cambridge: Cambridge University Press, 1952).

6. These lines from *The Frogs* are quoted from its English translation by Benjamin Rogers, *Five Comedies of Aristophanes* (Garden City: Doubleday, 1955), pp. 121–22.

7. Bernard Weinberg, "Castelvetro's Theory of Poetics," in R. S. Crane, ed., *Critics and Criticism* (Chicago: University of Chicago Press, 1952), pp. 354–55.

8. This translation is by James Meredith in Immanuel Kant, *Critique of Judgment* (Oxford: Oxford University Press, 1952), p. 14.

9. Søren Kierkegaard, *Fear and Trembling* (Princeton: Princeton University Press, 1941); and *The Sickness unto Death* (Princeton: Princeton University Press, 1941).

10. Leo Tolstoy, *What is Art?* Aylmer Maude, trans. (New York: The Library of Liberal Arts, 1960), p. 10.

8. THEMATIC PROJECTION

1. T. K. Seung, *Cultural Thematics: The Formation of the Faustian Ethos* (New Haven: Yale University Press, 1976), pp. 207–16.

2. This translation is by H. R. Fairclough in *Virgil*, rev. ed., Loeb Classical Library (Cambridge: Harvard University Press, 1935).

3. This translation is by A. T. Murray in *Homer: The Odyssey*, Loeb Classical Library (Cambridge: Harvard University Press, 1919).

4. This exposition of Dante's fourfold allegory is given in his dedicatory epistle to Can Grande, the authenticity of which has been disputed.

5. The investigation of what is generally presupposed and implied by our ordinary talks has been one of the main topics in pragmatics during recent years. For details, see Bas C. van Fraassen, "Presupposition, Implication, and Self-Reference," *Journal of Philosophy* (1968), 65:136–51; Robert C. Stalnaker, "Pragmatics," in Donald Davidson and Gilbert Harman, eds., *Semantics of Natural Language* (Dordrecht: Reidel, 1972), pp. 380–97; and Andy Rogers et al. eds., *Proceedings of the Texas Conference on Performatives, Presuppositions, and Implications* (Arlington, Virginia: The Center for Applied Linguistics, 1977).

6. Hans-Georg Gadamer, *Truth and Method*, Garrett Barden and John Cumming, eds. and trans. (New York: Seabury, 1975), p. 236.

7. E. D. Hirsch, *The Aims of Interpretation* (Chicago: University of Chicago Press, 1976), p. 32.

8. Stanley Fish, "Interpreting the *Variorum*," *Critical Inquiry* (1976), 2:478.

9. Norman N. Holland, *5 Readers Reading* (New Haven: Yale University Press, 1975), p. 12.

10. Fish, "Interpreting the *Variorum*," p. 483.

11. I have given a full account of this problem in my *Structuralism and Hermeneutics* (New York: Columbia University Press, 1981), ch. 8: "Relativity and Subjectivity."

12. E. D. Hirsch, *Validity in Interpretation* (New Haven: Yale University Press, 1967), pp. 61–67.

13. William K. Wimsatt Jr. and Monroe C. Beardsley, *The Verbal Icon: Studies in the Meaning of Poetry* (Lexington: University of Kentucky Press, 1954), p. 4.

9. THEMATIC COHERENCE

1. Charles Singleton, *Dante Studies*, 2 vols. (Cambridge: Harvard University Press, 1954–58), 1:91.
2. T. K. Seung, *The Fragile Leaves of the Sibyl: Dante's Master Plan* (Westminster, Md.: Newman Press, 1962).
3. *Ibid.*, pp. 29–133.
4. For details, see my "Bonaventure's Figural Exemplarism in Dante," in Giose Rimanelli and Kenneth Atchity, eds., *Italian Literature: Essays in Honor of Thomas Goddard Bergin* (New Haven: Yale University Press, 1976), pp. 117–54.
5. For further details, see T. K. Seung, *Cultural Thematics: the Formation of the Faustian Ethos* (New Haven: Yale University Press, 1976), pp. 77–89, 243–55.
6. In John A. Scott's review of my *Cultural Thematics* in *Italian Studies* (1978), 33:114.
7. Erich Auerbach, *Dante: Poet of the Secular World*, Ralph Manheim, trans. (Chicago: University of Chicago Press, 1961).
8. For the attempt to apply the New Criticism to the reading of the *Commedia*, see my *Cultural Thematics*, pp. 135–36.
9. I. A. Richards, *Practical Criticism: A Study of Literary Judgment* (London: Paul, Trench, Trubner, 1929).

10. THEMATIC TRADITION

1. Friedrich E. D. Schleiermacher, *Hermeneutik*, Heinz Kimmerle, ed. (Heidelberg: Carl Winter, 1959), p. 90.
2. *G.S.* 7:213–16. *G.S.* is an abbreviation of Wilhelm Dilthey's *Gesammelte Schriften*, 14 vols. (Göttingen: Vandenhoeck, 1913–1967).
3. Martin Heidegger, *Being and Time*, John Macquarrie and Edward Robinson, trans. (New York: Harper, 1962), pp. 194, 362–63.
4. Hans-Georg Gadamer, *Truth and Method*, Garrett Barden and John Cumming, eds. and trans. (New York: Seabury, 1975).
5. *Ibid.*, p. 264.
6. *Ibid.*, p. 245.
7. My critique of Gadamer's contextual relativism is given in my *Structuralism and Hermeneutics* (New York: Columbia University Press, 1982), pp. 198–212.
8. Heidegger, *Being and Time*, pp. 191–95.
9. Gadamer, *Truth and Method*, p. 261.
10. *Ibid.*, pp. 236–37.
11. *Ibid.*, p. 238.
12. *Ibid.*, pp. 324–31.
13. *Ibid.*, pp. 237, 239, 259.
14. *Ibid.*, p. 271.
15. *Ibid.*, p. xiv.
16. The traditional division of the hermeneutic domain has been threefold: *subtilitas intelligendi* (understanding), *subtilitas explicandi* (interpretation), and *sub-*

tilitas applicandi (application). For details, see Gadamer, *Truth and Method*, p. 274.

17. *Ibid.*, pp. 274–305.
18. E. D. Hirsch, *The Aims of Interpretation* (Chicago: University of Chicago Press, 1976), pp. 19, 85–88.
19. Gadamer, *Truth and Method*, pp. 289–94.
20. *Ibid.*, pp. 295–96.
21. *Ibid.*, pp. 278–89.
22. *Ibid.*, pp. 310–25.
23. *Ibid.*, p. 264.
24. Hirsch, *The Aims of Interpretation*, p. 40.
25. Gadamer, *Truth and Method*, p. 270.
26. *Ibid.*, pp. xii–xiii.
27. *Ibid.*, p. 270.
28. The title of Gadamer's book is usually taken as ironical. For example, Richard Palmer says that the title "contains an irony: method is not the way to truth. On the contrary, truth eludes the methodical man." See his *Hermeneutics: Interpretation Theory in Schleiermacher, Dilthey, Heidegger, and Gadamer* (Evanston: Northwestern University Press, 1969), p. 163. David C. Hoy expresses a similar view ("truth cannot be guaranteed by method") in his *Critical Circle: Literature, History, and Philosophical Hermeneutics* (Berkeley: University of California Press, 1978), p. 92. The authorial intention imputed by these accounts to Gadamer is quite different from the one my account postulates, which is concerned with the primacy of truth over method.
29. Gadamer, *Truth and Method*, p. xi.
30. *Ibid.*, p. 273.
31. For Rudolf Bultmann's program, see his *Jesus Christ and Mythology* (New York: Scribners, 1958).

11. THEMATIC DIALECTIC

1. T. K. Seung, *Cultural Thematics: The Formation of the Faustian Ethos* (New Haven: Yale University Press, 1976), pp. 189–216.
2. A. L. Kroeber, *Anthropology: Culture Patterns and Processes* (New York: Harcourt, 1923); and Ruth Benedict, *Patterns of Culture* (Boston: Houghton Mifflin, 1934).
3. Benedict, *Patterns of Culture*, pp. 79–80.
4. *Ibid.*, pp. 95–96.
5. *Ibid.*, pp. 173–80.
6. *Ibid.*, pp. 130–72.
7. *Ibid.*, pp. 159–72.
8. The following is a summary of my historical survey in *Cultural Thematics*.
9. J. N. Findlay, *Hegel: A Re-Examination* (London: Allen and Unwin, 1958), p. 76.

10. Gustav Mueller, "The Hegel Legend of 'Thesis-Antithesis-Synthesis,'" *Journal of the History of Ideas* (1958), 19:411–14.

11. W. T. Stace, *The Philosophy of Hegel: A Systematic Exposition* (London: Macmillan, 1924), p. 97.

12. Richard Kroner, ed., *G. W. F. Hegel: Early Theological Writings* (Chicago: University of Chicago Press, 1948), p. 32.

13. Findlay, *Hegel*, p. 353.

14. Marx's notion of historical dialectic is scattered all over his works. Kierkegaard's notion of existential dialectic is perhaps best articulated in his *Either/Or*, David F. Swenson and Lillian Marcin Swenson, trans. (Princeton: Princeton University Press, 1944). Weber's notion of cultural dialectic is also scattered all over his works. Louis Schneider gives a good account of Weber's notion of cultural dialectic in his "Max Weber: Wisdom and Science in Sociology," *The Sociological Quarterly* (1971), 12:462–72.

15. Max Weber, *The Protestant Ethic and the Spirit of Capitalism*, Talcott Parsons, trans. (New York: Scribner's, 1958).

16. Claude Lévi-Strauss, *The Savage Mind*, George Weidenfeld, trans. (Chicago: University of Chicago Press, 1966), p. 69.

17. For details, see my *Cultural Thematics*, pp. 231–43.

18. Hegel, *The Phenomenology of Mind*, 2d rev. ed., J. B. Baillie, trans. (London: Allen and Unwin, 1949), pp. 228–40.

19. Louis Schneider, "Max Weber," p. 467.

20. Weber, *The Protestant Ethic*, pp. 171–75.

21. Hegel, *Phenomenology*, pp. 681–808.

Index

Abelard, Peter, 196, 205

Adler, Mortimer, 111

Aestheticism: autonomy of, 121–22, 127; supremacy of, 123, 125, 127; quasi-religious role of, 124–25, 129; tyranny of, 130–31

Agnosticism, textual: as condition for emergence of textual solipsism, 3–4; and textual objectivity, 5; and contextual subjectivity, 8; and interpretative anxiety, 16

Alan of Lille, *De planctu naturae,* 195

Allegory: vs. analogy, 162; as resolution of thematic tension in twelfth century, 205

Appropriateness: as condition of speech acts, 107–8; and context grammar, 108; as uniquely pragmatic category, 108–9; as both means and ends, 109; as intrinsic vs. extrinsic, 109

Aristophanes, *The Frogs,* 114

Aristotle, 24; *Categoriae,* 55; *De interpretatione,* 55; *Rhetorica,* 56, 109–10; *De poetica,* 56, 109–10, 111, 118–19, 120, 121–22, 145; on poetry and generalities, 74; theory of mimesis, 92; on the notion of appropriateness, 107–10; and methodological difference between *Poetics* and *Rhetoric,* 109–10; and genre criticism, 111–12; his defense of poetry, 116; as father of intrinsic criticism, 117; on poetry as art of imitation, 117, 118; on poetic pleasure, 118–19; on mimesis, 118–19, 193; on quasi reality of art, 119; on univocity, 119; *Metaphysics,* 119–20; on substance, 119–20; *Nicomachean Ethics,* 120; on poetry as subordinated to ethics and politics, 120; *Politics,* 120; on didactic vs. mimetic functions of poetry, 120–21; and aesthetic autonomy, 122–23; and humbling of poetry, 125; and tragedy, 132; dualism of, 155, 161; and Gadamer, 183; on *praxis* and *techne,* 183; and communal view of human nature, 198–99

Auden, W. H., on tragedy, 132–33

Auerbach, Erich, on Dante, 169

Augustine, St.: on Holy Trinity, 160–61; on Pelagianism, 164–65; and secular ethos, 195, 210; and two semantic orders, 207

Austin, J. L., 32; his classification of speech acts, 85–86; on use of words, 86; *How To Do Things with Words,* 86, 223n6; on locutionary, perlocutionary, and illocutionary acts, 86–87; on felicity conditions, 87; on literary speech acts, 91; and John Ross, 96; his definition of illocutionary act, 100–1; Habermas' critique of, 104–5

Autonomy: of text, 11; textual vs. contextual, 37; textual heteronomy as by-product of linguistic autonomy, 37–38; of interpretation, 38; semantic autonomy as generating contextual indeterminacy, 38; of aesthetic function, 121, 122; of nonreligious values, 122–23; of human will, 165

Bacon, Francis, his instrumental view of knowledge, 197–98